MW00559281

PRAISE FOR *Touching the Art*

"*Touching the Art* is ekphrastic, intimate, historical, and proximate. The art of the title, paintings by Sycamore's grandmother Gladys Goldstein, appears only through description—and what description. We encounter the work, learn who Gladys was and who she was in relation to—how gentrification, redlining, and antiblackness shape space, and how 'family' organizes itself to refuse confrontation and to excise queerness. Sycamore employs diverging yet deeply related histories. *Touching the Art* is an education; a beautiful instruction in feeling and looking."
—Christina Sharpe, author of *Ordinary Notes*

"Mattilda Bernstein Sycamore braids humor, tragedy, and unabashed presence in every single sentence she writes. Blending history, essay, and memoir, telling her own secrets and truths through the lives of others. I adore Sycamore's writing and would follow her anywhere. Nobody touches the art like Sycamore."   —Catherine Lacey, author of
Pew and *Biography of X*

"Sycamore responds to the call for white artists to reckon with our pasts, our connections to power and privilege. The scalpel she takes to her own family is laser-sharp. In all the messily queer craftsmanship we've come to expect from her prose, she offers us a handhold and a way forward: Touch the art, fuck it up, get free. Art is a part of our liberation and our future, and Sycamore is trying to write us all free."
—Joseph Osmundson, author of *Virology: Essays for the Living,*
the Dead, and the Small Things in Between

"I love writers who take risks, who rattle cages, who overthrow the tables of the money changers, writers who can whisper truths or shout them fabulously from rooftops. Yes, I love Mattilda Bernstein Sycamore."
—Rabih Alameddine, author of *The Wrong End of the Telescope*

Touching the Art

ALSO BY MATTILDA BERNSTEIN SYCAMORE

The Freezer Door

Sketchtasy

The End of San Francisco

So Many Ways to Sleep Badly

Pulling Taffy

AS EDITOR

Between Certain Death and a Possible Future: Queer Writing on Growing Up with the AIDS Crisis

Why Are Faggots So Afraid of Faggots?: Flaming Challenges to Masculinity, Objectification, and the Desire to Conform

Nobody Passes: Rejecting the Rules of Gender and Conformity

That's Revolting!: Queer Strategies for Resisting Assimilation

Dangerous Families: Queer Writing on Surviving

Tricks and Treats: Sex Workers Write About Their Clients

Touching
the Art

Mattilda
Bernstein
Sycamore

Soft Skull　New York

First Soft Skull edition: 2023

Grateful acknowledgment for reprinting materials is made to the following:
Excerpt from "Why I Am Not a Painter" from *The Collected Poems of Frank O'Hara* by Frank O'Hara, copyright © 1971 by Maureen Granville-Smith, Administratrix of the Estate of Frank O'Hara, copyright renewed 1999 by Maureen O'Hara Granville-Smith and Donald Allen. Used by permission of Alfred A. Knopf, an imprint of the Knopf Doubleday Publishing Group, a division of Penguin Random House LLC. All rights reserved. Frank O'Hara, excerpt from "The Day Lady Died" from *Lunch Poems*. Copyright © 1964 by Frank O'Hara. Reprinted with the permission of The Permissions Company, LLC on behalf of City Lights Books, citylights.com. Selections from *Restless Ambition: Grace Hartigan, Painter* by Cathy Curtis (Oxford University Press, 2015) reprinted with permission of the Licensor through PLSclear.

Library of Congress Cataloging-in-Publication Data
Names: Sycamore, Mattilda Bernstein, author.
Title: Touching the art / Mattilda Bernstein Sycamore.
Description: First edition. | New York : Soft Skull, 2023. | Includes bibliographical references.
Identifiers: LCCN 2023019120 | ISBN 9781593767358 (hardcover) | ISBN 9781593767365 (ebook)
Subjects: LCSH: Goldstein, Gladys, 1917- | Sycamore, Mattilda Bernstein—Family. | Artists—Family relationships—United States. | Creation (Literary, artistic, etc.)
Classification: LCC CT275.G55763 B47 2023 | DDC 700.92—dc23/eng/20230506
LC record available at https://lccn.loc.gov/2023019120

Jacket design by Lexi Earle
Jacket art: Untitled candy wrapper collages © Gladys Goldstein
Book design by tracy danes

Published by Soft Skull Press
New York, NY
www.softskull.com

Printed in the United States of America
10 9 8 7 6 5 4 3 2 1

To Gladys, of course—

For JoAnne, 1974–1995
For Chrissie Contagious, 1974–2010
For David Wojnarowicz, 1954–1992

Touching the Art

I'm six years old, wearing a yellow sweater and a long pink scarf that goes past my waist, the tassels blowing in the wind. I stand very still inside a white rectangle on the left side of the painting, next to cartoonish flowers as big as my head that float in a dense green that covers half the canvas. There's a tulip growing toward my hand from the white ground, but I do not look happy. Somehow I never realized this until now.

This painting was in my grandfather's bedroom, the room that became mine when I visited. So it kept me company. Did I always just look at the flowers and colors and recognize the figure on the left as me, and find this comforting?

In that room I was still afraid of the dark, there were still monsters in the blankets, but when I look at this painting now I can tell that my grandmother actually saw me when she painted it. My mouth is a straight line across, eyes blurred into something like panic, I'm staring ahead but my whole body looks frozen. I'm there, and yet I'm not there at all.

I'm not saying Gladys meant to paint all of this, I'm just saying she was painting honestly. When you allow your work to express what you see, sometimes your work expresses more than you know.

When she painted me again at age twelve, long eyelashes emphasize my femininity—here I have softer features, hints of a nose and lips, my hand reaching into paper collaged onto the canvas. The painting is saturated in blues like I'm in the sky or the water but also I'm grounded by what I'm holding on to, these words. What do they say? The way my shirt becomes a collage but also everything is fluid—even in the brightness of my gaze I'm holding on with a stoicism that I didn't realize she recognized.

The relationship we have through her art. Through the process of making art. So I remember those seashell windchimes, and when one broke, and that's how she decided to use them in her handmade paperworks. She would take me and my sister to the button factory, that's what she called it, a store somewhere on the way downtown in Baltimore on a street of old buildings—was it Calvert Street, or Charles? It wasn't a large storefront, but I remember huge containers filled with buttons near the entrance, a scoop was twenty-five cents or you could fill a lunch bag for a dollar, something like that. It took me so long to decide on those buttons because I would find a single one that already felt like treasure, a gold filigree or a brass tableau or an astonishing matte chartreuse, everything was art, this was what I learned from Gladys.

There is art in a frame, but also there is the frame of art. You put it on a black background, on a white background, on a background of color—a touch of color or the color of touch, when you hold it up in the air you realize how strong it is, this handmade paperwork of so many delicate layers. You hold it up to the light or you place it down under the light—there is what the art does, and there is what the art does to you.

When I was a kid, Gladys encouraged everything that made me different—my sensitivity, creativity, softness, femininity, introspection. She was an abstract artist, and she wanted to set me free, that's what it felt like.

Once, my other grandmother bought me an instructional book on how to draw an airplane, and when I drew an airplane just like the book told me to, Gladys was horrified. I can't remember any other crime I committed as a child in her eyes. As an adult, the standards changed, and that's one of the things I'm trying to understand here. But even when I visited her after moving to San Francisco at age nineteen, ready to claim queerness with my body, she was ready to photograph it. Here I am with purple and green hair, standing in front of the painting where she reproduced part of a poem I wrote in high school—I'm looking at the camera like nothing can touch me.

Did Gladys say you look like a hustler, something like that, but also she photographed me with my shirt off, and I can't find the exact photos I'm looking for, or maybe they don't exist, not in the way I remember. The hustler pose must be this one where I'm leaning shirtless against the wall, hips pushed forward.

But the pose from behind must have been Gladys's idea—I'm reaching up the white studio wall designed with pegboard to hang her paintings for viewing. The white wall emphasizing my painted nails, a chain mail bracelet on the left wrist, a silver phone cord wrapped around my right, green-and-black polyester plaid pants, combat boots.

At least half of these photos are out of focus, but Gladys was always looking for the glorious mistake, the perfect error. How a broken circle is still a circle, how there can be so much motion in something so still, so much depth of field in neutrals, such an individuality between the two sides of this paperwork and so they pull you together. But also a hole ripped into the bottom right of the piece, an invitation to see the whole.

A whole is greater than the parts, that's what they say. But Gladys also knew that a hole could be greater. Nothing teaches more than absence, and if I'm feeling her absence now I'm feeling present. My pale skin in these photos, afraid of the sun in San Francisco I would cross the street to reach shade. Gladys, too, was afraid of the sun on her skin. But surely not the light.

How a photo of a person in front of a painting can either be a photo of a person, or a photo of a painting. Can it be both? In this photo my green hair melds into the blue-green of one of Gladys's Emotional Squares paintings, and the blue in the painting brings out the blue in my eyes. Between person and painting, between person and person. Or I'm dancing for the camera in several shots, and one of them is just a blur of green and blue and gray and Gladys's thumb in the frame, here we are together.

I'm moving between wanting to hold this person that was myself and wanting to see this painting again, all the vulnerability even when I'm projecting invulnerability, but can I tell you something else? When I was looking through my file cabinet to find these photos, I found a set of photos that an acquaintance took about five years later, in Seattle in 1997—in those photos I'm shirtless too because the photographer requested it, and my hair is blue blending into pink, and then shaped into perfect curls and swirls. But here's what I notice—the return address on the envelope that contains these photos, it's the same building where I live now. So Amy Rossman, who took these photos, lived just two floors down, and one apartment over, but I had no idea. Coincidence doesn't always tell us about history, but history always tells us about coincidence.

Suddenly I'm remembering the trip when Gladys took these photos—I think I was in Baltimore for ten days, which was the longest I'd ever stayed there. I went downtown one night and found an open mic at a café, and did I read something there? No, but I thought about reading something.

I remember sitting in the park by the Washington Monument, which was right near the café, and also near the Walters Art Museum, a landmark I knew from Gladys, and some cute boy came up to me. He said he went to MICA, and I didn't know what MICA was, oh, the Maryland Institute College of Art. Actually that was the art school where Gladys once taught, when it was just known as the Maryland Institute, in the 1960s. She was one of the first people hired to teach abstract painting there.

So this cute boy started talking to me in the park by the Washington Monument, right near a gallery on Charles Street where I went to a show of Gladys's collages sometime in the '80s. It was one of those moments that could have become a hookup, especially when he told me about the porn shop nearby, but then maybe it didn't become a hookup because we talked for too long. I mean I couldn't tell what he wanted, and I didn't know how to make it into what I wanted, because also I wanted to talk. I would have talked more. It's funny how I can start thinking about a conversation with a random guy I met in a park twenty-five years ago and still regret that I didn't get to know him more.

I want to let go of the need to describe the art, and instead describe the sensation, the mood, the shaping of emotion. But also I need to say something about how an oil pastel drawing is embedded in this paperwork, it's just a small part of the piece but you can't look away because the colors are so vibrant.

The frame is always important in Gladys's art, not the frame around the art but the frames within. I want to say something about this paper she made, how it's even but coarse and there are so many textures, your fingers tell a different story than your eyes.

When I was a kid, everyone in my family said I'd inherited Gladys's visual sense. The way the loop of the string pulls your eyes up, the movement of eyes versus the movement of texture and color and sensation. The brightness of a color, yellow, and how that can pull you off the page. How I say the page but I mean the artwork.

What does it mean to inherit a sense?

The way the arc of the brown follows the motion of the straw embedded in the paper, the motion of the hand. Gladys's hand. If I make this motion now it feels like anger, but if I do it slower then it feels like a welcome. Art is never just art, it is a history of feeling, a gap between sensations, a safety valve, an escape hatch, a sudden shift in the body, a clipboard full of flowers, a welcome mat flipped over and back, over and back, welcome.

How Gladys wanted to use her hands so much that toward the end of her life, when she kept falling and hurting her hands, still she would try to get up those steep stairs to her studio to make more art. Maybe this is a story of obsession. Maybe this is a story of love. Maybe this is a story of breathing.

But actually they didn't just say I'd inherited Gladys's visual sense, it was her sense of taste. Everyone said it. Sometimes it could be a question: How come you were the one who inherited her taste? But it was also always the answer. As if taste were something you could inherit. As if it were even taste we were talking about.

If art is a structure of feeling, it is also a feeling of lack. The paradox in writing about someone who's dead is that then they feel more alive. You want to call her up and say listen, I'm writing about you, I have some questions. In this light, how all the browns become pink. Suddenly I see the blue at the top corner, and oh, how is that even attached?

Wait, it's bent back, damaged. These paperworks are all in a cardboard box sent to me by my mother after years in her storage space. And, before that, years at the University of Maryland—after Gladys was approached by the university, she donated one hundred works to form a permanent collection of her work in 2004. This was a years-long process, involving documentation of her work, conversations about what to include in the collection, and the production of the catalog. Gladys donated an additional one hundred works that the university could sell to help fund the collection, and the ones I have are numbered so I wonder if they were originally part of those one hundred or just works that were also considered. They are individually protected in clear sleeves that must be acid-free because there's no discoloration. But the box wasn't kept flat in my mother's storage unit, or in transit. So there are bent corners and unintended creases, there is damage in this way. But not enough to make the art look worse, I don't think. Just more delicate. If Gladys were alive, we could talk about this. She would be interested in hearing my thoughts.

If the self is always a collaborative project, Gladys gave me what I needed as a child, this I know. What changed as I came into my self is one of the things I'm trying to figure out. How it changed, and why. Because if I look at these pictures Gladys took of me when I was nineteen, I can see the way we're collaborating. I remember her commenting on my hair, how she thought it was interesting. She liked my earrings, except the largest one that was like a horn. And in the photo where she asked me to reach my hands up against the wall from behind with my shirt off, the emphasis goes to my thumbnails painted black and the bracelets around my bare arms. We are making art together with my body.

The dynamic between thinking about art, and creating it. Experiencing art in the everyday, like you're walking down the street and you look up at the way the light hits those vines that cover the side of that building. Or when the vines start to change color, reds and greens and browns. Or when you go back by that building one night, and you look up, and the vines are gone, and now all you can see are the marks in the paint where they once were. Which one of these means the most depends on what you're looking for.

The way there's the art, and its history, and then there's Gladys's history in creating the art, and then there's my history in witnessing and imagining her creation.

And then there's my history of writing about Gladys—I'm thinking about *Pulling Taffy*, my first novel. Here it is, on the bookshelf right next to my desk. I open it up with Gladys's art on my walls above. In the book I changed her name to Rose Stern. Because she loved flowers. Because she was stern. Not to me as a child, but later. To the world?

When my father was in college, he decided he wanted to be a writer. But when he announced this to Gladys, she said simply: Then you support yourself.

So he decided to go to medical school instead. Gladys told this anecdote proudly, over and over.

I don't believe it, though. Not exactly. I mean I believe she meant this as a threat, but also I believe he wasn't brave enough to reject her.

I mean he wasn't brave enough to reject the world. And she knew this. Does this make her threat more cruel, or less? If art is a gap in feeling, it's also a feeling of the gap.

When I asked Gladys how she saw herself in the context of twentieth-century art, she said, "I'm much better than Jackson Pollock—I'm not as good as Mark Rothko, because he did something different. I'm like Richard Diebenkorn, only maybe he was a better painter. But there are things I can do that I don't think anyone else can."

So you see, she wasn't modest. She compared herself to the famous men of her generation, why not. Women weren't allowed in that hallowed realm anyway. Not in the public record.

Unlike these famous men, Gladys did not gain national prominence, she did not influence generations of artists around the world, her work is not widely acclaimed, and she barely exists now in official memory, even in Baltimore. But, "there are things I can do that I don't think anyone else can." Isn't this the goal of every artist?

How Gladys would pick up a leaf from the street and ask me what I saw. And we could marvel at this together. Every leaf another pattern undoing the pattern, color as a way of experiencing the brightness of feeling.

And yet I see her cruelty, when she said to her only child, who was telling her he wanted to pursue a creative life: Then you support yourself. I see Gladys's cruelty, but also I see it as a dare.

Later, my father did write books, about psychiatry. I've never read those books, but after I remembered that my father sexually abused me, I went to a therapist who asked if it was okay to read one of my father's books. So he could understand him. This seemed strange to me, but I said sure. And then that therapist came back the next session and said he didn't think it was possible that my father could have sexually abused me, because the book was so rational.

The falling apart and coming together, the rupture and fusion, to see it all in this contained space—how the arrangement of color and pattern and texture creates so much emotion. To contain it, and let it go. You hold it up close, and suddenly you see the hills and valleys. Far away and the shapes become clearer.

But did that therapist say rational, or logical? If you have logic on your side, you have everything. So maybe my father had everything.

In *Pulling Taffy*, I write, "It's his eyes I remember; when he took off his glasses I'd scream, like in Rose's portrait of him . . . I fell in. In Rose's house, the paintings sing. The critics say: 'catapult.'"

Am I the critics now? Every paperwork a new discovery—this one in simple primary colors—red, yellow, and blue, on white—four straw pieces pulled from a decaying placemat that I remember, forming a broken and open square inside the white square of the paperwork itself, and crossing the colored squares underneath the white inside the larger square. It's almost like a Mondrian, actually. Did she mean it to be in dialogue with his work, or is this just something the critics say?

Mondrian was one of the artists that never moved me, I knew he was supposed to be great but I didn't know why. I would see his work in museums or on postcards but it all looked the same. So when Gladys told me he was the artist that impacted her the most, I was confused.

Then Gladys said Mondrian taught her how to paint white. Or did she say he taught her how to see white? And I hadn't even thought about the white in those paintings, I was just looking at the patterns.

How white is always a relationship to what's around it, but also how white is composed of what comes through, not an absence but a presence.

You stand up, and you look inside one of these silver almost-squares, a frame inside the frame, and there's a whole other work of art there, a complete world of movement and stasis, pleasure and softness, darkness and light. "Contained in almost all my paintings, there are three or four other paintings that I'm wasting," Gladys says to me in *Pulling Taffy*, and in this painting there are more than three or four.

The more I look at it, the more I find. When you have a relationship with a piece of art, there's loyalty involved, but there's also a depth of feeling, the way it shifts every time you look. Circle over circle over circle, but then you get closer, and each circle isn't a circle at all—the geometry of art created by the frame, the geometry inside the frame, but also art as the undoing of geometry.

It's not just Gladys's paintings that contain multiple works inside them, but her paperworks and collages, no matter how small. Maybe it's the accumulation that allows the composition to flow. If you look very closely at this candy wrapper collage, you can still see the word INGREDIENTS.

Gladys wanted the ingredients to show, she was not in search of perfection. But the perfection of letting imperfection show, this was a skill she cultivated.

In Gladys's art, there are always so many places to focus your attention—I can disappear into this world of her creation, reappear in a different shape. Even just looking at her signature in the bottom right corner, gold on black and where are all these specks of gold inside the black coming from? And how did she make handmade paper look like paint as if it's splattering, maybe she splattered the wet pulp on like paint and then pressed it down? With handmade paper the hands are always there, paper emulating feeling.

I can hold this paperwork up to the light, put it on a table under the light, or place it on a box on the floor, and still I can't figure out how she did everything. Art is always a mystery, even when it's not a mystery. How it affects us, or fails to. How we fail. How art fails us.

I don't know if she got up in the morning and said this is what I need to do, or if she got up in the morning and said this is what I need. I don't know if I need to know. But I know that I need.

I picture her climbing those steep stairs during the last weeks of her life, after she fell and broke her hip, her hand, her wrist, her finger. I mean she kept falling. Still, against everyone's advice, she climbed the stairs, so she could make more candy wrapper collages.

She had already made hundreds of them. What else was she trying to convey. That she hadn't already conveyed. Or was making art simply the process of living.

Am I wrong to say that sometimes, when you carry a piece of art, the art carries you? When there is a difference, and when there isn't. Like the birch tree in the front yard of the house where I grew up, I would peel it just to see, imagining this was how they discovered paper.

Sometimes I can't tell which side is the front, and which is the back, and sometimes Gladys blurred this distinction on purpose, when she noticed that both were their own pieces. I have a collage like this, and I want to see both sides. So I don't frame it.

Gladys didn't title most of her collages, but she did title the paintings—*Checkered Life. Touching Light. Day Dusk. Plus A. B Series II. Dawn. Light Square. Spring Star. Pastoral. Day Scape. Magic Day.* These are some of the paintings I have now.

As a writer, I notice how vague these titles are. They can say everything, or nothing. But then there's *Child's Play*, a painting she made in 1974, one year after I was born. There's no way this isn't about me. And there's no way I would know if she hadn't used that title.

See how she's recording our relationship, even before I possibly could. Recording me. Something between us. The light. I have this painting now, *Child's Play*. I see spaciousness and loss. I see a bright central present, a presence, a swiftness in the lines, a chaos, a stillness in the corner, collapse.

How there's a chain of command between color and line but everything stretches everywhere at once—there's a center, but it isn't necessarily central. How the metallic silver collaged parts expand the field. How magenta or yellow or orange brings your eyes down but somehow the lines between or beyond still create the momentum.

This is not a work primarily formed by geometry—there are shapes, but they are more like doodles into one another and so your attention constantly shifts—see that purple and red rectangle with partial yellow border? Maybe you stay there a while, noticing the triangles within, how no color is just one color, the translucence of the paint, but then maybe you're in that space at the center of the canvas where everything and nothing dissolves. No, the orange and yellow over there at left or the bleeding red and blue in the top corner. No, the silver collaged parts on purple pushing through gray, the red in orange in gold at the center, yes, there could be a figure on the right with arms not yet formed and this is how you see that it's the lines that win, inside and out, where lines become unlined, wait, that careful orange coming out of gold in purple, into more purple, back to gray into mauve into teal into orange and I think this would be, could be, my belly.

Gladys believed that child's play was the most intricate perfection—the art of children. Primitive, she would have said, which to her was the highest compliment, and I guess if you're using it to describe your one-year-old grandchild then this isn't as problematic as when you're describing Mexican street art, which she also called primitive. She had a little book in her studio called *Children as Artists* by R. R. Tomlinson—she was mesmerized by the images of art by children reproduced inside. This was the one book I took from her studio after she died, it was so small I could carry it with me on the train.

Tomlinson says that when artists invoke the primitive, they are not using it in the same way as an ethnographer to describe people they see as uncivilized, but to describe the early parts of a school of painting that would eventually become more clearly defined. But the colonial gaze has always been a part of abstract art in the European tradition, and invoking the primitive is part of this. Gladys wasn't thinking about the colonial gaze, she was thinking about children. What a child could provide for her. And isn't this its own form of colonization.

The pressure to resolve pressure. How the paperwork can look ragged, but when you touch the surface it's soft. The cracked shell of a quarter moon, one small torn piece of paper that somehow looks tie-dyed, light gray on charcoal into pink and blue leading up. But then if you hold it in another direction, suddenly it's the squares you see. Turn more, and it's the horizontal motion. Another look, and it's the textures pressed into the background. Is that ink? Almost like a fingerprint right underneath her signature, leading into the lace decaying off the page.

I keep saying page. When it's not a page. And yet here we are.

I'm wondering if there's an archive of Gladys's papers as part of the University of Maryland collection—my mother read her journals after she died, but there wasn't anything she was interested in so she threw everything out—all the papers in Gladys's house after she died—her notebooks and letters and records and receipts and boxes of ephemera, everything went into the trash. But are there papers in the University of Maryland collection that Gladys gave to them before she died?

Then I remember that I have my own files, including a file of all the letters Gladys sent to me. It's actually a pretty big folder—I open it up, and I see so many of the addresses where I used to live, some of which I'd forgotten. I'm tempted to put them all in order, but also I want to resist this temptation.

Oh, look—here's a photocopy of one of my letters to Gladys—March 31, 1993, postmarked from Berkeley, where I stayed for a few days in between San Francisco apartments. At this point in my life, I photocopied my letters because I didn't want to forget, I didn't want to forget anything, not anymore. On the outside of the envelope, I've written:

> for gladys goldstein
> who must bare herself to me & I will do the
>   same (to/for her)

And, on the back of the envelope:

> <u>the deal</u>
>
> a week (yours/mine) in san francisco
>   for
> a week (mine/yours) in baltimore

In 1992, I dropped out of the elite college I'd spent my life working toward because I realized this wasn't where I would learn what I needed—I found what I needed across the country in San Francisco with queers and direct action activists and vegans and anarchists, sluts and whores and runaways and incest survivors, dreamers and outsiders and druggies and club kids and freaks and flamers, all of us together and apart, trying to create a world that didn't just reenact harm.

In 1993, I've enrolled in a class at City College called Lesbian/Gay Influence on Modern American Art and Culture, not for credit but to learn the queer history that I've been denied, and we're discussing Abstract Expressionism, and I realize this is Gladys's generation—she was painting at the time, and so I write to ask her "how were you influenced—& then of course connections you had/have & so this, you may consider your first (formal) invitation to visit me."

She never visited me in San Francisco, not once during the fourteen years that I lived there over the course of two decades—I'm not quite sure why. Maybe it felt too far? But she never visited me in New York, either, and New York for her was a familiar place. I wonder if she felt threatened by my life, what she might find if she came to me instead of just seeing me when I visited her.

In *Pulling Taffy*, I write about one of those visits—Gladys drops me off at the Jewish Community Center to use the gym. I tell her "I felt like an alien. I say it's like I dropped you off for a few hours at a nursing home in Wyoming," but Gladys "doesn't understand what it means to be straight."

I remember thinking about my wording here, the question of what it means to be straight—even though Gladys was around plenty of gay artists, I don't know if she ever struggled to fully understand their world. Which makes me more curious about Keith Martin, Gladys's best friend, his papers are archived at Syracuse University. Browsing the inventory of his papers online, I see Gladys listed in the general-correspondence box. But the only letter I see in the index is from "Gladys and Ed," both of my grandparents, so it's probably not personal.

In the biography for Keith Martin, it mentions a "reminiscence of Gertrude Stein," and correspondence with Alice B. Toklas, so he must have been connected to the queer intelligentsia of the time. Gladys always emphasized Keith Martin's prominence in the Baltimore art world. She gave my parents three Keith Martin drawings of ballerinas, and she had a sculpture of his in a glass case, also of a ballerina, but the rest of his work that she owned she kept out of sight. I found a few of his pieces when I went to her house after she died—my mother was planning to throw them out.

I kept two of them, one an abstract work of black ink on paper, *Letter to a Friend #3*, from 1956, and another a paper collage, from 1967, strips of paper cut vertically and pasted together with a movement formed by the layering, and taped together at the top, with the tape visible. It was on some decaying mat originally, so I removed it, and now it's floating on a white background with a black mat, and I love having these mementos of Gladys's relationship with this gay artist, someone she loved and presumably accepted. But I wonder if some of this acceptance had to do with the fact that his art did not connect in an immediately discernible way to his experience as a gay man.

So maybe when I say I wonder if Gladys ever struggled fully to understand Keith Martin's world, I mean my world. Because as soon as I came into my own as a writer, as soon as my work became noticeably queer, sexually and politically saturated, she called it vulgar. Why are you wasting your talent, she would ask me, over and over, until it became a refrain.

Gladys did visit me once, in Boston in 1995. She came with my other grandmother, Fran, even though they weren't friends. I write about this visit in *Pulling Taffy*, where Fran becomes Florence.

> Florence and Rose aren't drag queens, but they might be able to pass: Florence with the Chanel choker and Fendi bag, Hermès scarf which reads Chanel. Rose with pink-red hair and drawn-in eyebrows that don't quite match. You can almost see them saying *Honey*—these tits are *real*.

So this is probably what Gladys thought was vulgar. Although she started thinking this earlier, with the chapbook I made when I first moved to San Francisco, when I was nineteen, and I was working my way out of Language Poetry and into something that would reflect more of my experience.

But wait, I'm reading this chapter, "Florence and Rose," and then: "Rose guesses it, says Florence can't you tell he was raped?"

"Florence is shocked"—and now I'm shocked too, because I totally forgot this. I wouldn't have remembered this without this book. How writing can be a record.

"Rose is worried: Matthew are you sure you *know* who it is?"

See, Gladys already knows it's my father. Even though we haven't talked about it.

It's possible that when she visited me in Boston in 1995, I was getting ready to confront my father, and it's possible that I wasn't getting ready yet. I know I spent months writing a fifteen-page letter describing what I remembered, how the abuse had harmed me, how I was healing, and telling him I would never speak to him again unless he acknowledged sexually abusing me. And I sent that letter to my four grandparents and my sister by Express Mail the day before I planned to confront my father—he was a psychiatrist, a master at manipulation, so I wanted everything to be on paper. So he couldn't twist anything around.

When Gladys received the letter, she called me up and said: Are you sure this happened?

And I said yes.

And she said: How am I supposed to go on living?

She went on living, and she did not support me—it was my father's pain she was worried about. Fran came the closest to acknowledging his abuse with her immediate reaction, when she said: It must have been him, because there was never anyone else around.

But then she courted my father for a relationship—they would get together one-on-one for lunch, which was something they had never done before. She would call to tell me that things would be so much easier for me if I would just patch things up with my father. But her hypocrisy was no surprise to me. She had never pretended to care about much beyond money and status and image.

It did surprise me when I realized how much Gladys also believed in class striving and upward mobility. But middle-class security gave her the freedom to create. She was never going to leave that, and she didn't want me to leave it either.

It didn't surprise me that Gladys supported my father and abandoned me when I confronted him about sexually abusing me, since I knew that most families support the abuser. But this didn't mean it hurt less.

I didn't acknowledge this pain, because there was too much other pain. How do I acknowledge it now?

I look up at the painting above my computer, and there are ladders to climb to the sky. For a long time I didn't want any of Gladys's art, even though I'd always loved it, because I thought it would just make me sad. Because of who she became. Who she became for me. Just another barrier to overcome.

But then, on one of my visits, I chose a few of her candy wrapper collages, and she framed them for me, and when I put them up on my walls I felt that light in my eyes. How a piece of straw escapes the frame or the paper itself all shaky at the edges or just the imperfections remaining, the softness of an uneven border.

A world without borders is nothing Gladys would have invoked, but I come to it here anyway. The way the texture of light re-forms the visual experience which becomes sensual, the way a big motion of the hands becomes an expansion in the chest, or I step up to look at this one place where something that might be a pen-and-ink drawing, black lines in geometric shapes, or it might be a piece of wrapping paper, whatever it is unfurls on top of a gold diamond, a kite in the air about to lift into the sky, let's go.

The paradox of abstract art is that everything can be present when nothing is represented. When I study the texture, it's a dream unwinding. How I can feel so broken, and then look into the art and feel something else.

How you look again at the brown, and there's so much red that maybe it's more of a maroon, a burgundy, a purple, and suddenly I remember how Gladys would take the dryer lint and blend it in with paper pulp to create some of her colors. She was looking for beauty in the everyday, in every way, and yet she also felt like art had to transcend experience.

Gladys even sent me a letter when I was visiting JoAnne in Seattle for a month in 1994, a few months before I turned twenty-one. I'm struck by the first line, where she says, "Have a good vacation—you sound good——relaxed!" Because I always think of that month I spent with JoAnne as the first time I ever felt relaxed. But I don't think I would have told Gladys this. Somehow she just felt it. She heard it in my voice.

"That artist," she writes, and suddenly I remember going to a Basquiat show at the Henry Art Gallery at the University of Washington—I remember going to that show because it moved me so much. And here Gladys is telling me he was exploited, as if I didn't know, and then she mentions taking a photo of graffiti in Paris—why Paris? "It was gorgeous—as a child's work is gorgeous—as yours was. But we all have to grow up sometime. Only Klee grew up to equal his childhood work and still be a 'wonder' child."

She's lecturing me, but at the same time is there a kind of sadness that "we all have to grow up sometime," if only Paul Klee "grew up to equal his childhood work"?

Gladys liked to tell a story from my birth. They brought me into the waiting room to see her, and she was smoking. I started coughing right away. And that's when she decided to quit smoking. So our lives were connected right from the beginning. That's what she's painting in *Child's Play*—her relationship with my movement and the air, a cyclical progression, a succession. I'm already trying on selves—or, she's trying them on for me.

In *Pulling Taffy*, when Gladys says to Fran, "can't you tell he was raped," Fran is shocked. And then Gladys turns to me, "are you sure you *know* who it is?"

Fran is annoyed: "Of course he knows who it is."

So then Gladys changes the subject: "Where are we going for dinner?"

And it's actually a dinner I remember the most, one dinner in particular, or maybe it was lunch. I remember exactly what I wore—a tiny plaid polyester shirt that was purple, blue, and red on white, which matched and clashed with the colors of my hair, and then plaid polyester cut-off shorts that, now that I think about it, came from the same pants I wore in that photo shoot at Gladys's house a few years before. And then fluorescent plaid thigh-highs, and combat boots.

I remember the outfit, because both Fran and Gladys were furious about it. They asked why I was trying to shock them. But I wasn't trying to shock them, I was letting them in. At the restaurant, I showed them pictures from the photo booth at the big gay club where I went dancing every Sunday, and they asked if I was a transvestite. I told them that language was outdated.

Provocative, that was the word they used. Are you just trying to be provocative? That was a phrase my parents used when they were arguing. My father was always trying to provoke everyone in the family, that was his game. Provoke you until you completely lost it. This was what he wanted. So then he could act surprised. Surely you were overreacting.

Eventually I learned to gaze through him when he was screaming at me, maybe I was looking at one of Gladys's paintings on the wall behind him. I remember the shimmering one in the dining room that kind of looked like an abstract menorah, because of the ways Gladys used the foil collaged over the paint. It's in my mother's bedroom now. Although I don't know if Gladys meant is as a menorah, since she was never religious. We would drive past the Orthodox neighborhood near where she lived in Baltimore, and she would shake her head in disapproval at the people outside in their front yards or on their way to temple—isn't that ridiculous, she would say. Then we would drive through the neighborhood where she said all the rich Jews lived, it was hilly and wooded and you could hardly see the houses except when a driveway came into view, and you might catch a glimpse of sleek glass modernism. She didn't exactly approve of these Jews either, but she would describe their houses if they collected her art, which paintings they had on display and what else they collected, especially if there were famous artists on the walls beside her.

After Gladys died, my mother asked me and my sister to pick the paintings we wanted, so she could put them in storage until we had a place for them. And she sold the rest at auction—hundreds of paintings, collages, drawings, and paperworks. She thought she was going to make a lot of money, but it definitely didn't turn out that way.

Even if I would never have a place to hang some of those paintings,

I would rather keep them in storage or give them away to people who loved them than sell them for fifty or a hundred or two hundred dollars to art speculators. My mother even sold the painting I was most attached to, one of the ones I put aside. She sent me the catalog for the auction, and there it was, on the cover.

But just when I'm despairing about this auction, I come back to a sentence about Gladys in *Pulling Taffy*: "She's busy devaluing her art, wants the creditors to say what is this junk?" This conversation would have been from the late '90s, but I remember it from before as well. She was worried that my father would have to pay too much in taxes after she died. She was obsessed with this. Was he obsessed with this too, I'm not sure. There was this whole plan about getting the art out of the house before the auditors came, something like that. But do auditors really just show up at your house?

And then my father died of cancer while Gladys was still alive. After that, her ideas shifted. She wanted my mother to sell her art, which made no sense because my mother was not an art dealer. It was like Gladys was testing her. And my mother tried to play this role, because she thought she would make money. So they were both doomed.

Gladys had a long career that began in the 1950s, but she cut all ties with her dealer at some point in the '80s. I always assumed Gladys stopped showing her work in galleries because of the corruption of the art world, but then later, when I asked her about this, she said oh no, the people in the art world are the most generous people in the world.

How she thought I would believe this, I have no idea. Probably she just wanted another opportunity to tell me I was wrong.

This was on the same trip when I was on a book tour in 2004, and half of my belongings were stolen from the trunk of a rental car. So I went with Gladys to a mall in the Baltimore suburbs to buy socks and underwear, and of course people were staring, but then one of the salespeople complimented me on my style, and somehow this was what Gladys was appalled by. That someone liked what they saw.

The next day I remember standing in Gladys's bedroom, next to the mirror that took up a whole wall, while she told me that my earrings were ugly. My earrings arranged like a mosaic. I knew there was no way she thought they were ugly. It was just that she didn't want me to stand out in this way. It was my queerness that was ugly to her.

The way this paperwork is ripped at the top, and pieces of straw connect through the rip like thread. And then there's straw in the paper too, right beneath the surface, ground up inside, with glittery beads from broken necklaces tumbling down into the pale blue. I have some of those beads now, in a crystal jar. The jar was also hers, now it's on a glass shelf in my bathroom. When I sift through the sparkling beads I feel like a child again, not the child in trauma but the child who can still dream, in spite of the trauma, and this was the gift Gladys gave me.

Look at this paperwork above my bedroom dresser—it consists of four pieces, squares. The two at the bottom are separate, but the two at the top connect with one thin strand of paper. The unity of color and form—blacks and blues and reds, matte and shiny. The explosion of the circles inside the squares. The dialogue between each element. The way the elements are the same in every square, but used in different ways. How the shiny crinkled red foil might dominate in a particular light, or the blue in another. The way the red beads are still on the string, draped inside a circle while unraveling.

I open another card in my file of letters, undated. It just says: "All of the things you wish for—be happy."

And it does make me happy.

The meaning of abstract art is it's yours to imagine. If I recreate my relationship with Gladys from touching her abstraction, mesh embedded into white paper, decaying lace, straw spilling off the edges, marbleized tears, what meaning do I find in a stillness that creates calm, allows for breath, softens the air. You take in the colors, but it's the white that stands out. Gladys says to me: "I spent a year trying to make a white that was warm enough for the sun."

When I notice the black line of a scarf embedded into a paperwork, thin white paper on top and ripped at the center to reveal faded flowers, I gasp. It must be a really thin scarf because the paper still feels fragile, delicate, light. Or actually, when I pick it up I can feel a heaviness, even if it's an intentionally thin handmade paper. And there's a melancholy to this piece in a way that's different from the others. The ripped red of the scarf like a gash. The faded pink as if it's been slowly decaying over the years.

But what really feels disturbing, somehow, are the beads embedded inside the paper, trapped. And these two round shells at the top look like they're trying to get through stitches. Even the gold leaf that emerges in tiny places feels more like longing than celebration.

If I hold it up in one particular direction, I see a pink tone to the white shells that I didn't notice before, how it plays off the flowers in the scarf. How the rips in the paper allow the scarf to emerge, but also they hold it down. How there's so much tonal quality just in the black paper pulp, and I'm thinking about dryer lint, how I was looking at mine, and it keeps coming out gray—I remember Gladys creating whole pots of blue and red and pink, and did this happen randomly, or did she wash her clothes with that intent in mind, after discovering the possibility.

Actually I have a video of her making paper. When I watched it the first time, I was disappointed—it didn't feel like her. She was wearing too much makeup, and everything felt staged. And the quality of the video was so bad, even though it originally aired on public television—maybe something about the transition from its original format to DVD, I'm not sure.

But I want to see her hands in the wet paper again.

The video is called *Goldworks: The Art of Gladys Goldstein*, and it starts with some terrible classical flute music, and then there's one of her diamond-shapes. You can see the darkness and light of the colors, but everything is overexposed, distorted, which distracts me because I can't appreciate the art. Of course I have her work in other forms, other photos, and then I have the actual art, but also I want to see these pieces too, like this first one I don't remember, and I don't know where it is now—I want to experience it again not just from my imagination. But do you see how I've paused the video, after only five seconds? Probably this is going to happen a lot.

Okay, back to this horrible flute music. And then there's the same white pegboard in her studio that's in the background of the pictures she took of me, and is that one of the paintings she used then too? I think that one's in the University of Maryland collection, let me look in the catalog—oh, here's the one I'm thinking of, *Signals*, from 1981, it's another painting from her Emotional Squares series.

The university used *Signals* in the poster commemorating the retrospective in 2004, and then years later my mother decided she wanted it in her living room. So she tried to get them to trade it to her for another painting, but they weren't interested. They had already chosen the works for the collection. But my mother was very persistent. And this is what led to their falling out. Eventually they returned all the paintings on permanent loan. Which is how I have so much of Gladys's art now.

In the catalog there are quotes from Gladys's notebooks—I hope these aren't the notebooks my mother threw away, I hope they have them in the collection. Gladys says, "To get away from being too emotional I decided to be more geometric."

She wanted to get away from being too emotional, but then she called the series Emotional Squares.

What is too emotional, anyway? Especially when you're talking about a painting.

Gladys writes, "a piece of paper left to the elements will rot, but if gently handled, it can become a permanent part of a work of art." Which makes me feel better about the damage to these paperworks I have now. Like the one that's too crumpled at the center to be intentional, with one piece turned around, it looks like it's getting in the way. So I tear it off. I think it looks better now, more like she intended, but how could I ever know?

Now I have two tiny scraps of handmade paper by my computer—I put one in my mouth, and it feels like it's dissolving. But really it's just wrapping around my lip. I pull it out, and once it dries it looks the same. I put it back in my mouth. There isn't really any taste, only texture. The glory of natural materials.

Oh, a slight bitterness to this other scrap. Wait, this paperwork with the scarf embedded inside is called *Bethany X*. So this piece that feels so mournful to me is named after the beach town where we went on vacation as a family every summer. Did Gladys notice the family dynamics more closely then? My father's rage, how my parents were always arguing, the damage to me and my sister. Or was she only trying to convey the turbulence of the ocean? The faded scarf like that surprise you find when the waters recede, your hands sifting through the sand.

Oh, I see here, in the catalog, not just that she didn't want to be too emotional, but "too sky-bound."

Are we looking up, or looking away. Too external, or too eternal? How I keep stopping and starting this video, and then going back to the beginning, and today I even like this flute music, it's taking me somewhere.

"I don't believe in themes," she says, "you know, it just happens. I do believe in structure in painting, so I have to have the structure, and it's usually a geometric form. And after that, I can become emotional if I want to."

I wonder if this applies to the rest of her life too, how she utilized the conventional structure of marriage in order to support her art. Unlike so many of the women now known for trying to create an artist's life at the time, she was the dominant one in her marriage. Maybe because she wasn't in a relationship with an artist. Maybe because she wasn't in New York.

Oh, here's the painting called *Night Jazz*, with jazz playing in the video. My mother said she would send me this one, but then she couldn't find it. "The feelings of things are more real than the things themselves," Gladys says. "The sound is what happens. And a painting to me is what happens."

Wait, she's about to walk into her living room. I have to rewind this. Here she is now, paused on her way. To the living room. Her living room in 1988, when I was in high school. I'm getting chills.

And looking into Ed's bedroom with the door open, there's that painting of me at age six, wearing Fran's long pink scarf. It started with a photo. Was the photo from the same day when I walked out of Fran's building, and someone said you have a beautiful daughter. And she didn't correct them. Because she was flattered they thought she was so young.

And Gladys chose this picture emphasizing my femininity as inspiration. She even got the trauma right. I loved flowers, and here they surround me, but can I even tell? That tulip is so close to my hand, and yet I'm looking so far away.

And there's my grandfather's huge dictionary, sitting on the dresser in front of the painting. I forgot about that dictionary. What words did I find there?

And the living room, with the same furniture, I'm trying to get a closer look but then we're back in the studio, with *Pastoral*, which now I have in the lobby of my building. This is the first painting that really looks beautiful to me in the video, how you can almost see through the papers that form the squares on the canvas, all the layers of green.

Pastoral as a title for this abstract layering of green squares and the spaces under and between, as if to make an idyllic landscape from the light coming through tissue paper collaged onto canvas. Is this title meant as a critique, or invocation?

But let me go back to Gladys's entrance, her entrance in this video. She appears in a beige button-down linen shirt and gray trousers because she believed in wearing neutrals—she's wearing dangly earrings and sandals, saying "Painting is like a philosophy."

And here she is lifting paintings in her studio—I love seeing her doing something so habitual, picking up a big painting and throwing it on the wall, saying "So when you shift the light, the painting changes. And that to me is kind of exciting."

This is when I feel like I'm there.

What I see and what I feel and what I remember, but is there something beyond? The diagonals in this paperwork that make me want to go back to those other diagonals behind my naked chest. If there's desire here, looking at my chest in this photo so pale and soft and smooth, boxers visible above pants falling down, black nails and silver bracelets, yes, I can imagine myself kissing up the line between belly button and chest up to neck to lips and then pressing my whole body against my body, and what am I desiring? There's desire to hold, and there's desire to help, and then there's just desire that's desire, and this is all three.

The way language can open up, can open up to hold me. There's the light of the night, and then there's the light that conjures the night, and then there's just the night. How silver can be gray and charcoal and white and steel, gold hues quivering out. I put the paper in my mouth again, and this time it tastes really bitter. Maybe because I'm chewing on it, now it's a tiny little ball. How the moment in these photos was the moment when I was ready to let breath in. Maybe that's why I took off my shirt. Because I was no longer afraid.

But I realize I'm getting the date wrong on these photos. They're from a year later, when I'm twenty—I can tell now, because of the style of my hair, the style I chose after abandoning the fluorescent goth bob. I still have the fluorescent colors and the shaved part underneath, dyed black, but my hair is shorter, razor-cut into those jagged edges I wanted for everything.

But when did I remember I was sexually abused by my father, before this trip or after? I don't know the exact date of the trip, but I do know when I remembered I was sexually abused. It's in my journal— September 19, 1993. Zee, my first boyfriend, is writing that first flashback down for me. This is what I'm saying:

> layers of dots
> bright fluorescent blue, lavender, green in chains
> layers and layers round
> connected, thousands of them
> move 3-D not on one plane
> haven't seen them in 10 years
> couldn't go to sleep because of dots
> call my mother and I don't remember what she
> said. put my head in pillow and there
> would be more and more of them

everything in the room is flickering
everything in the room is shaking slightly really quickly
like watching a movie that doesn't work.
static dots here and there in clothing, etc
I used to think that it had something to do with the sun
when I learned about atoms somehow I thought the
dots related to that, I mean I knew atoms were much
smaller, but somehow I thought I was seeing the structure of things. I used to think that the dots had something to do with shutting my eyes too tightly.

How beautiful of Zee to write this down for me so I could stay in the
feeling of this flashback I didn't yet understand. And now I have this record. "I wish I had a tape recorder, because this isn't really working," I'm
telling him, but now I know it was working. September 19, 1993. There's
a question mark after 19, so it could be September 20 or 21. If I turn back
a few pages I see that I'm upset because Zee is suggesting I might have
been abused because I can't be touched in certain places. How beautiful
to have a boyfriend at nineteen or twenty, now we're twenty, we're both
twenty, how beautiful to have a boyfriend at that age who could identify
this. And then I continue writing after he stops:

I was looking at Zee, or the outline of his face and everything was shifting backwards although his face was
outlined by light and the eyes, the extra dimension
being the dots weaving around and through things
and the eyes on my wall, surrounding me—my worst
childhood experience—waking up screaming and crying and my mother would soothe me back to sleep the
faces in the blue/navy blanket the evil rocking chair the
night I was pulled off my bunkbed afraid of the dark
had to keep my head under the covers, run for the light,
thinking the dots had something to do with how I shut
my eyes too tightly. Feeling at first like this was a drug
flashback, but I couldn't identify the state—filled with
horror, so eerie fatalistic and then I realized it was my

childhood—completely blocked out—why? Something
is being hidden is something being hidden, is it something to do with my father his naked body . . .

Bethany X with those busted eyes, I realize that's what the buried
beads outside the circles make me think of, something growing rotting
something rotting growing. Still that scarf and memory submerged like
a wave. I wonder if, when Gladys numbered a piece, this always meant
there were others, or if the others were just ideas or discarded pieces. I
mean are there really ten paperworks in the *Bethany* series? I've never
found a series of more than four.

Another letter, from about a year before the photos. A year before
I remembered I was sexually abused. Gladys is trying to convince me
that I'm wrong to leave college. Even just for a semester, which is what I
would have said at the time.

"I can't believe that you discussed your decision to take time out
with anyone who cared about you," Gladys writes. She tells me she au-
dited a one-year class on propaganda in the 1950s, and accuses me of
being manipulated.

"The whole idea of college is to be able to gain knowledge that will
create a desire to 'think,'" Gladys writes, but this is the propaganda I'm
rejecting. I've finally found the friends who will hold me in all my beauty
and complications. I've finally figured out how to dream of unlearning
trauma. No one is going to tell me what to do. No one is going to tell me
how to be. I am not my father, who could be bullied. Who became the
bully. I am going to unlearn all of this.

So when I read this letter from Gladys now, all my anger at her returns. I can totally see myself on the phone with her while she's telling
me I'm ruining my life, telling me that my friends are worthless, telling
me that I don't know what I'm doing, telling me that she's learned her
lesson and she wants to pass this wisdom on to me, telling me that she
should have finished school instead of leaving to become an artist—all
of this condescension and manipulation just to try to get me to do something that is the opposite of what I need.

When I talked to my sister and my mother about this book for the
first time, they both emphasized Gladys's cruelty. My mother said flatly:

"She wasn't a good person." My sister talked about how Gladys controlled our grandfather, how she kept him subservient.

But when my mother and sister mentioned this, I felt myself shrinking away. For so many years I'd endured Gladys's judgment and dismissal—every time we talked on the phone, she just wanted to tell me that everything I was doing was wrong. When I started working on this book, I wanted to focus on the tenderness I was feeling.

I didn't want my father in this book, not at all. But where would I be without him. He was Gladys's prized creation, he gave her status in a world that did not believe in women or art—he was a Jewish doctor, in her mind there was nothing above that. She was mesmerized by his success, she kept his degrees framed in her bedroom, just to the side of her makeup table, so that every day when she got ready she would have his accomplishments with her. She displayed his books in her living room, where there were rarely any other books, among the minerals and treasures she collected, multiple copies on three different tables, even though no one was going to read them. They were only for practicing clinicians. But she needed to display them, to show the world that this was her son.

So if I write about her art without him I'm just telling a lie. When I was a child she gave me a way to imagine hope, but before that she gave me him. How else would we have met?

When Gladys told me that if she could do it all over again, she would have finished school, I felt like she was renouncing her entire life, everything I respected about her, in order to get me to follow a narrow path toward upward mobility and elitist attainment. I was shocked, because I had always looked to her as a model for something else. She had chosen the life of an artist as a woman against the odds. She had mastered her craft and spent decades perfecting her techniques of intuitive composition. She had developed a vast body of work based on endless experimentation.

When I was a child, Gladys offered me the tools to imagine myself outside of normalcy. And yet, once I came into my own self, she wanted to put me back in that stifling space. But it was too late. She didn't realize all she had given me.

So I want to mark this place where our relationship crumbled, even as I'm writing a book about how our relationship endures. But this is a relationship through her art. This book wouldn't exist if Gladys were alive, because I wouldn't have realized I missed her.

She wanted to control who I would become, but I wouldn't let her. So our relationship did not survive, not in a meaningful way. Still, when I look at her art, I feel an inquisitive sense of joy. Even just to look at how she ended the embedded texture in this piece just before the bottom, which is so smooth. And there's her signature, so careful in pencil here. Connecting with the pencil in the collage at the center, and that cloud of dryer lint that starts or ends in a pink tissue paper effect and if I press my lips to the paper I can feel the grooves.

What is it about Gladys's art that creates a sense of wonder? How, after looking at her art, I can feel this way when I look at anything—this is the place in me that she helped to create.

My mother says her impression of Gladys will probably always be entirely negative—for a while after Gladys died, she was in my mother's dreams—she wanted her out of her dreams.

Back to the jazzy music of the video intro—it's only an eight-minute program, but I don't think I've gotten past the third minute yet. It's almost a ritual, watching the way the camera introduces the paintings, and then Gladys's voice: "I don't believe in themes, you know, it just happens."

And here I am, searching through the themes. The screens. The screams. The self-expression beyond self-possession, beyond self, beyond "the feeling of things." Wait, I almost missed her entrance, just before two minutes in, let me rewind.

How art can be delicate, and art can be strong. How delicacy can be a strength. How this can be true of people too. Did I learn this from Gladys?

Even when you're not making art, you're seeing what will become art. How intuition is a skill that you can only develop if you are always paying attention. When I was a child, Gladys told me creativity meant everything. I believed this myth, and it saved me.

In the video, Gladys throws that painting in the air like it's nothing, she's been doing this for so long and it's not like she's about to stop now. How old is she here? I'm looking through the catalog, but I can't find her birthdate—probably she didn't want them to publish it. But by 1988, when this video aired on public television, she was about seventy.

She says, "So when you shift the light, the painting changes," and then they show the same painting in shifting light, and it really does look completely different every time the light changes.

And here she is on the floor of her studio, saying, "When I get that blank canvas in front of me I go crazy, I can't wait to get something on it." She says she's establishing the mood and the color first, while she throws color onto the canvas, and when I pause I look at that worn-out floor that she's used to make so many paintings.

I still miss that studio. The way I felt there. Maybe that's the way I'm feeling now.

Here she is moving her hands through a tub of wet paper pulp, now she's in the paper-making studio that she shared with other artists—I remember driving there with her, going up Falls Road toward down-town Baltimore, and then under an overpass and behind a bunch of warehouses, and there it was, something magic. She dips the paper mold into the tub, I love all that texture. What a soft blue in one, and then she presses it onto the table and it looks white.

"It's very hard to find anything new for a painter, because he still has a flat surface and he's still working in a flat manner across the canvas and I like the challenge of having the paper, it can give you another kind of feeling without being a sculpture."

And here we watch as she layers a circle on top of a square on top of a square, forming a V, with two rectangles at the bottom. Here she is in action in her white button-down shirt, sleeves carefully rolled up, a black striped scarf tied at the neck and a white apron with words across it in black. She looks exactly like you might imagine an artist might look for the camera, and here she is, for the camera.

She uses a bucket lid on top of the paper screen to create a circle, that's all, now I remember that. And then she throws gold leaf into the wet paper and creates one of those broken circles by placing two half circles onto a small square paper mold. This video is longer than I thought, almost nine minutes already and I want to get to the end, I want to get to the end so I can go back to the beginning and start again. So I can arrive at this place where I see her hands covered in all that goo, creating something magnificent.

"As the painting changes," she says, "you change with it. You start out with one idea, and then something else happens."

And that's how I write. The form emerges from the act of writing.

And here Gladys rips off some of the white paper, and then adds one of those number stencils we found at the button factory, and places the paperwork into the press. She turns the press to tighten it, and says, "The truth is that it doesn't make a difference how you do a painting, or what you use in it, as long as the end result is a work of art."

But what is a work of art? She doesn't tell us.

After I confronted my father about sexually abusing me, my parents became closer. My mother had been threatening divorce since my childhood. But no longer.

My mother found a false memory syndrome specialist to advise them, and then the whole family gathered regularly for sessions with him at Gladys's house. If my memories were false, then their lies could become real. For years, my mother tried to convince me to fly out to Baltimore for these sessions. Or even just to schedule phone appointments on my own. Because this therapist was so caring, that's what she said. He gathered them all together and assured them that I was the problem. They had to bring me back to the family.

Legacy isn't just what forms you, it's how the forms restrict.

To the right, the upside-down black letters from a margarine wrapper on the gold almost-square that dominates the center. Not all the letters, but enough for you to know what it is. So many colors and textures of gold inside this gold, how the layering of the silver wrappers that surround it creates a stage for language.

Not language, just words. Broken down, curling, unfurling.

So much of the art that enters hallowed ground once came from trash. Or it was described as trash, like in this photocopied advertisement from the New York Foundation for the Arts that Gladys sent me, which says, "Some art is controversial. Some unfathomable. Much of it is beautiful and sensitive and makes us feel deeply. Few people like it all, nor should they."

And also, "Artists aspire to create new forms, pursue emotional truth, explore the unexplored."

But still my work remained unfathomable to her. She never came to my readings when I was in Baltimore, and I don't think she read any of my books. I'm not sure if she even looked at them.

When I went to her house after she died, I realized how much it would have meant to me if she'd engaged with my work. As an artist. And I wanted to preserve this space where I still felt such a sense of freedom. Even though I knew my mother was going to sell the house, I started to fantasize about making it into an artists' residency. Wouldn't Gladys's studio be an incredible place for other artists to work?

And then there could also be a writer in residence, living downstairs with that separate entrance and bathroom, and a desk already set up by the window. And in the third bedroom, where I stayed as a child, would be the live-in artist caretaker. The living room and dining room could host artists' talks and discussions, and the house would exhibit a rotating collection of Gladys's work.

I knew my mother would never do this, but I suggested it anyway. And then she sold the house.

My mother inherited the house and its contents, including Gladys's art, but my sister and I inherited the rest of the estate. This inheritance changed my life because it allowed me to pay my basic living expenses without worrying.

After my father's death four years before, when my mother inherited everything, I asked her to create an account like this, and she said yes. I talked to her financial planners, and they said no problem.

But my mother never created this account, because she changed her mind. For two years, she kept saying yes, until eventually her financial planners told me she said no.

My mother was the executor of Gladys's estate, and so for a year I wondered whether I would actually inherit what was promised to me, but eventually it happened. While I have never aspired to middle-class ideals, financial stability helps me to write, because it helps me to live. In this sense, Gladys helped me to write this book.

When I was a kid, and I knew I wanted to be a writer, Gladys told me that many of the best writers never got published. So when I sent my poems to *The Paris Review* as a teenager because they said they wanted to discover new voices, and of course they rejected my work, this did not discourage me. Maybe it even made me more confident. Because so many of the best writers never got published.

I don't know that Gladys said this to encourage me, but it was probably the best thing anyone could have told me. Publishing was something extra, once places finally started accepting my work—it was exciting because I could connect to other writers and anyone who read my work, but it was not the primary reason for writing. That was just for me. It still is.

In a Maryland Public Television show called *Artworks This Week*, Gladys says, "I really cannot remember when I started to paint, because I've always painted."

This interview celebrates the opening of Gladys's collection at the University of Maryland in 2004. And here she is, painting in her studio on a canvas hanging from that same pegboard, now in her late eighties.

"I don't really feel that I'm an abstract painter," she says. "I think that I'm a realistic painter, because I'm painting what I see as a realistic meaning in art, which is the space that surrounds all of us. So that's what I'm painting, I'm painting the things between you and me."

She's painting a realistic meaning.

But how do you paint meaning?

Abstractly.

If I'm painting the things between Gladys and me, is this the space that surrounds us?

The title of Gladys's retrospective at the University of Maryland is *Capturing the Essence*, and she explains, "How do you paint the wind? You capture the essence of that particular thing, or you try."

I wasn't thinking about the wind, but then I put these two paper-works side by side, and I notice there's a similar shape that dominates, or not a shape, but a counterclockwise circular movement at the top left. In one the break is literally a rip in the paper, and in the other the break is where the paper darkens—does this look like a rip because of the other rip, because of the lighting in my apartment right now, or because of the light that Gladys wanted to come through?

Coincidence creates a conversation between works of art, but also art can be a conversation. If you're listening. And maybe even when you're not. As if paper can pull out of paper to become bark.

I have a collage in the entryway to my apartment that used to be in Gladys's entryway—it's one of her most elaborate compositions, the layers of paper and glue bending the collage up toward the glass. So you can see the shape, the tension and extension. Matte browns and tans with flowers and foil and shapes on top, words from cut-up labels, articles from magazines, at least four languages visible if you look close. But the language here is in the visual layering, the way each shape is cut apart to meet what it was cut from.

Sometimes Gladys fell in love with a collage, and realized oh, there's a painting here. So she used this collage as a model for one of her largest paintings in the University of Maryland collection, *Page IV*, a diptych that's 48 inches by 120 inches. I hold the image from the catalog up to the collage in my entryway that's about the same size as the reproduction, or half of the reproduction that spans two pages, and I can see how each segment in the collage is in dialogue with the matching segment on the left half of the diptych.

Art as a container of art. Or do I mean a container for art?

Another letter—this one Gladys sent to me in East Boston in the summer of 1995. Oh, no—the first sentence: "Please write and tell me that you are doing something meaningful."

I'm getting ready to confront my father about sexually abusing me. It's right around the corner.

When I confronted him, I thought I would feel relief, but actually where I felt relief was in the process of getting ready.

He was screaming, he was calling me psychotic, he was saying I needed help, and I handed him what I'd written, and said: Everything I need to say is here. And then I walked away. I was worried he was going to come after me. I was worried he was going to attack me. I knew this was a childhood fear, and so I did not look back.

Gladys writes, "There was someone in my life who really changed it. His name was Hobson Pittman. I went to Penn State to study with him, because I had heard that he was a wonderful teacher, and I was interested in the methodology of teaching. It was a toss-up between him and Hans Hofmann. Hobson was the more liberal in his views. He told me I was an artist—a bona fide artist!"

I like the exclamation mark here, marking the disbelief turning into belief.

Gladys continues: "Well—I had been to art school—been the best in my class—but that doesn't make one an artist. He was the first person—and the only person—who supported me in my beliefs. He asked to be the one to tell me when the university decided to buy one of my paintings. We became friends until the day he died.

"He was homosexual, but it never dawned on any of us to ever even think about that—the only thing that mattered was not only that he was a master teacher, but a wonderful human being and a very fine artist."

Surely Pittman's homosexuality mattered in the 1950s—to her, to the other students, to himself. Surely this could have been part of what made him the "wonderful human being" who told Gladys that her art mattered. And, since she wasn't a sexual object to him, maybe this allowed him to see her in all her potential. Maybe this was true for Keith Martin too.

To believe in the visual is a process that goes beyond the visual. Belief is a system, but it is also something beyond the system. Something beyond belief.

Gladys helped me to dream in everyday experience, to look at a flower and savor each element. To take it all inside. She helped me to imagine a world where everything else could and should be pushed away to make room for more imagination. She pushed the world away for me in those moments when we would go up into her studio like up into the dream when it's no longer just a dream. I was awake, and I was alive.

"I'm painting what exists between limbs of trees, space and sounds and everything that you can't really see with your naked eye. At least I think that's what I'm painting." And Gladys looks at the camera so seriously here, a subtle smile. There's something plaintive in her gaze, but it's also commanding. She knows what she's saying. She's in control.

Here's the painting that's on the cover of the catalog, *Day Remembered*. Gladys is talking about what I keep calling windows or a frame, a broken or an open fence, a chain, here she says, "Many many years ago, I did paintings that had lines in [them], linear movements all over, attaching things to one another.

"I felt that if you touched my life then you were a part of my life forever, that there was a string somehow or other that attached you to me.

"And I thought that if I could harness a geometric form within the feeling of my painting, then I would be able to be as emotional as I wanted, and still have good spatial relationships within the painting."

Is she talking about painting, or her life?

That string attaching—

Sometimes it holds the paper together, but just barely. Sometimes the string is beneath the paper, a gash, or hanging off as ornamentation. Or extending through a rip in the form at the top, like *Sea Grass III*, where there is the string inside, a cyclical motion undone, the string removed and only an indentation, the string covered and darkened, the string forming a border, the string bridging the rip at the top like hair, the string floating through, suddenly, a soft bright blue, delicate, there for us in all dimensions.

"Life is very exciting, but it doesn't stay the same all the time," Gladys says, "and I don't want to stay the same all the time."

And yet she wanted me to stay the same.

Now Gladys is talking about how she started making her candy wrappers after she had back surgery, when she couldn't do a lot of work standing. She says she wants to do something "a little bit different than anyone had ever done before . . . I like the gemlike quality of the candy wrappers, so I keep it small. But each candy wrapper, even though they are very very small, is a total painting."

How Gladys changed her artistic process due to pain, it forced her to innovate. And how this happened for me too—twenty years ago, when my chronic pain first became debilitating and I couldn't write like I used to, in frantic bursts trying to get everything out. So I decided to write a few sentences a day, with no intention of plot or structure, and after a few years I was shocked to find that I had over four hundred pages. And that text became my second novel.

I love the tone in Gladys's voice when she says, "I have candy wrappers, I'm going to do candy wrappers"—suddenly high with excitement, should I say childlike excitement?

This is how I want to feel all the time.

In the video she has the candy wrappers spread out on her table, and now I want to do the same thing. I can't believe how many of these collages I have in this tiny box, and how varied they are. This is what I'm struck by, every time I look at Gladys's art—how much variety there is, in the same techniques. Sometimes it's the colors that stand out, and sometimes all the layers, or the way the shapes collide and merge, and reemerge. And sometimes the composition, formal and humorous at the same time. How something so tiny as this one, three inches by three inches, can become such a complete piece. There's so much to look at, and also, you don't have to look at any one part.

"I don't like to put titles to things. I mean people have called me one thing or another in the critiques, but I just think I'm a contemporary painter, and I am a very contemporary person," Gladys says in the video, and it's true that her art can resonate as contemporary, even now, like when people come over to my house and they assume I'm the artist.

Oh, now Gladys is on her patio, where she made her oil pastel drawings—she's smearing the oil pastel with her finger, and I want to pause here, with the lush green of her garden in the background. Where it's just her fingers on the vellum surface, freshly manicured nails with clear polish—she uses one hand to smear the pastel and steadies the vellum with the other hand that holds at least two other pastels, I see a red and a blue and maybe a teal, she's ready to use them all. The way she cradles the oil pastels in her hand while pressing two fingers onto the paper, steadying it. And then the colors on the vellum, out of focus, blending into the white, the light, this is a softness I can feel.

"I really don't care very much what people think about me, or my art. I hope that it brings some kind of pleasure to some people, but that's something that I can't control. That's something that's going to happen, or it's not going to happen. Either the paintings will be more meaningful, or they won't be meaningful. I really don't know about that, and I really don't think about it. And you know what? I don't really want to think about it."

And then the video ends with her laugh—the glint in her eyes, even with all that makeup. How she's smiling in her living room, fresh flowers in the background, a painting behind her that almost blends with her lipstick, the branches of the pussy willows forming the other side of the frame, connecting with the black line in the painting. I'm struck by the emotion in this composition. Even the light in her hair.

Of course, we all care about what people think of us, and what people think of our art. But we can't make decisions based on that. Otherwise we're not really making art.

"It's a deal!" Gladys writes at the beginning of this letter from March 1993—she says she'd like to meet me in San Francisco for a week, and then we can travel back to Baltimore together. But she's waiting for the results of some medical tests. Since she never visited me in San Francisco, I wonder what those medical tests revealed.

And here she's telling me that "today it's a lot better for homosexuals than it was twenty-five years ago. My best friend for over thirty years was Keith Martin."

She writes, "He's the one who did the ballet sketches in your kitchen."

Those sketches were there my whole childhood. Now they are in my mother's dining area. Gladys tells me they were my father's bar mitzvah present from Keith at age thirteen—sketches of ballet dancers as a gift on the day when my father symbolically became a man, in 1956. What a hilarious queeny gesture.

And my father saved these drawings, even with all his comments warning me about homos and fairies. But he never mentioned Keith Martin. I didn't even realize he had known him.

Gladys writes, "Keith's lifetime friend Dave McIntyre was fired from his job as executive manager of a large firm when it was discovered he was gay . . . Fortunately, we all had enough influence in those days, and Dave was hired [by the] Baltimore Museum of Art."

And here I wonder about this influence, and who Gladys means when she says "we." I want to hear more details, but then Gladys spends the second half of the letter telling me that gay people are just people, she resents that artists like Robert Rauschenberg and Jasper Johns, "etc etc" are considered gay influences when "they are artists and their influence is there. I have many gay friends—lots of them couples," she says, "some I like more than others. Is that any different than other people."

Even though she mentions homophobia directly, and how it affected Keith Martin's lover, she's still offended that her grandchild is searching for a queer legacy. She even goes on to say that she was thrilled to hear a navy spokesperson say "women can fight as well as the men, gender has never been a problem with us."

"Gender should not be a problem—don't make it one," Gladys adds at the end. Part of me would like to just keep the first half of the letter, where Gladys is excited that I've invited her to visit me, where she's being candid to me about her gay best friend and the homophobia of their time, part of me would like to have stopped halfway through, so I could just feel her excitement. Before her need to control the conversation. The conversation that was really about me.

Here's another letter, undated, where Gladys is telling me that she's done a lot of research about Thanksgiving, "and nowhere have I found anything to do with war with the Indians." And then she goes on to tell me the tale of Thanksgiving as the time when everyone got along. As if I've never heard this before.

At the time I thought she was just losing it—she couldn't agree with me on anything—in one letter, she tells me my hair dye might be poisonous, in another she asks, "Are you physically ill? Emotionally ill? Are you getting help?" She's trying any tactic to put me in my place, and failing, flailing, in an obsessive furor.

But there's also the possibility, I realize now, that she actually did believe the myth of Thanksgiving. That this artist who inspired me in every way as a child, who was an intellectual and creative thinker on so many levels, that she had never really questioned the white supremacist foundations of everything. That this was another part of my life that was destabilizing to her. That she was not ready to challenge middle-class norms, this is now obvious. And what could be more foundational to middle-class norms than white supremacy?

I'm sure that I wanted to throw these judgmental letters in the trash as soon as I received them. Or rip them to shreds. Or burn them. And yet I saved all of them.

Maybe you were wondering if I ever wrote back, and so was I, but here I have a photocopy of a letter from October 30, 1993, starting with the envelope that says:

> Gladys Goldstein
> Who I Never Write to
> But I'm Writing Now
> A Shock to Both of Us

And here it all is, so much of what I'm thinking about now, but as I articulated it at the time:

> Gladys—I understand your frustration anger annoy-
> ance @ me for not writing I see the knots of intertwin-
> ing pains—but I cannot accept condescension as the
> result. You hope I'm "not involved in a mind-altering
> group" that might "corrupt [my] creative mind." What
> the hell is a mind-altering group? How would one cor-
> rupt my mind? Gladys: I am not a lost child vulnera-
> ble and prone to brainwashing. I have a mind, a strong
> will and I use them. Just because I use myself in ways
> you disapprove of does not mean that I have somehow
> allowed a parasite to enter my brain. Political activ-
> ist groups are not cults—they are groups of thinking

individuals dismayed with a world country city that systematically obliterates...

Gladys—I always looked to you for something different from the force-fed preconceived clone life of my parents Fran & Herb my friends my psychiatrist my doctors people I met on the street. When you feed me the same thing, or at least a variation, COLLEGE IS EVERYTHING DON'T WASTE YOUR LIFE, I am disappointed in you. I've heard this all my life—it's been sifted into my pores—and to hear it now, from you, makes me angry and sad and lonely. That is the shroud—societal mores covering our relationship like a black cloud.

I love you and I know you care about me as intensely as _____, but I wish you would free our relationship from **family** from **duty** from **right**. I want to talk to you as a human being, not as a grandparent. I want to hear about your life, your art. I want to know what you fear, what you embrace, who you really are.

But Gladys refused my invitation. In the middle of this collage there are almost wings—a round opalescent sequin, flatter and larger than the usual sequins, beckoning into a moon or an eye or a window, the gesture of the red in movement, a circle of white paper beneath brown. I can tell you about the way squares interrupt circles covering squares. I'm saying the frame collapses, and the frame expands. I'm saying it's cinematic. I'm saying we can imagine our way in, and we can imagine a way out.

Gold foil melts through the white of the paper, one imprinted pattern colliding into another, a diagonal line producing a broken star. And another—geometry wound and unwound, the pattern on top of the pattern undoing the pattern. To mold and remold the experience of the wall—what was it I wrote to Gladys? A shroud. Un-shroud.

I find a letter postmarked December 1993, where Gladys mentions the photos she just took, they'll be ready in about a week, "I'm sure you felt hemmed in while you were here, but unfortunately compromise is one of the things that we have to do when we really care about someone."

Compromise on what to do today, sure. But not compromise on who to be.

It would be easy to say that she couldn't grow, that she was already in her seventies and this was where she would end up. But I refused to believe this because I still wanted to believe in her.

Wait. If Gladys took those photos in December 1993, this was after I remembered I was sexually abused.

So I visited her after. Just months after realizing I was sexually abused by my father, just months after that, I visited her in Baltimore. To exchange a week of mine for a week of hers.

From my confrontation letter:

> For months in San Francisco, I walked around in a daze. Feeling this tension in my neck as if I were about to be stabbed, this tension in my abdomen so that I couldn't stand the feel of anything against my chest. I was in a constant state of wanting to scream or tear myself apart. Or tear everything around me apart. I'd look around me on a bus, and I couldn't figure out where I was, why all these people were around me, how they were going on with their lives. How I was going on with my life.

In the midst of flashbacks and flailing, feeling like I was feeling for the first time, making myself vulnerable, taking the anger out of my body, trying to relax, to dream, to heal, in the midst of realizing that leaving my body didn't have to be a part of sex, in the midst of learning how to say stop, learning how to say stop for the first time.

> Running out of the house one night after an argument [with Zee], he came running after me, and I screamed, shrieked, threw my whole body in the air, fell on the cement crying shrieking so loud that neighbors came outside and when I stood up, I thought *my father raped me then bought me* and it was so clear for the first time why I hated money so much. The way he kept me in that house because I believed in the lie, I believed in the lie

that I needed to outdo him on his own terms. I needed to go to a better college, to get married and live in the suburbs with someone I hated, buy a bigger house and get a better job, and then I would win.

In the midst of thinking my father was in my apartment in San Francisco, his eyes in the walls, he could be anywhere it was dark, I would be walking down the street and maybe he was behind me, even on the bus, in the midst of realizing why I was always unable to relax, why I had to be on guard at all times, why my body had always been in pain, why I couldn't even understand what relaxation meant. In the midst of waking up in terror, asking my roommates to check under my bed to make sure my father wasn't there. In the midst of asking my roommates to maybe check one more time, in case my father was hiding behind the curtains with an axe. In the midst of realizing why I had never been able to feel young, because when I was young and vulnerable sometimes I'd trusted my father and where did that lead.

In the midst of learning how to breathe, in the midst of learning how to stay in my body, in the midst of learning how to eat without feeling nauseous, how to eat without thinking about calories or conflict, how to breathe while I ate, in the midst of learning how to slow down so I could feel, how to feel without being overwhelmed, in the midst of all this I went to visit Gladys.

So I'm in Gladys's studio, and I'm dancing, I'm dancing for the camera.

Let me try this move, the one in the photo, I can feel it now, not quite comfortable but not completely unfamiliar and then there's this photo in profile, shadow on both sides, and yes my body still looks stuck—I'm frozen in a pose for the camera, but also I'm frozen in the pose I learned in order to survive my father, breathing only between throat and head, how memory works in waves, how knowledge builds and overwhelms, the way the same feeling is never really the same feeling.

Hands on hips, looking out at the camera like: Whatever. My hair an accessory to survival. Bracelets to hold me together. Learning how to create a present I can live with I mean a future. The gold leaf melts into the paper, the way you see oil in the sidewalk and it's all those colors at once but also it isn't really any color at all.

Beyond Gladys asking me, "How can you judge your family for wanting you to have an easier life? How can you judge them because they love you so much that they want you to have the advantage of learning from the best professors—how can you judge them for wanting you to make the most of your creative abilities."

At the time, I did not judge Gladys for raising my father. I only judged her for what she refused to understand.

Here Gladys is not yet telling me that my work is vulgar, that I'm wasting my talent. "I also know you feel disappointed in me," she writes, "but that's o.k. as long as you can tell me so."

Eventually I couldn't tell her anymore. Here's a boat made of HOHOHOHOHOHOHOHOHOHOHOHOHOHOHOHOHOHOHO-HOHOHOHOHOHOHOHOHOHOHOHOHOHOHOHOHOHOHO-HOHOHOHOHOHO, the letters going in all directions to form the repetition but actually it's not a boat because this collage goes the other way, vertically. The sense of play in the patterns that interweave with HOHOHO, and "choose" partially visible in white on black paper, with "from our" almost entirely ripped away, and then "ma   ork," and at first I thought it really should go in the boat direction, but now I realize no, this way there's a sense of falling and floating, a piece of a cartoon, flecks of gold leaf, and the sky, but it's sideways.

Can I tell you about the lobby of my building now that Gladys's art is there—how you even see all the colors through the glass of the front door, and then when you enter the small foyer maybe you notice the way the gray of the chain no what did Gladys call it, the structure, the lines, "linear movements all over, attaching things to one another," how it connects with the gray of the walls, the brightness of the colors peering out of the almost-boxes, and then across from this painting from 2003 that's forty-eight inches by sixty inches is another painting in a similar style that's a long horizontal rectangle, but only fifteen inches high, and the dialogue between these two pieces, *Plus A* and *B Series II*, so much motion in the continuum of shape and the way the skinny one leads you in, and then, in a little alcove that before had no purpose at all, a little alcove with a hanging light, a hanging light for no reason, now there's a reason because there's a small painting of Gladys's from 1964, the year this building was built, and maybe these are the lines Gladys means, white lines going in every direction, pulling through the blue—she was known for these white lines, and how it almost looks like the paint has cracked, but it's just the white on blue.

I want to say something about the excitement I feel every time I walk into my building now, like I'm on a journey—I can just stare, and stay, and then I turn the corner, and way down at the end of the hallway there's *Checkered Life* with its mayhem of pastel squares and what is that at the center, almost like hair falling from moonscape into a scarf that becomes light, the uneven arrow, and if you walk all the way down the hall to touch the life, yes, bumps. Look to the left, and suddenly all the textures of collaged geometry and then, above the glass table in the mail area, there's *Blue Moon*, another 1960s piece—1968, to be exact, so that's four decades of Gladys's history in art, in my lobby.

But I'm talking about the way my eyes open into softness—I touch *Blue Moon*, and, yes, I'm touching paper creating the colors and textures, and let me go back to *Pastoral*, the one in the hallway by *Checkered Life*, just to study how that huge wrinkle in the paper creates so much depth, what does it say in the catalog? "The papers on the surface of *Pastoral* are so thin that light penetrates through to the painted canvas underneath."

But the sense is that the light comes from inside. In between. That's where I go when I look at Gladys's paintings, step out of the elevator into my lobby and boom, you're looking right at *Touching Light*, see, we're touching light again, and the way I thought about these paintings for a long time, imagined them in these spaces before they arrived, the shimmering wash of metallic paint in *Magic Day*, the collage weaving in and out of the paint, the layers of color over color into color, and when this one went up in the lobby someone asked: Did she make this on acid?

But something I'm thinking about now, while reading the University of Maryland catalog, is that it's always focused on Gladys's art. "Even as a young child, Baltimore artist Gladys Goldstein was a painter" is the first sentence after the preface. It doesn't say anything about her parents or her husband, or offer any mundane details about her life. It only talks about her life in the context of her art.

The catalog tells us how she learned to paint—first studying at the Maryland Institute, later attending the Art Students League of New York, and then enrolling at Pennsylvania State University to study teaching methodology with Hobson Pittman. And this is as close as it gets to the traditional arc of biography. She must have instructed the writer in this way, right? She must have said: I only want to talk about my art.

I'm thinking, again, about the role of gay men in Gladys's life. Starting with Hobson Pittman. And then Keith Martin. How did they enrich her thinking? And how did her relationships with them influence her feelings about me, both as a child, when she supported everything about me that set me apart as queer, and as an adult, when she supported less and less.

Here in my folder of letters, I've enlarged a sentence from the end of one of her letters. Five photocopies, actually, making one sentence as large as possible, over and over. I must have been planning to use this in an art project of my own:

> There is life beyond sex you know.
> There is life beyond sex you know.
> There is life beyond sex you know.
> There is life beyond sex you know.
> There is life beyond sex you know.

What is a life beyond sex, and who decides?

Another letter, sent to me in Boston in 1995. The first letter she's sent to me on lined paper. This must be soon after I confronted my father, because it starts with "As you probably realize, I've written you umteen letters, none of which have been mailed."

And then: "I'm sure you realize all of the consequences of your actions; but I don't think you realize the full extent of the hurt that has occurred."

The hurt that has occurred—not because of my father's abuse, but because of my letter confronting him.

Do I really want to read this? Can't I go back to talking about how, at the center of this handmade paperwork, there's an oil pastel drawing where you see the title, partially covered, *Night Forest*. But it looks more like the bottom of the ocean—how the colors from within the drawing echo but never quite match the colors of the paper surrounding it.

Or maybe this paperwork where she uses the number stencil, and it's so subtle that I'm not sure I need to take it out of the protective sleeve, except then I do, and I see the juxtaposition between white and beige, how all the colors of white stand out on their own.

Gladys wants me to consider all sides to the story. As if there are two sides to the story of a father raping his child.

Gladys writes, "if others do not truly believe this, then why not try to find out why and how this belief or disbelief could have happened"—but I never actually thought she didn't believe me. So this made her betrayal worse.

She didn't want to talk about why or how the abuse happened, so instead she talked about belief. But it was her actions that mattered to me, not her beliefs. What didn't she want to see about herself?

Here are the numbers, side by side:

0112345678 0112345

0112345678 01123456

I can't show you all the gradations, all the ways the numbers hide from sight. The holes between the numbers, the numbers that barely emerge. Or, if I look at this other piece, the way I'm always drawn to the red circle in brown, or the shine of the wrapping paper coming from underneath. I could take out another paperwork, or just look up at these silver ladders, windows floating on chains or vertical tunnels, a pulley system.

"We all want to get on with our lives" is how Gladys ends the letter.

She meant I was getting in the way. The truth was getting in the way.

When she said lives she meant lies. The family wanted to get on with the lies.

In art, Gladys wanted the imperfections to show. This was where she found beauty. But in her life she wanted to conceal.

"In order to cut handmade paper and keep soft edges—I just take a brush and with water, follow your path. In a few seconds it will soften and you can quickly pull it apart." This is a note Gladys sent with the paperworks she mailed to me in New York, a few years after I confronted my father, when I told her I wanted to make art about our relationship.

I wanted to rip apart her art to depict our relationship, but I found that I couldn't, even when she gave me instructions.

In my confrontation letter:

Dream 6/2/94. 1: Someone is swinging an axe back and forth so that his whole body moves with it. This is in my room here or in my room at my parents' house and I realize that he is going to chop through me with the axe and I scream and/or the dream ends. 2: I'm organizing a video retrospective outdoors and it gets messed up, I'm watching a surrealist video with Mom, she's asking lots of questions. 3: I'm at Gladys's house and there are two men talking at a table in the corner of the kitchen. One is going to have two twins, he's very proud. The two men agree that they can't imagine anything more disgusting than giving birth. I say some women think it's incredible, there's no better high. I'm putting postage on envelopes which is my job, earlier I'd been doing it somewhere else and it was political, somehow similar to the activist group organized around the second Rodney King verdict. The phone rings and I go into the living room with Gladys and Poppop and the t.v. I'm between Gladys and Poppop and the t.v. It's my father on the phone and he says this is your abuser. I start crying, I want to say what did you say? because I'm not sure and my mouth moves but the words won't come out. I don't look at Gladys but I want her to see me so she'll know I was abused. I try to say what did you say, I can only say excuse me? He says something, maybe I got the letter, maybe he's crying. I try to say what did you say? Gladys is watching me, she can feel the pain. I'm crying and I'm trying to say what did you say?

My father is on the phone, and he says what he will never say, not outside of a dream. He will never say it. He will not say it before I confront him, he will not say it after, he will not say it during the eleven years when we don't talk because he will not say it. He will not say it when I go to visit him because he's dying of cancer.

He's dying, and I'm sobbing.

I say I love you.

I say I don't want you to die.

I say I wish we could have a relationship.

And he acknowledges nothing.

But in this dream, he says it. That's what dreams are for.

But also I want to say something about Gladys. How she's in this dream because I want her to support me.

Instead, she wrote:

"I'm sure you realize all the consequences of your actions; but I don't think you realize the full extent of the hurt that has occurred. You will answer, but what about 'my' hurt? I do—we all do—and we are treading lightly."

I just noticed that Gladys put "my" in quotation marks. Because even my pain couldn't be mine.

How to write about trauma without feeling the trauma, I guess there is no way.

I walk outside to look in windows, but no one's windows look like the spaces and places where language stops, not tonight. If feeling has an inside, and an out. How a scrap of foil becomes a field of sunlight, red encircling green next to orange above silver, a line of teal on top of a pattern next to words too small to read, a Dove candy wrapper in maroon and gold like a cape over the entire history of art, just look above, the northern lights, how the ingredients form a frame around an Easter egg wrapper crushed to pull open a simple line of gold leading us to the flowers beyond. How everything is organized and wild and bursting through, shaped into what meets the eye must really mean. Representation and presentation—the visual, the textual, the emotional, the sensual, the experiential, here we go again.

If I look closely at this collage, I see there are ingredients: palm kernel oil, cornstarch, cream of tartar, dextrose, sugar, xanthan gum. Oh, and here's some "information," a 1-800 number, "artificial." Like how if you look very close at *Checkered Life* at the end of the hallway in my lobby, you find:

> SEND TO
> NAME
> STREET ADDRESS

And then, collaged sideways in even smaller letters:

> custom
> shipping
> billed

How a circle can be broken into so many pieces, but you still see the circle in the pieces, and is this true of any other shape? That spiral at the center, it's from a placemat I remember from Gladys's kitchen table—is this what it means to grow up with an artist? Even after she's dead, still there's this living memory.

I rub my hands over the paperwork. Maybe rub is the wrong word. Or hands. When really I mean fingers. Or this collage that says:

SLEEPS
LEEPSLEE
PSLEEPSLE
LEEPS

in the bottom right corner but upside-down, handwritten, but I think it's from an image, fading out into

SLEEP
EEEE S
S L EE
S E P
L E L E
SLEEPSLEE

Next to the upside-down carriage paper or actually it's postage and a locomotive inside the shifting gold-and-white border, but then at the center, the abstraction of white, the gold tentacles of what has to be the sun, and you know I've always struggled with sleep.

And then I turn the collage over, on the back a reversal but also a whole different piece, where is this black on the front, oh, I see, just a sudden smudge on burlap and the way an opulent density of decay bubbles to the surface over another strip of burlap, the places where the leaf of the gold really looks like a leaf.

How music always carries the memory of when you first heard this music. How this can be a burden. How this can be glorious. How this can be suffocating. How this can make you shake. How this can make you sing. How this can make you dance. And can this be true of visual art too.

Sometimes, when the CD skips, I think maybe I should stop listening to CDs. And sometimes, when the CD skips, I think this is what it feels like to really love something.

In Gladys's work there's always a visible process that collides with the invisible, and is this how we learn to speak. Here the surface is so smooth that the layers seem almost impossible—

SLEEPS
LEEPSLEE
PSLEEPSLE
LEEPS

When I first told my mother I was working on this book, she suggested I talk to Helen, Gladys's childhood best friend.

Is she alive, I asked.

I don't know, my mother said.

Do you have her number, I asked.

Yes, my mother said, but then she couldn't find it.

Six months later, she found it, and I called Helen, and she answered the phone. She was 101 years old, and completely cogent. She told me so much that I would never know otherwise. Starting with the year of Gladys's birth—in her obituary, it says 1918, which is also the date used for the University of Maryland collection. But actually she was born in 1917—my mother found her birth certificate, and driver's license, which confirm this.

Helen and Gladys met in third grade, and they were very competitive—Helen was the president of the Latin club, and Gladys was the president of the French club. They were both straight-A students at the top of their class, and so they were sent to middle school number 49, an accelerated school where there were only four people in each class.

Gladys was sick when they first met—she had to stay home for a month, and Helen would bring her homework to her house and that's how they became friends. "We knew that we had something special, and we only talked about it with one another. After school, Gladys would go to the Maryland Institute to study painting, and I would go to the Peabody Conservatory to study music—it was a way of life."

They decided to be blood sisters, and Helen, who always wore blue to match her blue eyes, promised she would never wear green, which is what Gladys wore, and Gladys promised she would never wear blue. Helen swore she would never study art, and Gladys swore she would never study music.

They grew up twelve blocks from each other, near Western High School. Gladys's father, Sam Hack, was the manager of the A&P on McKean Avenue, and they lived in a neighborhood where everyone was Christian. Her family never belonged to a temple, so people thought she was Christian.

When they were twelve or thirteen, their friend Jane Oliver introduced them to her brothers—Abraham, or Abe, who was eighteen, and George, who was sixteen and a half. They lived in a huge mansion in Windsor Hills—allegedly it had been built for the Jewish gangster Bugsy Siegel, but then he went to prison and never moved in. When Gladys and Helen got to the house, "it was so beautiful, like nothing we had ever seen before. We were both stupefied. I came from a very wealthy family, but this was something entirely different."

Alex Oliver said to his sons: "These are exceptional young ladies, and when they grow up I hope you will still know them." After that, at school Gladys and Helen would pass notes back and forth: Do you like George, or do you like Abe? This was "at a time when the world was falling apart, and we were befriended by a millionaire."

Starting around age fifteen or sixteen, they would go out with the Oliver brothers. "Mr. Oliver was fascinated by us, he would take us to New York and take us to the theater and we began to live what we called our enchanted life."

The Olivers owned a hotel in New York, and took Helen and Gladys to stay there on the weekends. Helen and Gladys would share a room, and the boys would stay in another room. They still thought babies came from a stork. Helen's younger sister "thought I knew about something, but I didn't know anything. We knew nothing."

Alex Oliver ran the biggest network company in the South. "They were ahead of their time—they manufactured things half-price, and they were gorgeous." The Olivers became millionaires during the Depression. If you passed by something and said you liked it, they bought it for you. "When my friends were buying things for six or ten dollars, Mr. Oliver would buy me a dress for one hundred or two hundred dollars."

"Gladys was an absolute beauty, movie-star pretty, eyelashes four inches long. She was always insecure, and I never understood why. She always had somebody in love with her, and she didn't pay much attention to them. 'If I'm so pretty, why are you always the lead in the play?'" she would ask.

"Men were never a problem—we never had a Saturday night that we had to worry about having a date. Gladys fell in love with someone, but her parents wanted her to marry Abe."

After Gladys and Helen turned eighteen, Gladys married Abe, and Helen married George. "Gladys was unhappy from the day she got married," and got divorced after two years. Because of the divorce, the Olivers forbade Helen from associating with Gladys. Gladys moved to Florida, and she met someone there and fell in love with him, but when his parents found out she had been divorced they wouldn't let their son take her out anymore, and she was crushed. When she came back to Baltimore, she met Ed, the principal of Forest Park High School, and she married him a few years later. At the time, "If you were twenty, and you weren't married, you were an old lady."

After Gladys's marriage, Helen ran into Ed and found out that Gladys was sick, so she went to see her and brought her clothes. Gladys and Ed lived in a house on the second floor together, with her parents on the first floor, and she painted in the basement.

"By the time she was eighteen, when she was first married, she was already painting like Picasso." She hated doing portraits because nobody could understand—when she was twenty-seven, she painted a portrait of Helen while pregnant, with bronzy skin and darker hair and her mother hated it—she thought there was too much blue, that Helen's skin wasn't white enough.

"She never had the confidence in herself that she should have had—she was an absolute beauty, she was smart, she was talented, but she didn't have the confidence and I never understood it. I've always wondered about it. She had so much more than anybody I knew. And everything good was happening for her. Her career was doing well, she was gaining recognition in Baltimore. She was very busy, she was teaching at the Maryland Institute, and Notre Dame. She was very much respected by other artists. She never stopped painting. But she was never completely happy with what she did."

When Gladys was getting ready for her retrospective at the University of Maryland in 2004, they asked her to write something, and she asked Helen to help.

Helen said: Why don't you have Matthew write it for you?

Gladys replied: I couldn't, because what would people think?

What do you think she meant, I ask Helen.

She loved you, and she never stopped talking about how proud she was of you. She loved you, and she bragged about you.

But why do you think she never told me this?

Why do you think, I ask Helen, if Gladys was so sophisticated in so many ways, she thought my work was vulgar just because it was sexual?

Sophisticated was never a term I would use for her. She was absolutely unsophisticated. She didn't have the ability to think outside.

Why did she stay in Baltimore?

We didn't think like that. You didn't leave your family.

We had so many discussions about your homosexuality, Helen says, and I could never understand her. There are a few things I didn't understand about her, and that was one of them.

But what about Keith?

You're saying the same thing I did—Gladys, what about Keith? She didn't answer. I don't think she admitted that he was different. She never ever ever ever ever discussed it.

Helen says: She was brilliant in her art, and people were secondary.

If I say my writing is always placed-based, then you know I need to spend time in Baltimore in order to write this book. To find out what I can about Gladys's world, yes, but also to find my own world there too. A city for me is about coincidence, sensory perception, how you move and what moves you. To move to Baltimore temporarily, then, is about excavating Gladys's past, but it's also about seeing what will come through for me in the present. Writing a book is about letting everything in. "As the painting changes, you change with it."

I thought it would be easy to find a beautiful cheap place to rent in Baltimore for six months, but actually it's not easy, and it's not cheap. You can buy a three-bedroom turn-of-the-century rowhouse in a nice neighborhood for half the price of a studio condo in Seattle, but the rent for a one-bedroom apartment isn't that different. Is it DC commuters, Johns Hopkins University students, an artificially inflated rental bubble in the small sliver of central Baltimore where half the buildings aren't boarded up, a conspiracy of developers and city planners, or some combination of all of this, no one seems to know for sure.

Finally I find a furnished Victorian cottage from 1895, which costs the same as an unfurnished one-bedroom apartment nearby. I'm a half mile from Hopkins, and at night there are more Hopkins security on the street than there are pedestrians. They wear fluorescent yellow vests, and stand in groups on designated corners all night. Then there are white patrol cars that drive around in circles with their green sirens on, silent but flashing. The officers in the patrol cars wear blue uniforms like cops, but they also work for Hopkins—they patrol the whole neighborhood. Actually, several neighborhoods. Hopkins has a security force of over a thousand people so they can patrol the streets twenty-four hours a day.

Some of the security officers on the street look like kids just out of high school, and some look worn out from living, and occasionally they look like they're ready for whoever might be watching them to make sure they're doing their job. Almost all of them are Black, and yet their jobs exist to prove to white people that this is a safe neighborhood, without too many Black people. Not the wrong ones.

Sometimes an actual cop drives by in a police cruiser, and it's spookier than usual because you're so used to seeing the fake cops that the real cops are more jarring. You wonder what brought them here.

One night I'm walking down a deserted Charles Street, right near Wyman Park and just down the street from the entrance to Hopkins, and up ahead there's a car stopped in the middle of the intersection, the engine's running but the lights are off. I wonder if I should turn around, or walk past. I decide to walk past, and as I do I see that it's two undercover cops, watching me. One of them says to the other: No it's okay.

I smile like it's perfectly normal for two undercover cops to be stopped in the middle of an intersection, I mean actually it's not even an intersection it's just the middle of a block. I cross the street so I can watch the fireflies and lean against trees in Wyman Park. And I think about how people were worried about me when I said I like to go on long walks at night, people said you can't do that in Baltimore, and it's true that sometimes the neighborhoods change really fast, you cross a line and you don't always know where that line will be, and I live right near a line like that, but the most jarring thing for me so far is this duo of undercover cops.

On the outside of the Baltimore Museum of Art there's a neon light piece that goes like this:

VIOLINS
      VIOLENCE
            SILENCE

Every night I stand across the street and stare at the words wrapping around the corner of the building, the way they alternate and overlap:

VIOLINS VIOLENCE SILENCE
SILENCE VIOLINS VIOLENCE
VIOLENCE SILENCE VIOLINS

And sometimes the words are reversed, like you're looking in a mirror.

Sometimes the words start on this side, and continue around the corner, and sometimes they start on the other side, and continue in the reverse direction.

This is a permanent part of the exterior of the Baltimore Museum of Art, it's been there since a solo show of Bruce Nauman's neon works in the early '80s, after which he donated it to the museum.

I can't find any description of Nauman's intent, which must be his intent. The piece was initially commissioned by California State University, Long Beach, for its music department building, but then the school rejected it.

It was controversial in Baltimore too, for a while, but then I guess people got used to it.

When Gladys and Helen attended Public School 49, there was a German bund across the street, and Gladys and Helen went over there to dance to the music.

Helen says, "We were very limited in our scope of the world, I was good at what I did but I didn't know about anything else."

The official title of Public School 49 was the Robert E. Lee School.

The other accelerated public school in Baltimore at the time was Public School 1, the Edgar Allan Poe School.

"It wasn't until Hitler came that we thought about Jewish or not Jewish," Helen says. "Religion was never an issue. We lived a very small intellectual world. We knew nothing."

The best thing that's happened to me in Baltimore so far is this guy walking completely naked down the street—tan and tattooed, matted brown hair and beard, he smiles at me and I say hi.

Can I give you a hug, he says.

Sure, I say, and it's a real hug, emphatic and empathic—it's not sexual and it's not not-sexual. It's such a nice surprise.

He smells like a lot of pot and something rotten, but not too rotten. We're both covered in sweat, skin on skin in the hot sun and I kiss him on the cheek because it feels like the right thing to do. He says aww, and kisses me multiple times on both cheeks. You have beautiful earrings, he says.

What are you up to, I say, because I'm kind of wondering if there's a particular reason he's walking around completely naked, but also I don't want to make him uncomfortable by pointing that out, and he says I don't know, is there anywhere I should go?

I say I usually just wander over there to sunbathe in the park, and he starts to head that way. Good luck, I say, and he smiles at me again.

Is the point of art to bring us into ourselves, or out? I mean the Parkway Theatre is my favorite place to go to get out of the heat—I can even stare at the high-concept magenta wallpaper in the bathrooms, digitized popcorn kernels floating by. Or notice the shifting light outside as it settles over the decaying turn-of-the-century buildings across Charles Street, all those gorgeous reds and browns and look at those plants growing through the cracks in the bricks.

Usually when I go to an old theater I study the details, but with this theater you walk in and you just think: architect. Because the whole place has been gutted, and reimagined. Where did they get all this money?

Tonight I'm watching *Boom for Real: The Late-Teenage Years of Jean-Michel Basquiat,* which reveals nothing about Basquiat that wasn't already part of the public record—he was brilliant and wild, charming and manipulative, seductive and ambitious—he was homeless as a teenager, he did a lot of drugs, he became the toast of the art world, he died way too young.

Everyone already knows the myth that Basquiat was a lone genius destroying convention to create his own form. Yes, he was driven to remake himself as a lone visionary in order to become a top-tier art-world commodity, and this actually happened, which is rare for anyone, especially a Black artist, but we already know this killed him, so why portray posthumous canonization as a glorious path? Unless the movie is just about making more money for the ghouls of the art world who have already made millions and millions from Basquiat's death from an overdose at age twenty-seven.

I'm thinking about the Basquiat show I saw in Seattle in 1994, six years after his death—gazing at those paintings I felt an immediate sensory kinship with the dense layers of self-expression, the wildness, the raw beauty, the way language was interwoven with the visual, became the visual, until it was overcome by it. The movement, the free association that became a method and a system of organization, the disorientation that opens the mind.

The way we can create our own language, the symbols and the

strength, the bending, the mesmerizing nurturing scream. I left that show wanting to create, knowing I could create, knowing.

In the lobby of the Parkway Theatre there's a flyer for a new building across from the train station that says:

THE ART OF BALTIMORE
NOW LEASING.

In the photo, it just looks like your average prefab yuppie loft to me, so I'm not sure where the art is, but I guess they mean this neighborhood, designated by the city as an ARTS DISTRICT to change blight into bright lights. The marketing of Baltimore as a creative hub—artists as tools for displacement, a sad story that has obliterated so many neighborhoods over the last several decades, but here it feels more blatant. Maybe because these funded institutions sit in an area so obviously neglected by the city for so long. Just across the street from the Parkway there are Black people slumped on their stoops in drugged-out immobility due to decades of structural neglect, and next door there's Motor House, an art gallery/theater/bar complex with a design show called "Undoing the Red Line."

I walk out of the Parkway, and the graffiti on the street doesn't look that different than the graffiti in the movie. Is it on display? As if to say: We want what happened in New York in the '80s to happen here, now. There's even an alley behind Motor House where graffiti is legal, and all day long there are photo shoots and staged parties promoting multicultural consumption in a segregated city.

Back on Charles, where there's another movie theater, and then half a block of upscale bistros, and then everything ends at the bridge over the highway and there's the train station, illuminated. I turn the corner and there's some huge new building like a spaceship that's landed to promote gentrification, so much air conditioning that there's a giant puddle in the asphalt.

Oh, wait, that's the building from the flyer, the Nelson Kohl Apartments, this is it, with a wood-paneled entry and a white cube gallery in the lobby showing bland abstract art, two rectangular fiberglass planters in front, painted black and textured to look like cement. Two grasses planted to one side, and then four almost-dead grasses on the other. The entrance faces the parking lot over the highway, with the train station on the other side. I stand outside to watch for anyone going in, but they must all be inside with their air conditioning.

I decide to go to the show at Motor House—the bar in front looks like a suburban advertisement for urban living, but the show in the lobby is actually about redlining. It's mostly about New York and DC, although I do learn a few things about Cross Keys Village, where I went with Gladys as a kid, a sprawling gated housing development in Baltimore—a mixture of townhouses, a hotel, and mid-rise buildings in a leafy enclave, complete with a Frank Gehry–designed high-rise and a mall that includes Betty Cooke's modernist gift shop that Gladys loved. Apparently Cross Keys was marketed to both Black and white home-owners when it was built in the 1960s, unlike the whites-only history of neighborhoods nearby, like working-class Hampden and posh Roland Park.

At Motor House they have a sign thanking the city for funding the space—I look it up when I get home, and it cost $6 million to renovate, funded by an organization called BARCO, or Baltimore Arts Realty Corporation, dedicated to "creating working spaces for Baltimore's growing community of artists, performers, makers and artisans." BARCO also recently completed an $11.5 million renovation of another space in the area, Open Works.

I look up the Parkway Theatre, and the renovation cost $18.5 million, including a $5 million grant from a Greek foundation. So there was international funding involved. For a movie theater in Baltimore. Then there's the $19 million spent by another nonprofit developer, Jubilee, to renovate the Centre Theatre to house the Johns Hopkins and MICA film programs right around the corner. This is a staggering amount of money in a city struggling for basic services.

All this empty corporatized language promoting Baltimore as an arts hub, a creative crossroads, a robust creative sector, an incubator for the creative economy. Which fits right in with the marketing of the Nelson Kohl Apartments, named after two famous dead designers who had nothing to do with it, and claiming to be THE ART OF BALTIMORE, with studios starting at fifteen hundred dollars, "surrounded by art, music, restaurants, bars, movie theaters, and one of the world's premiere art colleges. When you live here, you can paint your own canvas—differently every day."

Fifteen hundred dollars for a studio, in a city that's mostly in collapse.

Walking back up Charles, there's a performance space in a former dry cleaner's where everyone looks like the people in the Basquiat movie—the same '80s outfits, only now everyone's wearing all black, you can't even have fun anymore with your studied indifference.

Crossing the street to walk home—past the Crown, where I danced my ass off to terrible '80s music and campy projections on white sheets, and everyone stared at me but no one approached. Past the Eagle, another old building gutted and renovated with a surprising amount of money—usually a leather bar doesn't have an upstairs cabaret and dance floor, a leather shop with an art gallery, and multiple streamlined spaces on the main floor. Not that anyone in the bar was friendly, but at least there were nice bathrooms.

And then I go into the convenience store where the register is behind bulletproof glass, my usual place to get an unrefrigerated bottle of water. A trans woman shaking a bit from drugs is ordering knock-off perfume, chewing gum, talking on the phone: "I'm on the stroll." A drug dealer steps in front of me to count out a huge stack of bills. I get my bottle of water, and then back on the street I'm thinking about all the contrasts—the NPR studio with signs out front that say WARNING DON'T SIT HERE WALL IS UNSTABLE, the members-only jazz club that I assumed before was a Black space, but when I walk by now it's all white guys outside, in between sets.

All the businesses that are never open, but the storefronts still advertise what was there before. The rehab center is the fanciest building on the block—across the street there's a new art gallery featuring Black artists, in an old brick building. And I find myself invigorated by the contrasts, the possibility for something surprising to happen—only this is how gentrification works. You look for what you can't find elsewhere, in neighborhoods where people are having trouble finding anything, and then eventually there isn't any neighborhood except the one that replaced the neighborhood.

At the Baltimore Museum of Art, there's a brochure featuring "5 ART-WORKS YOU CAN GENTLY TOUCH."

The first one is Felix Gonzalez-Torres's *Untitled (Water)*, a floor-to-ceiling curtain of blue plastic beads that I saw once before at the Tacoma Art Museum, in an exhibit of art by artists who died of AIDS. Apparently there are several museums that own this piece, and each museum owns multiple copies, so that when the beads are damaged they can quickly make a replacement.

You walk through the curtain, the beads hitting your skin and flinging side to side. At the Tacoma Art Museum this felt mournful, but at the Baltimore Art Museum it's pure celebration, bringing me back into my body, a delicate force. But also not so delicate—the way the strings of beads are so long, given the height of the ceiling, and if you walk through fast then the beads fly right back at you.

Then there's Carl Andre's *Zinc-Magnesium Plain*, which consists of slate tiles arranged in a checkerboard pattern on the floor. The brochure says, "Step onto this flat artwork and notice how your steps feel. Does it change your ideas about everyday objects, such as tile floors?" But is it possible to walk over anything Carl Andre made without thinking about feminist artist Ana Mendieta—they were married, and during an argument he pushed her out of their thirty-fourth-floor window and she fell to her death. He was acquitted of her murder—even after years of protests, he remains canonized. Why isn't this mentioned in the brochure?

Then there are two giant tubular Franz West sculptures in different shades of pink—they must be made of some kind of durable synthetic material but they feel like papier-mâché. Yes, the tension in my body starts to release when I lean against these sculptures at different angles—this is a much better way to appreciate the art on the walls, rather than standing, or sitting on a hard, uncomfortable bench. All museum seating should have options like this.

But are these sculptures supposed to evoke women's bodies? One of them is called *Violetta. To the song of Gerhard Rühm: I like to rest on aquatic corpses*, and we are invited to "Rest on *Violetta* and think about the meaning behind West's evocative title."

Maybe it's time to go outside. The last piece of art that you can gently touch is *Rock Chair*, by Scott Burton, located in the sculpture garden. As I walk down into the garden, I notice a marble sculpture with such smooth cylindrical angles—I know it's not *Rock Chair*, but I can't resist brushing my hand over the surface until a docent or security guard or whoever this is comes over and says NO TOUCHING, even though all these sculptures are exposed to rain and snow and sleet and hail and bird shit and squirrels and all the insects of the world, but no no no no no touching.

And the truth is that as soon as this person tells me I can't touch the sculptures, all the sculptures become ugly.

But I'm looking for *Rock Chair*, I'm allowed to touch *Rock Chair*.

I can't find it, so I sit on a wooden bench and look out at the landscaping that before I thought was gorgeous, but now all I feel is the overwhelming humidity and the approach of too many mosquito bites.

Joey is at his grandmother's house, trying to pick up his 16mm camera and shoot, and I'm telling him about the 16mm film by Chick Strand that I saw at the Parkway—the character can't get into the house, but the film is shot from inside so the camera looks out—all the glowing light seen through the windows, the trees and everything that's growing outside.

I keep saying Joey, just pick up the camera, you need to get out of your head, just pick it up and start shooting. You can even load the film while I'm talking to you, you might not have another opportunity to be there, this might be your only chance.

Eventually, Joey does pick up the camera. He picks up the camera, and shoots. A camera is not a gun, and yet.

What matters isn't the camera, but the gaze. Who is looking, and who is not.

No. Who will allow you anything.

Maybe you need more context—Joey is visiting his grandmother, and this might be the last time.

No. Joey is visiting his grandmother's house, this might be the last time. He's not allowed to visit his grandmother, even though she was just diagnosed with terminal cancer. He's not allowed to visit, because he's trans.

Let's back up, to get a wider angle. Of all my friends, Joey is the only one who has had a consistently supportive mother the whole time I've known him. Emotionally and intellectually and financially and intimately—supportive about queerness and polyamory, shifting relationships and relationships with the body, that's how it's always seemed.

Until. Until Joey came out as trans. When was that, a few years ago?

I can't even tell you the whole story, it's too much. Too much to tell. Joey only got into his grandmother's empty house because of a neighbor who had the spare key. So against the wishes of an unsupportive family, Joey is staying there—to archive memory, to imagine history, to feel, to feel what?

To feel.

Against structural violence, feeling may be our only hope. I keep saying don't internalize their bullshit, if you decide you want to visit your grandmother, you should feel free to do it at any point. She's not going to die because of something you tell her. She's not going to die because you are you. This has never happened.

Joey says he wants to look it up on the internet.

Don't look it up on the internet.

But this story has a happy ending, or happier, because Joey does visit his grandmother. In spite of the aunt who has power of attorney, Joey spends three hours with his grandmother, after waiting three hours for the hospital to let him in. Joey tells her stories about the relatives he visited in Italy, while they look at photos together and chat in Italian—Joey is the only other family member in the US who speaks Italian.

After Joey visits again the next day, he says he still feels uncomfortable being there because he's worried someone is going to tell him to get out. When his grandmother's eating, he's worried she might die—she might die while he's there, and then everyone will blame him.

The thing about dancing is it's when my body can finally dream. Or let go of dreaming. Or just let go. There's nothing else like it for me, and it took me fifteen years of moving through chronic pain to get to the place where I can move in the ways that I need to. Yes, I'm back at the Crown again, even though I thought I was going to the Eagle but when I got there I remembered the last time I went inside and I couldn't imagine going inside ever again.

Every scene is a bad scene, it's when we create something else that matters. And that's what dancing can provide—your body can keep you company. This time I'm in the blue room on the second floor with no windows which means no smoke from outside, and no smoke machine either, which is as good as it gets in these spaces, as good as it gets for me. The music is weird and glitchy with a bounce, so I let it bounce me—yes, watch me crawling across the floor into a roll and up to a spin through the air, now I'm on the other side. The way your feet can fling you anywhere with the beat in your body, when it keeps changing you just adjust. The wall a source for grounding and then I'm off into the spinning the flailing it's that moment when you realize there's no gap between you and the air I mean your body is air. So you can fly.

And just when I think now, maybe now I should leave, because it's always good to leave before the crash, don't wait for more because more could be too much, but just at that moment two people enter the dance floor with a flourish, I mean they're taking charge, planned dance moves they're young maybe dance students and then I'm right with them we're exchanging moves in and out of each other's eyes and this is what gets me high. I mean I was already high from dancing, but I was alone, and now we're flying together, yes, I think about giving them my number and saying let me know when you're going out, let's dance together, but then they're gone, just like that.

Now I've crossed into the next level of freedom, the one when your body really lets go, and how do you let go of that, so soon—when I finally leave I look at the time and I see it's been an hour and a half, probably my outer limit for dancing without overwhelming my body and the walk home does feel long and late and exhausting but also there's that extra space, that extra space in my body, sitting on this stoop to stretch my legs and leaning against that railing to let my hips go and bending around this tree to release everything, and yes, the next day I'm too exhausted, I mean every day I'm too exhausted but I'm even more exhausted than usual but also maybe there's something else.

I'm searching for Public School 49, which I know doesn't exist anymore, so I'm searching for the building. Why not map the physical whenever you can, a memory of someone else's memory.

Whenever I cross the highway into downtown, I lose my sense of direction, so I circle around until I find the right block. This must be it—next to the medical something-something building. Yes, it looks like this could have once been a school, from when schools were designed to look majestic, but it's impossible to imagine what this neighborhood was like because across the street is the hideous Symphony Hall, a redevelopment catastrophe. So it feels like the city just ends.

And maybe the empty storefronts and college-ready bars for the University of Baltimore amplify the emptiness, since so many of the major streets are closed off to make way for the white tents of Artscape, promoted as the largest public art festival in the country. And I'm thinking about something Karen, my Feldenkrais practitioner, a Jewish woman who moved to Baltimore in 1974, said when we were suddenly talking about Baltimore—she said: There's no money here, the only way to increase revenue is to bring it from outside.

I was telling her about walking around in Charles Village, Remington, Hampden, the intersections across the lines of identity that sometimes feel more possible for me here, and she said: That's not Baltimore.

She said: In the early years of AIDS I worked with babies with HIV, back before there were any medications, and their mothers were all addicted to drugs and many of them died, and that's Baltimore. And then I worked for years in the schools, and there was no hope in those schools, kids graduate from high school without even knowing how to read and that's Baltimore. Do you know the statistics on how many people are in poverty?

And she said: I was trying to bring yoga to the schools, because there's nothing external for these kids in those schools so I wanted to give them something internal—it was a program funded by a research grant and the woman in charge knew nothing about what actually happened in the schools, she had never even been there. But she got her paper published, and that was the point. And then the program was over.

Hopkins basically owns the city, Karen said—do you see all that work on Charles to make it look nice—that took years, and it was all for Hopkins. Have you been to their Bayview campus? They tore down everything in the area, everyone was displaced, entire families and neighborhoods, all torn down, and what for? My son went to see a psychiatrist there for a while, and it was just a machine. It's a racket. They call the shots. They're the only industry. That's Baltimore.

I'm sitting on Charles Street after the Crown, and some middle-aged redhead with a red face asks me if I've seen a tall Black guy with white hair, I'm guessing she's looking for heroin because she has that look in her eyes. No, I don't think so, I say, and she keeps walking. Then a little later I'm walking home, and there she is again, coming toward me with someone who must be the guy she was looking for. She wraps her arms around me and says I just realized, I just realized you're really sweet.

Once I asked Gladys if she ever went back to the neighborhood where she grew up.

You can't, she said.

What do you mean, I asked, does it not exist anymore?

I knew what she meant. She didn't say it, but still I knew she meant it had become a Black neighborhood. That's why she never went back.

It was a very nice neighborhood, Helen said, there weren't any Jews. Helen was also Jewish, so she was just pointing out what was most striking to her—that Gladys's white Christian neighbors might not have known she was Jewish.

And here the neighborhood is, a century after Gladys's family moved there, and seventy years after white flight began—block after block of old rowhouses where half the buildings have been boarded up. In many cases there's just a brick façade with nothing behind it, since the rest of the building burned down long ago. Only a few people are outside, nodding off in boarded-up doorways. Little kids playing on their own in the middle of the street, staring at our car like who or what or why.

The story of white flight and disinvestment. The story of Baltimore.

Occasionally there's a cheerful, freshly-painted building with flowers outside—oh, a liquor store. I'm with my friend Jules, a filmmaker who lives right near me in Charles Village, and we're driving back and forth on McKean Avenue, where Gladys grew up—it's a small street just off Fulton Avenue, a major thoroughfare. There's one block with a nice park, and on that block there are trees and the houses look well-kept and cheerful, but then it's back to half of every block boarded up. Nothing growing, just cement and desolation. This is Baltimore, block after block like this for miles, once you leave the white enclaves or the neighborhoods in the process of gentrification.

To gaze out at all this devastation feels too close to tourism—but we're looking for anything that might have been the A&P where Gladys's father worked, which was just a few blocks away from their house. If we find the A&P, then I'll know we're in the right place, since Helen didn't remember the address. But besides the liquor stores and the drug economy, the only business that looks active is someone selling sneakers and snowballs from a stand on Fulton Avenue as cars speed by.

We drive west on North Avenue—past more boarded-up buildings, more liquor stores, a flea market that says it's open once a week, a tag that says LOVE, which I recognize from my walks in Charles Village. Past a university and a community college, both '60s redevelopment projects, past a dump and a few strips of stores, some open and some closed, and then after a few turns we're in a wooded area on the edge of a huge park, how could this still be the city, and yet there are a lot of areas like this in Baltimore.

This is Windsor Hills, where the Olivers lived in their mansion with marble steps. I imagine that somehow I'll recognize that house—it was so monumental that it must have survived, right? But that's not how white flight works. There are still some mansions in the neighborhood, some beautiful but decaying, some subdivided, and some literally falling down. There's a huge one on a dirt cliff that's been stripped of everything so that only the façade is left—so much has been removed that it looks like the house is floating several feet off the ground.

Liberty Heights Avenue is more active than North Avenue—larger strip malls, discount chains, more people shopping. We drive farther, past a golf course, and then we circle back around to the house where Gladys moved when she married Ed in 1941. This is the house where she raised my father, I have the address because I found it on a flyer for an art show in her scrapbook in the archives at the Baltimore Museum of Art. It's a small, well-maintained craftsman house, with flower pots hanging on the porch. I can picture Gladys making art in her basement studio—and Gladys and Ed, my father, and Gladys's parents all living on the main floor—it would have been crowded, especially after Marvin, Ed's younger brother, moved in after his parents died. Someone must have lived in the attic too.

We walk around the neighborhood and it feels so tranquil, mostly small or medium-size houses from the '30s and '40s, I think, with incredibly plush grass everywhere. I imagine this is what it felt like when Gladys lived here, except now the trees are bigger and it's a middle-class Black neighborhood instead of a middle-class white neighborhood. People stare at us as we're walking around, they look a bit surprised but they're not unfriendly—when I wave, they wave back.

After a few blocks we get to the golf course, and on the edge there's some wilderness. It feels like such a peaceful place to grow up, and I wonder about my father. Then we wind back down a street with larger trees and older, larger houses, and when we're back at Gladys's former house I kind of hope the people living there will be outside like their next-door neighbors were before, so I can see if they want to chat about the house, but no one's out now. And I wonder if Gladys even knew the difference between the neighborhood where she grew up, which has been destroyed by structural neglect, and this neighborhood where she raised my father, which still feels entirely intact.

Yeah, that's the way you do it, I can FEEL the confidence, this woman says to me as I'm walking down Charles, past all the shade, there's a lot of shade today but she's right, I am feeling something else and I think it might be the change in air pressure because it's starting to pour out, yes it's pouring on my sunhat with the purple flower, my bare chest and purple shorts with rhinestone-studded translucent pink belt.

I'm getting soaked and I love it, two tank tops tucked into my back pocket and I put one on to go inside the train station.

In the bathroom, they're playing it's too late baby, baby it's too late.

And baby, what do I do?

I turn right back around, after I'm done with that bathroom.

So, honey, it's not too late.

Then there's the shirtless teenager who looks me up and down with his friends on bikes, and says where the FUCK is your shirt? Something tells me he's not really wondering about my shirt.

I keep seeing the same people on Charles, especially the ones who harass me. Like the guy I first saw after Pride when I was dancing with everyone in the street—I found a fun crowd on this one corner, mostly Black femmes, with a few butches or transmasculine types, and then some older interracial gay male couples who you could tell had been together a long time, and a few raverish weirdos of all races.

And then there was this young Black guy standing in the middle of the crowd and just staring at me. At first I thought he wanted to dance with me so I said hi but he just stood there staring at me with a strange look in his eyes, and I couldn't tell if he wanted to fuck me, or kill me. So I kept dancing in the blazing sun, it was the best house music I'd heard in a while.

Anyway, now I've seen him a number of times on Charles, and whenever he spots me he scowls and yells BITCH, so I guess he lives right around here. It's a Black neighborhood, so I'm the one who doesn't belong. One night he was with his girlfriend or maybe just friend, and he said: She wants your number.

And she said: He wants your number.

As long as the harassment stays at this level, there can be something almost friendly about it, right? Because there's a familiarity.

But then one night I'm walking home from the Crown, and the police have cordoned off this block—you can't get through, because someone was just murdered.

I'm here at the Store Ltd, Betty Cooke's gift shop, but what am I here to see? Maybe the brightly colored clear-plastic cube containers that used to be in front, now in an alcove in back—I still love those colors, purple and green and pink and yellow and all the combinations you can create by mixing them together. Or the vinyl change purses that turn into duffel bags when you unzip them and pull out all the fabric to turn them inside out—I remember the first time Gladys gave me one of those, and showed me how it worked, and it felt like such a magic trick.

One side of the store consists of cases displaying Betty Cooke's famous jewelry, mostly silver pieces connecting modernist sculpture with wearable art. And, when Jules and I go into that area, two middle-aged women come out from the back, one with sleek gray hair and the other with big glasses, they don't say can I help you they just watch.

There's a preppy fag at the front desk who gives a detailed description of everything else we look at in the store—this is the only thermos that will keep your coffee hot all day, those globes run on solar and wind, the tic-tac-toe set actually has three functions—it's a game, a set of coasters, and a set of trivets. I wonder if he's telling us all this because it's his job, or if he's just excited to see queers.

I actually don't know what a trivet is, but I have a brass tic-tac-toe set that Gladys must have gotten here. I'm struck by how much of her personal aesthetic must have been formed or informed here—the loose cotton clothes, the contemporary-yet-not-flashy, the dash of color among soft whites, the updates on minimalism, modern as a specific thing that evolves and yet remains the same.

And I'm thinking that this is what Gladys saw as sophisticated—a gated community inside city limits, not quite posh, but not quite not-posh. It was posher then, but now it's too dated to be exclusive. And Betty Cooke was seen as a design maven for much of Baltimore, someone bringing the flair of the Museum of Modern Art to Baltimore consumers. She created her own image with her silver jewelry, and borrowed from designers in the big destination markets to create her own niche.

An older woman wearing a huge pink sun hat and big silver earrings comes in with her daughter, who's helping her to walk, and for a second

I wonder if that's Betty Cooke. But after it becomes clear that she's a customer, I wonder if she might have known Gladys.

Cross Keys is such a strange place, huge trees and an open field on a hill, different housing developments arranged around what's described as a town square, but there's not much that's practical here—you can't get groceries or hardware and the different developments don't even connect to one another, so you have to drive in circles if you want to get from place to place.

On our way out of the store, I ask the guy at the front if Betty Cooke still comes in, and he says oh, how do you know Betty?

I say I'm working on a book about my relationship with my grandmother, who knew Betty, and he says what is her name.

Oh, he says, that name is very familiar.

He gives me a pad of paper, and I write a note for Betty—I'm Gladys Goldstein's grandchild, I write, thinking maybe I should say grandson, but shouldn't this be on my terms?

He reads my note, and says what's your name?

Mattilda, I say, and I point to it at the bottom.

I think of asking for his name, but why, when he says something like that.

Yes I'm walking shirtless in the rain again down Charles again, not even sure where I'm going exactly, and a crowd of women in green work scrubs yells get it, get it, GET IT!!!

And I throw my hands up in the air and smile back at them, and then a woman a few doors down yells hey, HEY, do you like to dance to house music, and I turn around to see if she's talking to me, yes, yes, and I say I love house music, where do you want to dance?

And she says not here, we have to go to a RAVE.

And I say okay, I'll meet you there.

The rain stops as I get to the bridge to downtown and I'm wiping the water off my chest so I can put my shirt on to go to the Jewish Museum—before I thought I might go to a movie, but then the rain cleared my head.

I decide to take the subway—it doesn't go anywhere near my house so it isn't generally practical, but now that I'm already downtown it's only a little out of the way. There are about ten turnstiles to get in—they were planning for something big and then they just stopped. It's open but it feels closed—a '60s dream of mass transit abandoned a decade later but then completed anyway, but only one line of the original six.

It's not crowded, and it's not empty, and I'm the only white person on the train, even though my stop is basically in the tourist district, right next to the Power Plant, a complex of bars where suburbanites get smashed. But white people don't generally take the subway in Baltimore.

I get to the Jewish Museum just in time for the synagogue tour—I learn that the Lloyd Street Synagogue is the third oldest synagogue still standing in the country, built in 1845 and saved from the wrecking ball in the 1960s. Now it's a museum. And then next to it is B'nai Israel, built in 1876 and still in use for worship today.

But this is no longer a Jewish neighborhood—the synagogues were saved, but not the rest. I ask when Jews left the neighborhood, and where in the city they went.

The tour guide doesn't really answer my question. He talks about how segregated Baltimore was in the 1950s, but I think he means segregated against Jews, because he emphasizes the Falls Road line that prevented Jews from living in posh neighborhoods like Roland Park, and the restrictive covenants elsewhere in the city. And he says the bad thing about this segregation was that Jews couldn't live where they wanted to, but the good thing was that Jewish communities were very dense, so that even though there are about the same number of Jews in Baltimore as in DC, the community here is much more developed.

I want to ask whether Jews were also part of enforcing segregation even as they were victimized by it, but I stop myself. I think it's because I'm already the odd one out—one of the families has a Black child but she's obviously Jewish too because they're talking about whether she would want to get married in one of these synagogues. And I get the sense that everyone is wondering about me. Whether I belong.

My mother calls on her way to visit me—she says she's at Cross Keys, and it doesn't look good.

What do you mean?

I mean it was already changing while Gladys was still alive, but now a lot of stores are closed, and the stores that are open don't look that good—Betty Cooke is still there, of course, but it doesn't look that good. But, you won't believe what happened. After taking a necklace in to be restored, and looking at all the jewelry, and walking around to look at the other shops, but there was nothing there, I went back to Betty Cooke, and guess who walked in the door?

Betty Cooke?

Yes.

Did you talk to her?

Yes, I said hello, and she said hello, but she didn't have a clue who I was.

But how would she?

You're right, how would she? And I said you may not know who I am, but I know who you are.

And she said Gladys used to come in all the time, she made some nice work. There's—and there she went way over my head, she was mentioning another artist, and she said: But she's nothing compared to Gladys. But what does that mean? She made some nice work, that doesn't sound nice at all, does it? She just wanted to get away from me, I could tell.

I think she just had a hip replacement.

You're right—she told me she had a hip replacement, and she could barely walk, but what was she doing coming into that store?

That's her routine, it's probably just what she does.

Anyway, I said to her, you've really survived. And she said what do you mean?

And what did you say?

I don't know what I said, but she looked offended.

It does sound kind of offensive to tell a ninety-four-year-old woman that you're impressed that she's survived. Now she's definitely not going to want to talk to me.

Oh, give her some time, I'm sure she won't remember.

I'm sure she'll remember—I just went in last week, and now you were there.

Just give her some time. I just couldn't believe how depressing Cross Keys was—I remember going there with Gladys, and she didn't want to run into Betty Cooke.

Why do you think she didn't want to run into her?

I don't know, because I always thought they were close—I know she designed some pieces for Gladys, and one time Gladys took in some beads, and she made a necklace for her, but maybe that was just business? Gladys really did seem concerned about running into her, and I was surprised. It might have been because she didn't think she looked that good, and she didn't want Betty Cooke to see her that way.

Well they knew each other for a long time, at least since the '60s, so Gladys probably went to that store since it opened.

I know, it's a part of our history—all of us, she would get us things from that store, ever since you were a kid.

And we would go there together.

Yes, all of us. But going there this time, it was really depressing. The three women working there, one of whom I would describe as beautiful, I mean to me, for an older woman, they weren't friendly at all, even though one of them said she remembered Gladys, and I just wanted more.

What did you want?

I guess I wanted to be entertained.

But that's not their job. I'm sure they're doing exactly what they were trained to do, I mean I'm sure they've all been there for years.

You're right—that one woman, the one I thought was beautiful, she said she had been there twenty years. But the whole place—I walked around the mall, and it looked like an Edward Hopper painting.

What do you mean?

The emptiness, the barrenness, like there was no one there—how does it still exist?

But now I learn that before Cross Keys became a gated community and a shopping mall, it was a Black village named after an inn. As early as 1802, not long after Baltimore became an incorporated city, Black people owned property in Cross Keys, and some of their homes were stops on the Underground Railroad, with hiding places sheltering people escaping from slavery on their way north.

After the Civil War, this was a village of several hundred people, including property owners and renters, churches, doctor's offices, a Black chapter of the Workingmen's Party, a nearby freshwater spring for bathing and laundry, grocery stores, a dairy, a café, and public schools. It was an intergenerational community of extended families connected with other Black communities along Falls Road to the north. Many families were of mixed heritage, including Black, white, and Native ancestry.

In the 1890s, when the Roland Park Company purchased the estates of former enslavers nearby, and began building exclusive whites-only neighborhoods, developers considered Cross Keys an unsightly nuisance. And yet, Cross Keys residents were hired by their new white neighbors to maintain their sprawling homes and enable their suburban lifestyles. Slavery had ended, and yet the pattern of race and class stratification persisted.

In the 1950s, the federal government funded highway construction across the country that destroyed Black communities as part of urban removal. In Baltimore, this wave of urban removal displaced at least ten thousand people, more than 85 percent of them Black. Half of Cross Keys was demolished to make way for the Jones Falls Expressway, including the churches, the doctor's office, and all but one of the stores.

Looking at a picture before the demolition in 1956, I see a charming street of storefronts with large awnings facing Falls Road, houses tucked behind mature trees. In a photo after the demolition, it's as if none of this ever existed.

Four years later, much of the remaining village was torn down by the city to relocate Western High School, which my grandmother had attended many years before, and Baltimore Polytechnic, where my father graduated in 1961. These were two successful public schools that had been whites-only until desegregation in 1954, and the city hoped that a new campus would keep white middle-class people from moving so rapidly to the suburbs, even with new highways built for that purpose.

When developer James Rouse purchased adjoining land from the Roland Park Company in 1961, he decided to name his new gated community after the Black village that had been destroyed by urban removal. He consulted with white residents of Roland Park because he needed their approval for permitting, but he didn't meet with anyone who remained in what was left of the Black village of Cross Keys.

Rouse was known as a proponent of integration, and his new "village" did not have any official racial or religious restrictions, but he initially planned for a quota on Black residents similar to one he enforced for Jews in an apartment building built by the Roland Park Company near the Johns Hopkins campus in 1951. When Jews protested that quota as anti-Semitic, Rouse responded that they should be grateful he was giving them access at all, considering that the developer had not allowed Jews before.

Perhaps Rouse felt similarly about Black residents in Cross Keys—his new development never instituted a formal quota but made sure only to allow a small number of carefully vetted Black residents, so that neighbors across Falls Road in the white-and-Christian-only Roland Park would not be too offended. Was this the kind of integration Gladys believed in?

I keep thinking about the narrative at the Jewish Museum about the neighborhood downtown where Jews first settled—the narrative that Jews moved there in the 1800s, and everyone got along. They established a thriving marketplace on Lombard Street, and everyone got along. Around the turn of the century, Italian immigrants started moving into the neighborhood, and into some of the stalls in the market, and everyone got along. In the 1930s and '40s, Black people started migrating from the South, and everyone got along.

In the 1950s, city planners decided that the area was blighted, and tore down much of the neighborhood to build high-rise housing projects, after many upwardly mobile Jews had moved into Northwest Baltimore and middle-class life. But people were optimistic about the process, and everyone got along. Then there was crime, but everyone still got along. Eventually city planners decided that the projects were blighted, and demolished the buildings in 2001. The city built new mixed-income housing to mimic the old housing that they had torn down. So maybe everyone didn't get along with the city planners, but they got along.

While I guess this narrative is better than an overtly racist one, or one that exceptionalizes anti-Semitic persecution, there's so much left out that it's hard to tell what is really being told. I'm not even sure whether they mention that Jews arrived in Baltimore because they were fleeing anti-Semitic pogroms in Europe. How strange that a Jewish museum wouldn't mention that—is the intent not to alienate non-Jews?

And then there's the fact that if and when Jews, Italians, and Black people did in fact get along, a lot of this probably had to do with common persecution, and racist and anti-Semitic housing covenants that existed in Baltimore until the 1960s. And then there's the role of Jews in white flight, in upholding structural racism. What a missed opportunity not to talk about all of this.

When I came to visit Gladys in 1993, and she was so completely frightened of me going to Mount Vernon, the downtown neighborhood with gay bars and cafés and thrift stores and galleries and gorgeous old buildings, this took me by surprise. This was not an unfamiliar neighborhood to her, but she was terrified of me walking around alone. To her, downtown meant violence.

In the 1970s, Gladys went to Mexico for several months alone, so she could study the Mixografia printmaking process Luis Remba had developed for Rufino Tamayo to create prints in relief. She called Tamayo the greatest living artist. She was also fond of saying that the self-taught artists who sold their work at marketplaces in Mexico were just as good as anyone in the galleries in the US.

In the 1980s, when Gladys was in her sixties, she went on a trip to Egypt by herself, and was enthralled by the pyramids and the art she found there. But in her own city, she didn't venture out of her comfort zone. She believed too much in the racist narratives about crime in Baltimore. She wasn't willing to look beyond her fear.

I get off the train in DC and I'm startled by the crowds of people rushing everywhere, the giant hall that literally sparkles—the calculated grandeur of everything. Baltimore and Washington are only forty miles apart, but this is a tale of two cities—DC is a boomtown, and Baltimore has been left behind.

I wasn't even sure I was going to DC today, I just got up and felt horrible, and walked to the train station in the heat. I knew I wanted to visit my grandmother Fran in assisted living in DC at some point, so I called her from the train. But she wasn't feeling up to a visit.

So I decide to go to the University of Maryland to see the collection of Gladys's work. Even though it's a half-hour drive heading out of DC, when else will I be here so I jump in an expensive cab and I'm on my way. We're driving through all these areas that used to be poor Black neighborhoods but now I see renovated houses and newly built condos and high-end apartments, mostly for white people. When I was a kid, DC was 80 percent Black, but in 2011 that percentage went below 50 percent for the first time in over fifty years, and the Black population has declined ever since.

My mother lives in an upscale loft in a neighborhood most white people were afraid of when I was a kid, but now if you stand on her corner around 5:00 p.m. you can watch hordes of white people in their business attire heading home from work. The Whole Foods across the street is so crowded that they changed the system for the checkout counter to the one they use for busy stores in New York, where you stand in designated color-coded lanes until your check-stand number flashes above.

But the art collection, it's a little depressing. At first I get to the building and I'm lost because they renovated it so everything looks different— Gladys's painting that I wanted to see the most, *Boy with Universe*, isn't in the lobby anymore, there's just a gray wall. Am I even in the right place? Oh, there's the sign marking the entrance to the collection, pointing downstairs, and then here I am in the current exhibit of Washington Color School painters, and then I walk to the end of this gallery, which is really a very wide hallway, and there's the sign for the Gladys Goldstein

Gallery, which is another hallway. These are fancy hallways, but they are still hallways.

This is the largest collection of Maryland artists in the state, and it's displayed in a conference center with bright geometric carpet that Gladys would have hated because she would have thought it competed with the art. Her collection starts with a bio, and then about twenty elegantly framed paintings, starting with one she painted when she was seventeen—I can tell they want to show a progression over seventy years of her life as an artist, but I wish they would tell us that. It's disappointing to see only one of her handmade paperworks on display, and there are no candy wrappers at all.

The other thing that's jarring is that in place of *Page IV*, maybe the largest painting in the collection, and one of my favorites, there's a giant painting by another artist. It's the exact opposite style as hers, and the largest piece in this gallery that's supposed to be dedicated to Gladys's work—couldn't they have hung this painting elsewhere? It would actually look great in the lobby.

Gladys thought her collection would be housed in a museum the university was planning, since that's what the director of the arts program told her, but that director is dead and all it says in the contract is that there will be track lighting for all the work. And there is track lighting.

But here's a piece I don't remember seeing before, *Magic Jar*, a mixed-media collage on canvas, the colors like a tablecloth of muted blues and pinks and gold foil, so many patterns contained in one pattern, how your eyes move in and out of focus as you travel from one to the next.

And now that I'm in a more contemplative space, I can go back to look at everything else again, like *Forest Song*, where the shape of a small wooden airplane wing Gladys had on her living room floor becomes trees. Or *January Blossom*, with all the colors coming through the white, and then there's a diptych where one canvas is half the size of the other, and I'm wondering how she decided to do it that way, the diamond shapes crossing over. And *Always*, where she must have thrown a translucent wash over the whole canvas, black brushstrokes dancing over gray and white and, yes, the light coming through.

Then I'm back at the big painting by Raoul Middleman at the beginning, which is also the end, and yes, it dominates—it's brash, it's figurative, it tells a story, and if it were upstairs on its own or somewhere else I think I might love it, the sensuality and blurring of gender. It's everything that Gladys took out of her art, and now her art has to deal with it anyway. For a moment I can appreciate this.

And then there's the added irony that Raoul Middleman wanted to study with Gladys in the 1950s, when he was a young abstract painter who found out about her work from a collector, and he followed the glowing reviews in *The Baltimore Sun*. But she turned him down as a student.

After Gladys's collection, there's an entrance to the Joseph Sheppard gallery, which is housed in an addition to the conference center. It cost $6.5 million to build, funded by the founder of the largest property management firm in the Baltimore-Washington area and other private donors. There are three rooms—one is an atrium with plants and trees and Sheppard's sculptures, which are bronze or marble and look like imitations of Greek or Roman sculptures. And then some of them depict baseball players.

Then you enter the painting gallery—glass doors, a towering ceiling with a skylight, beautiful wood floors and paneling, red cloth walls. The gallery is so over-the-top that it overwhelms the paintings, some of which contain satirical elements that draw my attention, and some of which just look like more imitations—still lives, portraits, whatever.

The third room of the Joseph Sheppard collection is a small, elegant library with his drawings on the wall. You can exit to the landscaped grounds from the sculpture atrium. There's a large sign incorporated into the glass entryway of the brick building that announces the "center for the art of Joseph Sheppard," with the name of the benefactor much larger, of course, but nowhere is there any mention of the rest of the art on display, just beyond the doors that lead to the conference center. There are four permanent collections hosted there, including local and international artists, and three galleries dedicated to single artists, as well as the main gallery hosting rotating shows, but there is no information about any of this. Sheppard gets the space that looks like a museum because a collector donated money on his behalf, of course this is an old story.

I go back through the collection of Gladys's art, and I can't help noticing the huge trash cans in the hallway, are those necessary? At least the bathroom is beautiful—gray walls matching the slate floor tiles, marble sinks, long thin mirrors with wood frames, Gladys would have appreciated this bathroom.

Back in the lobby, I'm looking at three works by contemporary Japanese artists, but wait, one of the title cards says Gladys Goldstein. I look at the works again—oh, that one at the top, a black box on white paper, and inside the box there's an explosion of color. But really it's all only black ink. And on the table there's an arrangement of succulents in a clear square glass container, green and gray plants and driftwood reaching up through white rocks and sand, with soil at the bottom—I look back and forth from the succulents to the drawing, and this is when I enjoy the collection the most.

I go outside to take off my shoes and walk in the grass to cool my feet. There's a lot of grass back here, and more of these fake Colonial college-campus-style buildings, but is there a campus here? What's this building with a gated driveway? Oh, it's the president's residence.

This branch of the University of Maryland was founded in 1947 as the College of Special and Continuation Studies, with locations around the state, and in 1949 it became the first university to send faculty to Europe to teach active-duty military personnel. Now it's called University of Maryland Global Campus, and it describes itself as the largest public online university in the US, with eighty thousand students and a presence on military bases all over the country, as well as in 120 locations around the world. There are huge banners on the building that advertise the university's connections with the Department of Defense. So essentially it's an arm of the military-industrial complex.

I need to eat something, so I decide to take a cab to the Whole Foods across the street from my mother's place on the way back to the train station. Generally I avoid Whole Foods for all the obvious reasons, but when I'm traveling it's one of the only places where I know I can get something to eat that might not make me sick.

Do I want to see my mother?

I actually think I do. So I call her, and ask if she wants to meet me in a half hour.

Are you serious, she says?

And when I get there, she says: I can't believe this is real.

And then when we're shopping for food, she says: This is the biggest surprise of my life—it's a great surprise, I don't usually do anything spontaneous.

And then later, after I've been over at her place for a while, she says: I think I'm finally realizing this is real.

My mother's selection of Gladys's art inspires me much more than the display at the university. Here you can see the full range of what Gladys could do, and every piece looks perfect in its space. In the loft, there are custom-made shelves to display ten framed candy wrappers, and they shine. And there are collages mounted in the lit backsplash in the kitchen. In the bathroom, there's a stunning candy wrapper on a white wall above the toilet. In her bedroom is the one piece of Gladys's work that I had in my room as a kid, a collage that I chose, and I can see why I chose it. All the layers of foil, reflective chains, one on top of the other. So many shimmering colors, so much movement within a deceptively geometric composition. Nothing is even, or straight, it's the layering that creates the organization, the continuous movement of your eyes.

The two large paintings next to one another in my mother's loft are different in style, but the colors intermingle. In the living room there's a painting that used to be in my father's dimly lit basement office at home, now displayed on a wooden easel that allows the winding forms to emerge on their own. And in the dining room are Keith Martin's drawings of ballet dancers from the 1930s, the ones he gave my father for his bar mitzvah, facing Gladys's abstract oil pastel drawings of female figures that she gave my sister for her pink-walled bedroom in the '80s, and the colors of the clothing in these drawings connect with the colors of the big painting on the next wall over. And then a tiny white collage on a white mat in a silver frame on a white wall, right by the balcony.

I can't credit my mother with this arrangement, not exactly, because she hired someone to do it for her. But it's a beautiful tribute.

Gladys was always the one that decorated my parents' houses, so I wonder what it meant that she never visited my mother's new home. It was just supposed to be a city home for my mother and father after they sold the beach condo. My father planned to pay for the new condo in cash with the proceeds, but apparently he forgot about the taxes on the sale of a second home and didn't have enough cash on hand to pay in full as he'd planned. So Gladys lent him the money.

I've never really understood this, since my father had much more money than Gladys, but it must have been something about access to cash right away. No one knew about my father's cancer yet. He would die before the condo was finished. After his death, Gladys told my mother that she knew that if my father were alive, he would have paid her back right away.

And my mother said: You're right.

That was all. She was keeping Gladys's money, even though she didn't need it. How Gladys must have resented this. How this must have doomed their relationship, if it wasn't already doomed.

But, I almost forgot—in my mother's closet, she has the autobiography I made for Hebrew school, with a laminated cover of collaged letters and photos, and inside, on one of the pages, there's a little square of handmade paper. And above it I write, "This is the first piece of paper I made. It is made of chopped up orange peels and orange juice."

You can see the grain of the orange rind and the subtle hue of the juice. I don't remember making this, but now I remember the feeling.

In my childhood autobiography I say that my favorite place was the Three Sisters, which was the name my sister and I gave to a clearing between three pine trees in the area between the edge of our backyard and the neighbors'. It was a lair, a hiding place, and a dream world, where deer and rabbits lived, and sometimes we did too, collecting pine needles and playing house. I remember my mother calling us back in for dinner, and we would try to ignore her for as long as possible.

And also I remember my father saying to me, just on the other side of the Three Sisters, where we had a mulch pile: You could chop up a dead body and put it in the mulch, and no one would ever know.

So it was better to stay in the Three Sisters.

Now I'm back by the trees at the edge of the golf course in the neighborhood in Baltimore where my father grew up, and I can't help imagining him running through the woods in search of treasure. Trying to escape his mother's perfectionist gaze. Trying to outrun the loneliness he felt as an only child—when did he start to resent his mother, a resentment that would build and build?

But I'm trying to imagine something else, something else in those woods. What might my father have found, if he found something else?

I'm on the phone with Brian Young, a former curator at the University of Maryland, who says his favorite work of Gladys's might be the candy wrappers—because that's when she's going out on her own, he says, she's not looking at anybody. He says he likes her paintings from the '50s the best, but maybe that's just because they fit in a recognizable lineage of Abstract Expressionism, maybe there hasn't been enough time for us to appreciate art of the '60s or '70s in the same way. Or, because the colors in her earlier work are darker, so you're conditioned to look at shape and form. He thinks her later works are more decorative because of the brighter colors and the lyricism.

I'm thinking about a conversation my mother had with a collector for the Phillips Collection, who took a look at the catalog for Gladys's retrospective and dismissed her entire career by saying that her work was "purely decorative."

I look at Gladys's paintings from the '50s, and I can recognize their skill, but they don't move me because she hasn't yet figured out her own style. And I always love color, so I never thought this would remove a work of art from the category of art, but Brian says critics are conditioned to see work that's moody or brooding as more accomplished.

Sometimes, when art is dated, it becomes canonical. And sometimes, when art is dated, it's just outdated. When you look at a Rothko or a Mondrian or a Pollock, how much of what you see is conditioned by the critics? If we're going to talk about whether art is decorative, let's talk about whether it's decorating oppression.

Joel and Norma Cohen became Gladys's next-door neighbors in 1986, but they didn't see that much of one another until 2004. That's when Joel retired from his job at Gimbel's and was working from home, and he got depressed because he had too much time on his hands. He volunteered to help Gladys catalog the work in her studio for the collection—eight hundred pieces or more, and that was just the paintings and paperworks. On most of the paintings, the title, date, measurements, and sale price were on the back, but many of them Gladys couldn't reach on her own, so Joel would hold up each one and dictate the details so Gladys could write them down.

Joel went over to her house every day for two years—he would ask a million questions about every painting, and Gladys liked answering. This was how they became close.

Joel and Norma were always going to flea markets, and after about three months Gladys asked if they could bring her back a wooden stool to collage. And Joel said how do you do that? And Gladys said it's easy—you take Elmer's glue, and you dilute it with water in a bowl, then you select the paper you want to use, you dip it into the glue, then you scrape off the excess glue, and you apply the piece of paper to the surface.

Why don't you do this stool, Gladys said, and at first Joel was hesitant but once he started he couldn't stop. He worked on it for about six hours, and then he came back the next day to finish it.

There it is in the corner of his living room, the first stool he collaged. I recognize Gladys's papers, but the borders are more defined between the pieces. I rub the top of the stool, which is red and uneven, and Joel says do you see that, at the end I asked Gladys if I could leave it like this. And she said: You can do anything you want.

And then there was the second stool, and the third stool, and Joel points to other stools in the living room. And pretty soon he was collaging on anything he could find.

Joel would go to Gladys's every day, for four hours a day—cataloging, looking at everything in her studio, and talking. After Joel had been doing collage for six months, they were at a restaurant and Gladys said you should start painting.

Joel said Gladys, I don't know the first thing about painting.

She said here, draw on this, and handed him a paper napkin.

Joel drew two stick figures with a dotted circle in between them, and Gladys said what is that?

Joel said it's two men walking a breast.

Gladys started laughing—she handed him the pen, and said why don't you title it, and sign at the bottom.

Then she took the napkin with her, and a few weeks later she handed it to Joel in a frame.

He takes me into his studio, and there it is, in a black frame with a black mat, a white dinner napkin with his drawing.

And that's how Joel became a painter. Gladys never told him how to paint, she just told him what to get. She never told him how to hold a brush, or how to mix paint. He said how do I start, and she said all you do is put paint on a canvas, move it around with a brush, and it will give you some sort of inspiration.

Gladys looked at every painting—Joel made one or two per day. She said Joel, you're a fast painter. He said is that good or bad? She said it's neither.

A lot of Joel's paintings were either titled with puns or were depictions of popular sayings, like *A Bird in a Hand Is Worth Two in a Bush*. He would bring every painting over, and Gladys would laugh, and she might say something like: This is a sky, but you don't have to just use blues, you can use any color. Or she might say: Is there anything in this painting that you would have done differently?

One time Joel knew exactly what she meant, because there were these weird figures all slanted to the right, and he hadn't noticed that before. He knew that Gladys liked horizontal and vertical, so he said it's called *All Right*, which he hadn't known before, he just said it as a joke, but then it became the title, and that was one of Gladys's favorite paintings—he tried to give it to her, but she said oh no I can't.

Gladys would never tell him what to do, but she would offer advice. She said: You're going to do things that you didn't intend on doing, and you're going to want to keep it that way. And he said give me an example.

And she said you're going to accidentally spill paint on a painting and decide you like it better that way. And she told him about spilling as a technique, but that didn't work for him because he didn't know how to mix color, it was better just to start with something.

She told him: You can take any abstract painting, and change the direction, and you might like it better that way. Or, you might like it both ways. One time he brought in a painting, and she said what do you think of this one? And he said I'm not crazy about it. And she said just redo it. And he said what do you mean? And she said just paint over it, you'll get some surfaces that you didn't know were there that come through. And now he does that all the time, because when he starts he never knows what he wants, so sometimes he ends up with three or four layers.

Gladys was different, Joel says. She laid out her paintings, more often than not. She would start with a white gesso over the whole canvas and then map it out with pencil. She would go over and over, he would see her agonizing over the smallest details for months on end. She always wanted everything to be balanced, so if something threw it off then she had to keep thinking about it until she found a solution, like adding a collage in the corner or some color in the center. It wasn't a traditional balance, not a symmetry but a balance of where your eyes would go.

He used to see her up in her studio at three in the morning, he could see her light on. But still she'd be up early in the morning and he'd ask her about it—were you up in the studio late last night? And she'd say yes, that was me, I was up in the studio, and they would share a laugh.

She had a painting group of seven students, all women, they had met for years. They came over every week for critique. She invited Joel to join, and he went over once, but he didn't feel comfortable, they all had art training so they were using a vocabulary that he didn't know. Joel said oh, so you don't like the background color? And Gladys said never say background—it's a negative, not a background. And that stayed with him, now he corrects other people, and they always say you're right. But at the critique, his feedback was totally the opposite of everyone else's. And Gladys said you know what, he's right. But that was the only time he went over.

Norma was there too, she went a few times. Gladys would always have cake, and cookies. During the critique, Gladys would walk over to a painting, and hold her hand over one particular part, and say what do you think of that? And they would realize it was better without that part. Or she might say if this was this, do you think you would like it better? That's how she would ask questions. She said she painted all her life, and painting was her life.

At the critiques, everyone had to start with something positive. And then after the critique, the artist would respond. It was a conversation. One time someone had a painting with a lot of weird bumps under the surface, and someone said what's that? And the artist said that's a prescription I don't take anymore, and I didn't know what to do with it, so I put the pills in the painting—I learned from Gladys that you don't throw anything away because you can always use it in your art.

Norma said she never heard Gladys say anything negative about anyone. But then one time they read the same book, and had the exact opposite opinion about one of the characters, and Norma was shocked because she had never heard Gladys talk about anyone that way. But then she realized it was because it was about a work of art. And I ask if she ever heard Gladys talk that way about other art, or other artists. And Norma thinks about it for a while and she says well, one time, I did, but I don't want to say who it was about, because I'm not totally sure, but what she said was "She gave up her child, and moved to New York to paint." And the implication was that Gladys could have done that, but she stayed home.

And I say was it Grace Hartigan? And Norma says yes, I think so.

When I asked Brian Young about the Baltimore art world of the '50s, '60s, and '70s, he said: There was one artist that really dominated, and that was Grace Hartigan, after she moved from New York in the '60s—and then she taught at MICA for decades—all the dominant artists in Baltimore taught at MICA, or at least that's what MICA would like to think.

And I remember opening up this coffee-table book about MICA at Betty Cooke's store, and there it was, a whole page on Grace Hartigan, talking about how she arrived in the '60s, and I wondered about Gladys, who also taught at MICA in the '60s, after she was recruited to teach abstract painting there. But she was there for only four years, 1960 to 1964. And, if MICA was the place where all the big artists taught, I wonder why she left. I mean, it could have been for any reason, but I look up when Grace Hartigan started teaching there, and it was in 1965.

But also there's Gladys's self-righteousness about staying in Baltimore to raise her son. I wonder what would have happened if she had moved to New York to pursue her career—if my father would have had more freedom then. If he wouldn't have built his life around impressing the mother he grew to resent. Maybe then he wouldn't have felt so trapped. Maybe he wouldn't have felt the need to trap the rest of us.

Gladys told Joel and Norma that it was because of them that she was able to stay in her house. How their relationship went from one of casual acquaintances to mutual support. And it started with generosity, and curiosity—Joel's offer to help Gladys catalog her art, Gladys's covert plan to make Joel into an artist. She wanted to make everyone into an artist, but with him it worked.

How often do neighbors really become neighbors?

The new owners of Gladys's house found a sketchbook of hers when they moved in, and they gave it to Norma. And Norma gave it to me—on the cover, in Gladys's handwriting, it says "Autobiography, Book 1." The paper has yellowed with age, and the pencil may have faded, but still, this is thirty pages of Gladys's life story, in her own words.

The first sentence is: "I can't remember my childhood."

Gladys describes pushing her baby brother in a carriage, and her older brother sitting on the steps with a gun, "A toy gun, no doubt, but to me it was very real."

Gladys's older brother is taking care of her while her father is at work, because her mother has gone to Philadelphia to visit her sister Rose, who is very ill. Rose is in love with a married man, and after Gladys's mother brings her back to Baltimore she dies of a broken heart on her twenty-first birthday.

"Does that really happen," Gladys asks, "it seemed like there was more to the story than when I was less than three, I wish my mother was here now to tell me what really happened between Rose and Alex, and why Rose had to die. And that must have had something to do with my growing up because although Lon was taking care of me during the day, I knew that I was no longer a child."

So this is something else that Gladys and I have in common—we felt like we were adults when we were children. By age three, Gladys is already walking for miles with Lon, her five-year-old brother, going downtown to travel agencies so he can collect brochures "to far away places." When Gladys mentions her first boyfriend, Roland, it's as if her sixth birthday celebration is also their engagement party. Gladys's father decorated their house with butterflies he'd made from crepe paper that were "all the colors of the rainbow; they filled the living room and the dining room, and balloons floated next to them." There was a magician, and there were lots of grown-ups.

Roland gives her a ring—"it was very grown up and I loved it."

The word "engagement" is crossed out. What does this engagement at six years old mean, crossed out?

Gladys describes her childhood walks with Helen in the

neighborhood, their adventures in the nearby woods, "Long walks, mostly for silence; somehow my memory feels most of all Helen's being there."

"Trips to the beach, picnic lunches, our first dates, our first trip to a nightclub we both almost choked trying to smoke a cigarette." Gladys thinks all the boys are in love with Helen, but it sounds like she and Helen are in love. "I thought of her then and think of her now as a daffodil!"

Gladys's father works for A&P, which is still a tea company in the 1920s, and "We weren't poor but we never had enough money." When A&P starts carrying produce, her father gets promoted to produce buyer, and he purchases a car for the family. He gets up early in the morning to go to the waterfront to buy produce, and he always brings home a sweet cantaloupe or watermelon or other exotic fruit. They rent out the upstairs of their house to different families, until eventually they have enough money to live on their own. Gladys remembers getting very sick, first with an ear infection and then with shingles. For months, "the walls and the ceiling seemed to be closing in on me."

Gladys's bedroom is in the back of the house, which faces the back of her friend Doris's house. Doris is a tomboy who "skated better than the rest of us and was always running, but Doris died. She must have been ten or eleven then. They said she had a hole in her heart, but I couldn't understand that then. I couldn't quite figure out what happened. I had nightmares of someone taking her out of the house wrapped in brown paper, and she wasn't around anymore."

And then another Doris, who is hit by a car. And Donald, whose twin brother is hit by a car. And then "later, much later, the son of the Chinese laundryman was drowned when he went swimming and I recall his father saying 'the neighbors won't complain about my boy anymore.'"

Gladys's mother loves to dance, but her father thinks dancing is "just a cheap lug," and so he forbids it. But when he works late on Saturdays, Gladys's uncle Aron, her mother's brother, comes over, and they pull the shades and turn on the record player and dance the Charleston, which they teach to Gladys, until the neighbors tell Gladys's father, and after that they can't dance anymore.

Then Uncle Aron disappears, "and it wasn't until recently after he died we found out anything about him. Mom never knew why and she used to cry. We knew he was alive, because he called me during the war and wanted to know if his mother was still alive, that he was in the army. But he never came over and wouldn't give us his address. I think Lon said he saw him once in a while—that he was a bartender at the Belvedere, but I never saw him again. After he died his widow was going through his things and she came across a birth certificate with another"

And that's how this volume of Gladys's autobiography ends, in the middle of a sentence. With the sudden deaths of all these children, the strictness of Gladys's father, and the disappearance of her uncle. But did he actually disappear, or was he banned from the house by her father? There must be more to this autobiography, since this is "Volume 1," and it ends in the middle of a sentence, but I don't even know where to look for the rest.

Sometime in the 1970s, when Effie Gereny was in her thirties, she saw one of Gladys's paintings at a gallery show in DC, and she was so taken by it that she looked Gladys up. She found out that Gladys was teaching at Notre Dame, so she signed up for the class. At the time, Effie was a realistic painter—the class was such an eye-opener, she says.

Gladys invited Effie to come to her house for the Monday critiques that she hosted, but Effie couldn't afford to pay. Gladys invited her anyway.

Effie says: She took me under her wing. As time went on, she was a tough customer. She wasn't prepared to work with you unless you were willing to work hard. She recommended shows and books—we went to a Richard Diebenkorn show together, and at first I wasn't that taken with his work, but the more she spoke about his art, traveling, and experiences, the more important he became to me. It was a slow but steady learning experience. There was no nonsense with her when it came to art. She was doggedly serious in our learning from each critique—you couldn't just miss a critique, this wasn't allowed or she would think you weren't taking your art seriously enough. If she felt that you weren't painting as much as you could, or if she thought you were losing a real interest in painting, she would say something. She was very direct.

I wasn't sure I could continue painting, because of responsibilities at home, Effie says, and Gladys kept urging me to continue no matter what. I went to Japan for a year when my husband got a teaching job there, and I thought I was going to have to give up painting, but Gladys sent me money to buy art supplies. And then I had a very successful show when I came back, and Gladys was there to support me. She was the reason I became an artist. She understood what painting meant to me.

Gladys only taught seniors at Notre Dame when Claudia DeMonte was a student there—Claudia was intimidated because she knew all the other art teachers at the school, and had already taken several classes with each of them, but Gladys seemed like she lived in a different world. She was very confident and sure of herself, sophisticated—she wore simple but elegant clothing, and she was a working, exhibiting artist who had a studio practice.

Gladys said you have to do this all the time, not just at school, artists make art all the time, you have to have your own style. If I remember correctly, Claudia says, she was adding sand to the paint at the time, and I never thought of something like that.

This was the late '60s, and the world was in the midst of the sexual revolution, but this wasn't happening at Notre Dame, which was a Catholic girls' school where you had to get permission to see boys in the lobby. Claudia was dating a guy who was four years older than her, and a student at MICA, and the nuns were scandalized. They didn't say anything, but they probably knew more than they were letting on. In her age group, women either got married and had kids or had a career. And she eventually got married but never wanted kids.

The way the class was set up was that everyone would paint on easels, and Gladys would walk around and talk about the paintings. She would ask questions—Why is everything in the middle of the canvas? Or: Have you thought of painting all the way to the edge? She would ask about using thinner paints, or thicker. She wanted to encourage all the different ways to put paint on the canvas.

Claudia says: She knew all the technical things about painting, and she was more aware of art that was being made at the time, and I think that was because she was making it. At the end of the class, everyone brought their work in for critique, and people had about three paintings each, but I brought in a huge amount of work, it took up a quarter of the space in the room.

All these drawings—they weren't very good, Claudia says, but Gladys didn't say anything like that. She saw the ambition, and she was impressed.

Gladys invited Pam Berwager to join the group of students she taught once a week in the basement of the church down the street from her house, and Pam was flattered, but she wasn't sure what the rest of the women thought, since they had been with Gladys for years. Pam was about fifty, and she was the youngest. They would get together in the morning, and paint for several hours, and then they would have lunch together and critique each other's work.

Pam says Gladys was very generous and very honest, if she thought you were working below your capabilities she would tell you, and she would tell you why, in both technical and ethereal terms. She told Pam that she had excellent taste and a sense of color, which made her paintings pretty, but it didn't necessarily make them good.

Pam could paint something realistically, but she was trying to unlearn this, and it was very difficult. Pam had finally made a painting where she thought she had left realism behind, she thought she had finally painted something that was Abstract Expressionism, but then Gladys said I want you to stand back and look at it and tell me why it's not Abstract Expressionism.

And she pointed out that there were two styles in the painting, one where there were images that were just shaded in a single color, but then there were a couple places where she had used shading to paint a piece of fabric or something like that, so the realism was still there.

As Pam got better, Gladys would get tougher, she might say the forms are great, and the colors are lovely, but I know you can do better. Or, she might say: What in the world are you doing?

Everyone in the class knew that Gladys loved apples, so they tried to impress her by bringing in apples that no one had ever heard of, carefully sliced into pieces. And then they would go around the room, and critique the apples.

Pam says Gladys stayed young no matter what, she was intensely curious and not dogmatic, she was interested in all forms of art, everything that was new—like computers, she wanted to hear about it. Everything except realism.

Pam would drive her to the University of Maryland when they were getting the collection ready, or to doctor's appointments, and Gladys would look out at the branches of the trees, and say: Do you see that negative space?

Gladys adopted me as the daughter she never had, Pam says. She was very private, and I respected her privacy. She would tell me what she wanted to, and not the rest. Sometimes she would tell me that she had painted me into a painting. She would ask what I thought of her work, and where it fit into her work as a whole.

Gladys thought conservative art was an oxymoron, Pam says—she was interested in anything new and different, and this is what all of her students embraced.

My mother says: Gladys saw herself as a feminist—she was a strong believer in women's rights, and her right to do as she wished. Always. This was totally consistent all the way through, that she saw herself as a strong feminist. She married Ed because he was going to allow her to shine, to have her own career. She was a pipe-smoking feminist, everything, the way she dressed—her clothes, she never wore tight clothes. The way she handled herself. Everything. She believed a woman should be independent, have her own career, make her own income. She went to Egypt without Ed. She went to Mexico by herself to study art, for months. But she wanted me to cater to her son—she said a few times to me that if you and Bill are that unhappy, both of you would be better off if you got a divorce. Even my mother, no matter how invasive she was, she would've never said something like that.

I say: But don't you think that's because all your mother cared about was propriety? And part of being a feminist, if that's how Gladys identified, is to go against propriety when necessary.

I thought it was none of Gladys's goddamn business, my mother says. Because I wasn't asking for an opinion.

But do you think it was true?

Oh, yes. But she certainly wasn't saying it for my benefit. I don't think she saw me as separate from being Dad's wife, from being a mother. I was there to be a good wife, a good mother, and to include Gladys and Ed as grandparents. Gladys idealized Dad. He was like a god. As long as he was achieving, she was enamored, proud, over-the-top. She would have never said anything to Bill.

But maybe that's because he wouldn't have listened.

When she said it, it wasn't from a caring point of view, she was irritated.

But do you think it could have been both?

My mother says: Bill would have loved to go to a museum with her, but I couldn't tolerate it because I felt like I would be invisible, dehumanized, in the shadow. It would be totally between Gladys and Bill, and I would be dismissed, alienated, so I didn't want to be a part of it. I told him he could go anytime, but he refused to, because he couldn't deal with being alone with her.

Do you know why?

No.

Was he angry at you for not going?

I don't know. I was stupid. I had a lot to gain from learning from her, but I didn't want to hear her opinions or her expertise because to me she would be showing off. I was thinking of her as a rival, as someone who would overshadow me.

My mother says: At times, there were some unhealthy things going on between Gladys and Bill, like they were boyfriend and girlfriend.

Do you mean they were physically affectionate?

No, there was no physical affection.

Do you mean their relationship felt romantic?

No, it wasn't romantic.

Then what do you mean?

I'll have to think about it.

My mother says: I was the only one who noticed, but when you were eighteen months to two years of age, I thought something was wrong because you were interested in ribbons and in women's fashion magazines. And Gladys would take you into her bed, and call you a pretty boy, which I thought was totally inappropriate. You wanted to play with girls and not boys, and at some point, I don't know when exactly, but you were very young, Dad and I took you to see a therapist, and she didn't see any concern.

But don't you think the real problem was your homophobia?

I wouldn't call it homophobia.

What about when I came out to you, and you suggested that I go to conversion therapy?

I wouldn't call it homophobic, I wanted you to have an easier life.

My mother says: The first time I went over to Gladys's, I was wearing a pale blue pants suit that was my mother's, and a ton of makeup, and Ed got all excited, and said Bill's bringing over a girl. But Gladys wasn't out yet, and Dad was very impatient, he said if she's not out here we're leaving. And they didn't even know we were coming over, so I thought he was being ridiculous.

And then Gladys came out, this tiny woman with a pipe. And I thought she looked like a little kid. And that's what I said, I said you look like a little kid.

And right away she liked me. I was a sweet girl, from a good family with well-known doctors who Gladys had heard of, she was very impressed by doctors. She loved that I was Jewish, but I didn't look Jewish. Her friends would say so your son is dating a gentile, and she would totally get a kick out of that.

Right away, I was the total opposite of who Bill and Gladys thought he would marry. He didn't like blondes. He didn't like curvy women, he liked flat-chested, dark-haired, super-thin tiny women like Gladys. He liked Asian women, he liked educated women, and I was none of that. I knew nothing. Gladys wanted to connect him with women majoring in art history—both Gladys and Bill thought he would marry someone who was an art historian. But right away we hit it off. She made a huge effort to get along with me. Anything that I ever said I liked that she was wearing, especially jewelry, she would take it off and give it to me. I had never had that experience, ever. I think she was worried that he would never marry, that he wouldn't have kids, and when we got married she said to me: I know that he can be difficult. But you're taking over now. I don't have to be responsible anymore. You're the one that's responsible. I think she thought I was going to save him.

Gladys was not perceptive, she was not intuitive in any way about people. She would ask me what a painting needed, and I had no idea. She had very strong opinions about things, but she would do the total opposite. What you saw was not what you got. She would always work and paint until she dropped, she did this every day, this was at the end of her life. She would wear herself down to the bone. She would continue moving paintings around even when she had severe back problems, which was very self-defeating.

Gladys stopped showing her work because Ed had heart disease. Because she wanted to take care of him. She treated him like a baby. And he was fine with that.

Gladys taught me so much. She taught me about art, she taught me taste in jewelry, she taught me the art of cooking and the enjoyment of eating. Dinner at her house was very special, and you were expected to be ready, to be dressed, and I had never experienced that before. She taught me that the presentation of the food mattered as much as what you served, the table settings, how to be a hostess. She had a great respect for food and how to handle it, just watching her hands work was so enticing.

She was a great believer in saving everything—she didn't throw it away. She would save anything. She did have an obsession with being thin and not eating too much, I don't know if she had an eating disorder, but she ate like a bird.

And then design, I've never met anyone with an eye like hers. She could put things together that you would never think belonged together, and they looked great. She didn't like expensive, she was definite about that, but she would buy something very inexpensive, and it looked expensive.

My mother says: Gladys knew from an early age how difficult Dad was. She took him for psychological testing. The psychologist said he needs a lot of love, a lot of attention, and he'll be okay.

I say: Do you think they gave him that attention?

I don't know. She never accepted him for who he was as a person, she treated him like an object to attain for her.

That was exactly how he treated me.

My mother says: Gladys knew that Bill had an unbelievable amount of energy, like her, and there had to be an outlet for that energy. She knew that Dad wasn't nice, he was just not a nice person. And I don't think she was either. I'm not sure if it was before or after he had cancer, before or after he died, but she said: I didn't think you two would last a year.

But I do remember she gave up smoking, which she loved, she loved the pipe, and cigarettes too, it was a big part of her personality. She gave that up because she didn't want any smoke around you as a kid, she thought that would be a terrible thing, and it wasn't even something that I had ever thought about. People just didn't think about it. But she gave that up, and I think that was very hard for her, but she did it, right when you were born.

I don't know what she felt about me, what she really thought. She knew that I didn't love her. The first time I met Bill, I went over to his place on Capitol Hill, and he said what do you think about the artwork? And I said it doesn't mean much to me, I don't know. I don't know that I really care. And I think he loved that.

Janet Mishner started studying with Gladys in the late '80s or early '90s. Her mother had taken Gladys's classes, and she said if you want to learn about color then study with Gladys. After several years, Gladys invited her to join the critique group at her house, which felt like a great honor, to have another opportunity to be in her world.

If there were eight people in the room there were eight very different styles of art, this was what Gladys encouraged. Her shining talent as a teacher, Janet says, was that she was tremendously intuitive—she would tell you exactly what you needed. A lot of teachers just see you as a student or an acolyte, but that wasn't true of Gladys, she wanted you to be great.

I had absolutely no idea how to make an abstract painting, Janet says, and Gladys would say just have fun. When she was teaching from ten to two at the church down the hill from her house, she would walk around the room and observe while you were agonizing. She showed me how to build composition with color—she would hold up one of her minerals and say look at all the colors in this, and you would see all the different layers, even in whites. She would say a color is only a color when it's next to a color.

Everybody in the class was Jewish, and sometimes the priest from the church would come down to say hello. There was so much camaraderie in the class—we would talk about books, movies, art—nobody painted from setups, we would paint from emotion. Gladys was always very interested in aesthetics, and that included herself. She was beautiful at ninety-two.

Janet sends me a picture of Gladys with wrist braces on, still making collages in her studio at the end of her life. The pail of glue sits in front of her on the table, and behind her is the giant door to her studio, which she collaged when she moved in, swirls of reds and oranges and whites. Behind her there are paintings arranged on the floor with strips of bubble wrap between them. There's a small black square one with a gold collage in it—even though it's not in focus, you can sense all the textures. Gladys is looking right at the camera, and you can see the determination in her gaze, but also a softness.

Bobby Donovan was hired to write the catalog copy for Gladys's retrospective. He went over to her house for months, first to have tea, then to go in the studio and talk about art—and he says Gladys never mentioned her career. She never even showed him her scrapbook of articles.

Gladys saw herself as a contemporary artist, so she didn't want to be defined by the past. She wanted her art to be considered on its own. But then Bobby wrote the catalog copy, and she rejected it. So someone else was hired to write it.

Bobby says Gladys was not a risk-taker, she was fiercely competitive with herself and how she saw herself among Baltimore artists, but she turned her back on the professional art establishment, and after that she didn't pursue a professional career, and you can't expect the world to come to you. She enjoyed the process of painting, and put that above anything else.

Like many artists of her generation, Bobby says, Gladys made the mistake of thinking that genius will be discovered.

One of my favorite things about living in Baltimore is watching my neighbors across the street, a father and adult son who sit together on the porch on most nights and some days, shoulders touching. They actually look like they get along, they look like they're friends, they look like they enjoy living together.

It's strange to look at a painting in search of yourself, especially when it's an abstract painting about you, *Boy with Universe*, dated 1976, when you were three. You can't search the face for clues, not even the body.

You can search for a body—is that one there, the movement of color into form?

This painting used to be in the lobby of the University of Maryland conference center, right by the entrance, but now it's only accessible on a prearranged tour with staff. It's upstairs by the offices, in an expansive hallway with a lot of other interesting art—one thing I like about this collection is that so much of it is on display. Even if this part of the collection isn't publicly accessible, at least someone gets to see it. And what is the point of a painting in a collection if no one sees it?

Boy with Universe is on a wall by itself, a gray wall like the walls in the lobby. It feels strange to be standing here with the curator, there's so much intimacy in the dripping of orange through peach—a yellow halo—not-quite-stars emerging through black or purple or brown or white. All the little paintings inside the bigger one, the way you don't notice this in a reproduction.

But shouldn't I be naked and pressing my lips to the paint to see what I can feel, or rolling on the carpet to experience the movement in the painting—how does the body remember the body?

It's my second time at the Mark Bradford show at the Baltimore Museum of Art. The first time I walked in knowing nothing, like I walk into most of the shows at the museum, maybe I was thinking about this notion of art that's decorative versus whatever the other thing art is supposed to be, and whether abstract art at this point can ever be anything but decorative. And does this matter.

So then I walked into the Mark Bradford show and right away I went somewhere deep into the texture and shape and form, the repetition and the breaks, the ripped apart and pressed together, the torn up and torn out, the inside out, the opening up, the softly screeching, the surface as containment and the surface as everything beneath the surface and the surface as not a surface at all but a depth of feeling.

And now I'm in the room with three huge black paintings formed by shimmering rectangles covering the canvas from side to side and top to bottom, and someone says: It reminds me of a film reel, where all the frames are slightly different.

And I hadn't thought of this before—the way the light comes through, what are we watching here.

Medusa is the tangled form in the center of the room, surrounded by the Sirens in those shimmering rectangles on the walls, and I notice that Medusa's snakes are held together by bungee cords, some of which look like tongues. Or do the bungee cords create the surface around which the snakes are formed?

In the next room there are three huge canvases in red, pale blue, black, cream, beige, tan, the colors formed by industrial paper mushed into a texture between paint and collage. There's so much energy in the one in the center for me today, I keep standing up and sitting down and moving around to look at it from different angles, just so I can feel the explosion of form out of form and into form.

The description says the work invokes the unfulfilled possibility of Reconstruction—the title, *Tomorrow Is Another Day*, comes from the final line in *Gone with the Wind*, and I'm wondering whether this adds to the painting or distracts from it.

The colors of the flag, and the colors of flesh and blood and sky.

And then you walk into the next room, and it's such a simple video, a Black queen shot from behind, wearing just a white tank top and orange exercise shorts, walking slowly. I say queen because of the movement of the hips. The video is called *Niagara*, and it recreates a scene from a Marilyn Monroe movie, but now it's not Marilyn walking away with a swish of the hips it's this Black queen.

I decide to go back through the exhibit from the beginning, starting with the giant rounded pockmarked papier-mâché mass protruding from the ceiling to the floor of the first room—you have to walk around it to get through. I'm gazing up at all the textures and the grooves, feeling its hollowness with my hands when the security guard isn't looking.

Then, when I'm staring at one of the Sirens again, a docent comes over, and says what do you think?

I love it, I say.

And she tells me she's about to give a tour for someone's eightieth birthday. No, seventieth, she says.

She looks like she's somewhere between seventy and eighty.

I say I'm thinking about whether the work is more impactful without the titles. And she says I tell people to go through one time without looking, and then to go back through and read everything.

She says have you noticed how the sculpture is held together? And I say yeah, with bungee cords, and she says zip ties too.

And there's a barcode, she says. And then we look for it.

Oh, there it is, but what does it say on it, handwritten?

New Medusa.

She says it came in parts, and when he was directing the staff, he said you assemble it like a hairdo—a little this way, a little that way.

Have you seen him in person, she says. He's like twice your height, and he has so much energy.

I was looking at the names of the Sirens, she says, and those aren't the names. I can't find them anywhere. I was looking at a book this big, she says, and she holds out her hands about a foot wide—I even took out my phone, and asked Alexa.

The free museum is the museum that matters. I mean matters for public space. I mean I'm back at the Mark Bradford show, and it's only a day later. I'm here because it's so cold outside that my morning walk, which is really in the afternoon, it can't take me any further until I get warmer. So I'm here to use the bathroom, I'm here to get warm, and I'm here to see this show again.

I ask about his poem at the entrance, is it really carved into stone? The staff person says it's cement, but it's a cement panel, maybe an inch thick, so that it's not so heavy that one person can't carry it on their own. And this time I notice how the art in each room is visible from the room before, like you see *Spoiled Foot*, that's what the first piece is called, you see it before you get into that room, glowing inside, and this time it actually feels like a giant standing above, formed from everyday scraps, fixers and fasteners holding us together.

And then I'm back in the room with the Sirens, and this time I notice the scratches, or what look like scratches on the film of the canvas that's really created with paper, layers of shimmering paper, and here I'm thinking about Gladys's Emotional Squares formed by torn pieces of canvas and paint, or hand-dyed papers and other collaged materials over the canvas so the light comes through, and is that what's happening here too. I mean it's happening, it's happening for me. Two artists who never knew one another, and almost surely never knew one another's work, but still a potential dialogue across time and space and identity and experience and how I'm here in the middle of it. How abstraction can create this.

Then I'm in the next room with my three favorites, the way the one in the center opens up my chest because of the scratches moving outward, stretching horizontally. How the dialogue between these three pieces feels different today, because I feel different. How that queen's ass is visible from this gallery too, if you look in that direction—the mundane and the extraordinary, the extraordinary in the mundane, and I realize I'm wearing the same colors as the papers that make up these works of art, and I'm all by myself today in this exhibit, except for the security guards, and it's so quiet, and how that affects how I'm feeling everything too.

Then I turn around and there's Medusa with her Sirens, and I'm thinking about how Medusa turns men to stone, and the Sirens seduce them into throwing themselves onto the jagged coastline. So you're walking past the bodies of all these men. None of them can harm us, not anymore. We can't even see them.

And then downstairs on my way out, past the gold sculpture with the alarm, through the contemporary Asian photography and then the plundered remnants of past civilizations and into the entrance with a gilded elevator, and this woman stops me to say I wish you were here for my talk, it's a talk about patterns, and you would be perfect.

She says the talk is for four-year-olds. And I kind of want to go.

On my next trip to the museum I'm fascinated by the moment in the Ryan Trecartin video installation where this drunk high school kid says to Ryan when he's in high school, holding the camera: "They all suck because they're all being gay to me. Nothing but love for them and I get nothing in return." The homophobic cliché voiced without cliché in mind, and what is the developing queer person behind the camera thinking? We see the layers of irony, but what do the kids in front of and behind the camera see? The way this installation is set up with rows of plush sofas on thick orangish carpet—the suburban family room, and are we in the basement, watching the kids of the suburbs saying let's fuck shit up. Let's fuck shit up. Let's fuck shit up. They know what they're imitating but still they're imitating.

Through the night-vision setting of a video camera from 2000 or before, edited with all the current tools available, we watch the drunken suburban antics that aren't exactly a re-creation, I mean this is actual footage of drunk straight boys smashing mailboxes with a sledgehammer, throwing TVs out of speeding cars, pulling a flag off a lawn and burning it, and is this porn, I mean it might be porn for me.

They've trashed the neighborhood, but they're still talking back to the cops. Do they get away, it seems like it. White privilege, class privilege, straight privilege, it's all here unadorned. The way the video is edited so that it circles around itself, the layers melting into one another, the sound looping, everything distorted and clear. Drunk glee, drunk frustration, drunk horniness. Sitting on the sofa in this museum I wonder if anyone's going to have sex here. The lights are dim, we're watching porn, are you ready?

Whenever I walk through Mount Vernon in search of a density of desire, but it's not there, not really, I walk down Charles Street, and I pass the Afghan restaurant where I went with Gladys twenty-six years ago.

Yes, it's still right there in the same place, and this time I decide to go inside.

At first I'm disappointed when they seat me in the main dining room that I'd forgotten about, but then I realize this is where we were, at one of those big tables in the middle. I remember I was surprised that Gladys liked the painted screen on the wall, abstracted tree branches with white flowers, a mother touching her daughter's shoulder as she climbs a tree. And then, at the far right, a girl playing the flute while facing away. I think I was surprised because the figures felt cheesy to me, but now I see the sharp delineation between positive and negative space—the green in front, and then the brown of the horizon into the white sky. Is something burning, or is it just the boundary between the lushness of this landscape and a more desertlike place beyond?

The child playing the flute reminds me of a Grace Hartigan painting on display at the University of Maryland when I first visited the collection—the flute player ruins everything, that's what I thought.

Are you vegan, says the waiter when I ask about dairy in the vegetable soup, which contains eggs, and so he recommends the vegetable platter. And I wonder if this is the same dish I ordered twenty-six years ago. It has a lot of flavor, but it's a little too spicy, and it's making me sweat.

Yes, I think I remember this.

How time circles around us, and then we're back. I'm watching the people sitting at the table where we were sitting—I came with Gladys and Ed, I keep forgetting he was with us because usually he made himself invisible. Or Gladys made him invisible?

We argued about something, but I can't remember what. Maybe that I was staying out too late—yes, that's what it was. Ed took Gladys's side, I don't think I had seen him get angry before and I liked him less.

The waiter wants me to know that the green sauce is vegan, are you allergic to walnuts?

No? You will love it.

And he's right.

I'm inside the inside of the Baltimore Museum of Art, through the offices and into the painting vault—oh, there's a Barbara Kruger on the floor, by the door. I've visited the archive a number of times, but this is my first time in the vault—it took a while to arrange an appointment, so it's useful that I'm in Baltimore for so long.

Most of the paintings are hanging on giant steel doors that slide out with some difficulty, and Gladys's painting, a huge diptych from 1967—each panel is seventy inches by fifty inches—is up high, in fluorescent lighting, so it's difficult to see all the details, but still there's something meditative about gazing upward at the brushstrokes, the places where the paint gets thicker and thinner, the two rectangles of a deeper texturing, and I'm surprised when I look at a Polaroid of the painting in the museum archive, and it's white that dominates, whereas in the vault it's the browns and yellows.

In the viewing room, I look at three of Gladys's works on paper—two are from 1955, and described as opaque watercolors, but the curator points out that they look like oil paint applied to paper with a palette brush. Both are abstract, but one looks like a variation of a landscape, with tree branches stretching into geometry. And in the other I recognize some of the movement she would later use in her collages, like the one from 1973 that I have hanging in the entryway of my place now that I keep thinking looks like a seaside scene although everything is a shimmering and layered white.

And the third piece looks a lot like a Miró, actually—he was an artist that I know she admired, but I hadn't seen his impact directly before, in the color palette and the gestures. It reminds me of when I went to an exhibit of Miró's drawings, and I sent Gladys the brochure, and then when we talked about it there was none of the usual tension between us.

They also have a number of Keith Martin's works on paper, so I can look for the relationship with Gladys there. Unlike Gladys's collages, his are intentionally flat—they almost look like illustrations. Everything looks evenly spaced, but when you get up close none of the forms are actually squares.

There's one collage of his from 1968 that looks almost exactly like some of Gladys's handmade paperworks that she made later, where the centers of the squares collapse or explode. And also the way he's cut up something that looks like a cartoon in black lines on white, making it into abstraction. If someone told me this was Gladys's work, I would believe it.

Keith Martin died in 1983—Gladys always said he died of cancer, but when you hear that a gay artist died in 1983, it's hard not to wonder if he died of AIDS. The *Baltimore Sun* obituary doesn't mention a cause of death, and when I asked Helen if she thought he died of AIDS, she said: I don't know.

An earlier *Baltimore Sun* article describes Martin's blindness as a result of diabetes retinopathy after cataract surgery, and then his triumphant return to the gallery scene when he decided to continue making collages anyway, using the small amount of sight he had left, which sounds so similar to artists with AIDS who developed CMV retinitis, and continued to make their work as they lost their vision.

Keith Martin died at age seventy-two, which was the average life expectancy in 1983. I don't have any evidence that he died of AIDS, I just think it's impossible not to wonder.

On February 14, 1983, Gladys wrote a short note to Brenda Richardson, curator at the Baltimore Museum of Art, on a card featuring a drawing she made that pictures a dove and the word PEACE. She asked if she could come to the museum to sign a large diptych that had become part of the collection many years before.

"When the museum acquired it," Gladys writes, "it was supposed to have been returned for me to varnish and sign, but they wanted it for an exhibition, and somehow or other it was never done."

Richardson responds with a typed letter on formal letterhead, dated three days later, saying that the painting is currently inaccessible, since, "as you know, as a result of a renovation program, a good bit of the collection (especially large-scale pictures like this one) had to be moved out of the museum building and placed in outside storage."

Six months later the painting is ready, and Gladys goes in to sign it.

The museum acquired the painting in 1967, and it may have been on display for many years after that, perhaps up until 1982, when the museum began the renovation process. It's the painting that's now in the vault. And I wonder if it was ever on display after Gladys returned to sign it.

I also wonder what made Gladys decide, sixteen years after the museum first acquired the painting, that she wanted to come in to sign it, especially since she'd already signed the back.

And then I remember that Keith Martin died in 1983, just a month after this letter, and five years after Brenda Richardson organized a show of his collages at the museum. Perhaps, in the face of his illness, Gladys realized her own mortality.

My grandmother Fran is dying. She's ninety-seven, living with escalating dementia. I wish someone would help her to understand that she's not going to leave the assisted living facility, so she can try to enjoy her time now, whatever she has left. Instead she's waiting, waiting until she feels healthy again. So she can go on with her life.

But this is her life.

At least her living quarters are comfortable, even somewhat spacious, and she has a nice view of the trees outside. She has one of Gladys's paintings on the floor, leaning against the wall in the corner—it's a painting I'd never seen before I visited her, green and purple on white, one of Gladys's later paintings. Fran bought it at the auction after Gladys's death. But she doesn't want to put it up now, because this might mean she's staying.

It took me a while to convince my mother to get Fran a stereo so she could listen to music, but when she finally did, she called me to tell me how much Fran appreciated it. Now she listens to Frank Sinatra when she's awake, and when she's sleeping, my mother says. She gets up, and turns it back on.

She still goes to dinner, my mother says, which is good because this is the only time when she socializes with the other residents. Otherwise she's in her room, or on a walk down the hallway with an attendant if she feels up to it.

Growing up, my parents were wary of either grandmother exerting too much influence. Gladys was too idealistic, and Fran was too materialistic. When adults would lean down and ask me what I wanted to be when I grew up, doctor or lawyer, Fran wanted me to know I had another option: stockbroker.

Gladys died at ninety-two, living on her own. She became more and more fixed in her ways, more and more judgmental, but her mind was intact. She died after she refused an operation that could have prolonged her life—she wanted to die on her own terms.

Fran has lived longer, but she does not have her autonomy. She will die of congestive heart failure, that's what the doctors say. I don't want her to die, because I still want her to experience joy—that's why I asked my mother to get the stereo.

Now at least she has the stereo, and she dances, she dances in her room.

When you're writing a book called *Touching the Art*, and you see someone's discarded art on the street, what do you do? Yes I'm touching it, but should I bring it home?

I'm not home, I'm in LA on the way back to Seattle, but now I have a pile of art on the living room sofa in the place I'm renting. Art by someone named Ian Aguilar—most of the pieces that are dated say 2016—abstract watercolors and colorful prints, drawings for sculptures and lamps, his sketchbook and color chart. I have about fifty pieces, and there were many more on the sidewalk. Did Ian Aguilar throw all this away because he felt his art got better, or did he give up?

There's a bill from the gas company, a disconnection notice for nonpayment, I hope this doesn't mean that Ian is no longer around. In the sketchbook, there's a draft flyer for a silent auction to pay for cancer treatment for Rose Aguilar. The benefit is called "Curate Cancer." Maybe Ian gave up because he couldn't curate Rose's cancer.

Ninth Street Women, Mary Gabriel's book about the women of Abstract Expressionism, starts with Grace Hartigan—in 1990, Mary Gabriel returned to MICA, the school she'd attended years before, to interview Hartigan. Gabriel was nervous because she remembered Hartigan's imperious presence on campus and the notoriety of her withering studio critiques, but she found herself entranced by Hartigan's stories of the formative years of Abstract Expressionism, of the cross-pollination in the emergent New York School between painters and sculptors, poets and musicians and composers creating their own world basically invisible to the dominant culture, their own ways of thinking and living and dreaming.

As someone inspired by Jackson Pollock, Willem de Kooning, and Franz Kline to paint abstractly, Hartigan is considered part of the second generation of Abstract Expressionists. Like the first generation, she labored in anonymity for years, but she rose to fame before her predecessors had received much commercial success. She was the first woman among her cohorts to be hailed in the New York art world, just at the point when abstract art of the US avant-garde was being commoditized. This work had been pilloried by the establishment, but now it was brandished as a tool for cultural imperialism as New York replaced Paris as the center of power in the art world.

Once art is canonized, it becomes an instrument of war. Think about the legendary misogynist men of Abstract Expressionism, blasting away at their canvases to claim a place in history. But before they arrived at the center of a speculative market their art helped to create, they existed almost entirely on the fringe, collaborating and fighting with one another in cold-water flats and all-night cafeterias in the shadow of the Great Depression and World War II. As the world around them coalesced into militarism and the nuclear family, redbaiting and nuclear war, Mary Gabriel writes, "It wasn't apathy that made them seek a world apart but disgust."

They struggled to reimagine the physical, emotional, intellectual, and spiritual act of art as a necessary means for survival. They wanted to free the self by claiming a place and space apart from what came before, even as they drew inspiration from their more storied European prede-cessors, many of whom fled to New York to join them as fascism fueled the Holocaust.

They argued about the future, and they argued about the future of art. Could there be? Would there be? Who would inhabit it?

Abstraction offered a way out because it was a way into the psyche.

These are the giants of Gladys's generation. When I asked her to place herself in the context of twentieth-century art, this is who she mentioned. Some of these artists she respected, and some she did not. But when she named her influences, she pointed to a generation before—Picasso, Mondrian, Klee, Kandinsky, Miró—some of the same artists that the men of Abstract Expressionism pointed to.

Gladys never compared herself to women artists, it was the men that mattered. In this way she was a product of her generation, and exactly in tune with the women of Abstract Expressionism. Almost all of them have a story they tell over and over about how some famous critic wrote that they painted like a man. Gladys has this story too.

This world of New York artists in the 1940s and '50s was tiny, just a few dozen at first—overwhelmingly white and male, it was still some-what porous. At the Ninth Street Show in 1951, which ended up defining Abstract Expressionism, there were at least eleven women artists among the sixty or so included—newer arrivals like Joan Mitchell and Grace Hartigan, as well as those who had been around longer, like Elaine de Kooning and Lee Krasner.

Elaine de Kooning was born just one year after Gladys, and, in 1936, when she first entered Willem de Kooning's sprawling Chelsea studio as an eighteen-year-old painter in awe of his work, Gladys was nineteen and also a painter, stuck in a marriage that she wanted to escape, dis-illusioned by the Maryland Institute, where they pushed tradition as the only path for an artist.

Lee Krasner was a decade older than Gladys and Elaine, and already an accomplished artist, but after marrying Jackson Pollock she dedi-cated her life and her talents to promoting his singularity. Both Lee and Elaine had their own careers, but they believed more in the work of their husbands.

After two years of marriage, Gladys divorced Abe Oliver, and moved to Florida, where she fell in love with the son of a Jewish department store owner, but when the scandal of her divorce followed her, this man's family banned him from seeing her. She returned to Baltimore to live with her parents, painting portraits for an income, and a few years later she married Ed, a schoolteacher. After that, her life would remain moored to middle-class stability. She would not live the countercultural life of Elaine de Kooning, Lee Krasner, or the other women who became part of the New York School, but also she did not have to compete with a man for her autonomy.

By all accounts, Grace Hartigan was a towering presence. "I never knew anyone, male or female, who appeared to have more self-confidence and determination," writes Joe LeSueur, in *Digressions on Some Poems by Frank O'Hara*. O'Hara was Hartigan's best friend, and a major promoter of her art while working at the Museum of Modern Art, and LeSueur was Frank's roommate, friend, sometime lover, confidante, and devotee, and he describes one night out with Grace when they're walking home from a party, and some stumbling guy is following them, and Grace turns and hits the guy so hard that he falls into the gutter.

Frank helps him up, but Grace continues walking straight ahead, while Joe struggles to catch up, asking why she hit the "wimpy little guy."

And Grace says: "I can't stand a man who doesn't act like a man."

The offhand remark, and when it enters history. When it becomes part of the story, and when it is kept out. Gossip as the story that is told versus gossip as the story that doesn't deserve to be told.

I'm searching through Grace Hartigan's history, in search of Gladys. Grace Hartigan was the one Baltimore artist of her generation who became canonized. Of course, she made her fame before Baltimore, but she lived there from 1960 until her death in 2008, and is the only artist consistently mentioned whenever I talk to someone about Gladys, even though they were not friends.

There is a story about Gladys and Grace, and this is what I'm looking for, in the gaps.

"I love men, why shouldn't he!" Grace Hartigan declares when asked about Frank O'Hara's homosexuality. I find this quote in the prologue of *Ninth Street Women*, where Mary Gabriel adds, "That he preferred men sexually didn't trouble Grace a bit." And this makes me wonder whether Grace Hartigan was a more liberated version of Gladys, more like the Gladys I imagined.

Except then there's this moment described by Joe LeSueur in *Digressions on Some Poems by Frank O'Hara*, where Grace says to Joe, "It's nice that Frank has a sex life, but does he have to bring his boyfriends around?"

According to LeSueur, Grace never hesitated to bring her own boyfriends along, but more disturbing to me is when Grace cuts off her relationship with Frank because her therapist tells her that he's getting in the way of potential intimacy with Win Price, her soon-to-be fourth husband, the one for whom she leaves New York. LeSueur describes the letter like this: "Grace, upon counsel of her cornball shrink, decided that there was no room in her brave new life for neurotic fags like Frank O'Hara and John Bernard Myers, both of whom received Dear John letters."

Mary Gabriel describes the same incident, but without the implicit homophobia. When I look at my notes to *Ninth Street Women*, I see that I've written, "Grace's analyst says break off ties to Frank and John Myers for a new start AND SHE DOES."

Six years later, Grace decided to restart her relationship with O'Hara, and a few months after that he was hit by a dune buggy on Fire Island, and died at the age of forty, in 1959. At the time of Hartigan's death almost fifty years later, Gabriel mentions that she had only two photos on her mantle, both of O'Hara, which was touching when I first read it, except now I can only think that she destroyed their relationship for marriage and a life in Baltimore that was just as tumultuous as her life in New York, except without the joy among friends. Was this worth it?

And I'm thinking again about the difference between gossip and history. Because Joe LeSueur's book is undoubtedly gossip, and Mary

Gabriel's book is a meticulously researched biography. Yes, Gabriel relies on Joe LeSueur's book for some of her most revealing anecdotes, but apparently not enough to trust his judgment about Hartigan's discarding of her close friends.

In the 1950s, Hartigan was so immersed in a world of queens that when she first began to show her work—at John Bernard Myers's gallery—she used the name George Hartigan as a gesture of camp solidarity with her fag friends. Joe LeSueur describes her as "headstrong, stubborn, contentious, intractable, self-indulgent, irrepressible."

And I'm thinking about Gladys, whose mentor, Hobson Pittman, was gay, whose best friend, Keith Martin, was gay, and these were the two people who supported her as an artist more than anyone else. And, after Dave McIntyre, Keith's lover, was fired from his job in the 1950s for being gay, Gladys says she joined with her friends in the Baltimore art world to find him a position as registrar at the Baltimore Museum of Art, where he became assistant director of administration until retiring in 1975. And, my mother tells me, throughout the '60s and '70s, Gladys and Ed would go on trips with Keith and Dave.

I don't know what they did and did not talk about. They must have talked about why Dave was fired, right? And yet to Helen, her best friend from childhood, she couldn't even acknowledge that Keith was gay.

Gladys supported everything that made me queer as a child, but as an adult my queerness made me vulgar. Maybe her way of thinking about homosexuality—as a vacation with friends—might not have been that different from Grace Hartigan's. Sure, Hartigan's world was wilder, but at least Gladys didn't abandon her best friend for marriage. She was already married when she met him. Already living a middle-class life, so this wasn't something she needed to aspire to. But Grace came from the middle class, and had rejected that path to become an artist.

After Grace's betrayal, Frank writes a review where he criticizes her for the first time, describing her new work as containing "a vulgarity of spirit which is quite disheartening in that it employs illusionistic devices to further apparently unfelt ends." And I'm thinking about the word *vulgar* here, the word Gladys used to dismiss my work, although she never described it as unfelt. Probably it was feeling too much, and this was part of its vulgarity.

But could O'Hara, who worked at the Museum of Modern Art and was instrumental in Grace Hartigan's career, have forgotten her artistic statement for the Museum in 1956, where she wrote, "I have found my 'subject,' it concerns that which is vulgar and vital in American modern life, and the possibilities of its transcendence into the beautiful."

Mary Gabriel found the Grace Hartigan quote about Frank O'Hara's sexuality in the footnotes of Marjorie Perloff's biography of O'Hara, *Poet Among Painters*. She pulled it out from the footnotes, and moved it to page ten. Was this a gesture of love?

The full context is that in a letter to Bruce Boone, the editor of a special O'Hara supplement in *Panjandrum*, a 1973 poetry magazine, Grace Hartigan writes, "that Frank was a homosexual was very understandable to me—I love men, why shouldn't he? It never—what would?—interfered with our love for each other. I'm not the first person to say that sex isn't necessarily love and vice-versa."

This is Grace Hartigan, more than a decade after O'Hara's death, rewriting their relationship as if nothing interfered. For whom was she rewriting the story?

Maybe I should say something here about the exhaustion of searching through texts for the moments when sparks arrive. But then I'm sobbing at the end of Joe LeSueur's book, the four pages about his and Frank's slutty interlocking sex lives, until Frank's shocking death after the accident on the beach.

Frank's friends, when learning that Frank has a 50 percent chance of living, and will have to quit drinking if he survives, wonder how that could ever be possible. Because so much of his life consists of drinking. So much of their lives. Alcohol as the bond that feeds and destroys people.

And then there's Bill de Kooning at the hospital, handing over a blank check: "I want the best for my friend."

And the way everyone comes together to mourn Frank's death—is this a family?

The way a book filled with gossip can still be reverent. The way Joe says he could never have a serious boyfriend because of his connection with Frank, even after their breakup. Even that word, that he calls it a breakup, while never naming their relationship exactly as one of lovers. The way friendship can hold so much. So much more. So much more than friendship.

And wasn't this true of Frank O'Hara and Grace Hartigan?

How I'm reading about this world in order to understand something about the time. And I didn't expect to learn so much. Or maybe what I mean is that I didn't expect to feel so much.

Grace Hartigan was hired to teach grad students at MICA in 1964, and she started teaching there in 1965—she says she contacted Eugene Leake, the president of MICA at the time, and said, "I have never taught in my life but I have to have contact with someone. Do you have anything I can do that won't take too much time?"

Gladys left MICA in 1964—was this because they hired Grace?

Grace "was a diva," according to Fred Lazarus, the next president of MICA. "She loved the diva role, and she mastered it well."

Gladys would not have tolerated this, although she was a diva in her own ways.

When Grace planned her move to Baltimore in 1960 after marrying Win Price, a Hopkins professor, she imagined creating a salon of artists and writers, a place for camaraderie and debate. But when she arrived, and, according to Cathy Curtis in *Restless Ambition*, there was "no contemporary arts scene to speak of," she abandoned this idea. But surely there must have been many artists in Baltimore who would have been delighted to socialize with Grace and exchange ideas in her fancy Roland Park home with Win Price. It's probably just that she didn't think they were worth it. "The notion of meeting a 'local' artist—someone whose name was unknown beyond the city—was meaningless to Grace," Curtis writes.

I'm wondering what would have happened if Grace and Gladys had become friends. Gladys knew every artist in Baltimore, and her career, while not as storied as Grace's, did extend to New York, Philadelphia, Washington, Paris, and elsewhere, and surely there would have been many insights she and Grace could share. I can imagine them going on a walk together, and marveling at a shiny piece of discarded foil in the street, an over-the-top window display, the layers of paint peeling off a decaying brick façade.

Grace and Gladys shared an obsession with getting the light to come through their paintings, they both thought the light was the most important thing, and I wonder what techniques they could have exchanged. I wonder if Gladys would have agreed with Grace that Mark Rothko was the most successful painter at bringing the light through.

Both Gladys and Grace made grandiose statements about art, so surely when Gladys said Picasso was the greatest artist of all time, Grace might offer her opinion that Picasso was the "greatest image-maker," Matisse was the "greatest colorist," and Bill de Kooning had the "greatest hand." Would Gladys have agreed?

Both Grace and Gladys were women artists who didn't think much of other women artists. They could only compare themselves to men, since men were the only real artists. Could they have eventually seen the silliness of this stance by glimpsing it in one another?

Before moving to Baltimore, Grace lived in a bohemian world where divorce was commonplace and artists created their own worlds. Could Gladys have learned from her risk-taking? And would Grace have learned from Gladys's unabashed love of the mundane beauty of gazing at the flowers in her garden, the birds arriving for the season, the falling leaves, all things that Grace appreciated as well, but she was suspicious of this calm. Could they have been calm together?

Grace said that the difference between abstraction and nature painting was that "one is working out of nature, the other into nature," and Gladys said, "Nature is art, that's what it is. It doesn't know any boundaries. It can do anything, and it does what it wants to do, and it's always beautiful." What if they had talked to one another in this way?

Both Gladys and Grace rejected the push to continue making the same kind of work once it attained a degree of renown. Grace did not share Gladys's disdain for showiness, and she reveled in success. Although she had left the New York art world, she was still notorious there, and even once she was knocked off her pedestal she would return in search of the same fame. But surely no one could have agreed more with Gladys's statement that "I can't keep repeating the same thing over and over again . . . I have to change, and I have to think."

Both artists embraced change, and both embraced the intellect. I wonder if Grace, who was famously direct, could have pushed Gladys to be more honest about the world. Would Gladys have pushed Grace to stop relying on the paintings of the past to imagine a future?

Both loved to read—would they have talked about books? Maybe Gladys and Grace could have gone to the Symphony together after Ed's death, so that Gladys could still use her season tickets. And maybe Grace would have introduced her to Joseph Meyerhoff, the patron of the Symphony. Would this have helped Gladys?

Would Grace and Gladys have gone to galleries together? When Gladys said, "You can't be judgmental about art," Grace would have laughed, oh how she would have laughed.

When Gladys is asked by an interviewer at the Jewish Museum of Maryland to talk about the permanent collection of her work at the University of Maryland, she says, "It's embarrassing." Even though she's about to turn ninety, she sounds like a little girl. Surely Grace could have taught her to let go of this false modesty.

When Gladys had her first solo show in New York in 1957, Grace was becoming a star. Did Grace see that show, and, if so, what did she think?

When Grace moved to Baltimore to marry Win Price, she lost her place within the New York art world. This was the inevitable effect that her friends warned her about. In her new marriage she was searching for what Gladys already had—a husband who would support her, and give her total freedom to create art on her own terms. Yes, Grace did want something more lavish and extreme, and Win did give her that, but also there was his early death from injecting himself with an experimental vaccine for encephalitis, and her resulting alcoholism that almost killed her. Probably she would have been too brutal for Gladys to support her at this point, although Gladys was loyal to her friends. And, like Grace, she probably demanded loyalty. Would they have found something in loyalty to one another?

I'm thinking about their relationships with gay men. Grace discarded Frank O'Hara, her closest friend, in order to live a life with the man of her dreams, or so she thought. But Frank already was the man of her dreams. What would Gladys have thought of this abandonment?

Gladys was married when she met Keith, and she welcomed him into her life as an artist, and into her life. Would Grace have learned something from this? Neither she nor Gladys liked promiscuous gay men, but it's likely that Gladys didn't really know what was going on in Keith and Dave's relationship. What would Grace have pointed out? Certainly she would have been much more direct in talking about it. Would this have helped Gladys?

Both Gladys and Grace found continued excitement in changing the style of their work when their interests shifted. Gladys was a dedicated abstractionist who wanted her work to stand on its own, which Grace would have found dull. And Grace was reworking the masters through an engagement with the figure, which Gladys would have found derivative. And yet, even if they didn't appreciate one another's work, I wonder what ideas would have come up in conversation.

As they got older, both Gladys and Grace struggled to continue making art, as their bodies grew more fragile. Could they have offered each other suggestions? Maybe Grace would have said to Gladys: You need to hire someone to help. And maybe Gladys would have told Grace to let go of her obsessive need to make everything so large. After all, Gladys perfected her tiny candy wrapper collages because of injuries.

In many ways their teaching styles were the opposite—Grace would tear her students to shreds, and Gladys, while sometimes critical, wanted to coax their best work out through compassion. Gladys was hired by MICA specifically to teach abstract painting, and Grace decided she only wanted to teach figurative painters. Wouldn't it have been interesting if they were teaching at MICA at the same time, with their opposing methods and preferences, their respective groups of fiercely loyal students? Maybe, once in a while, they could have stepped in the hallway to chat.

Existentialists are the greatest drunks in the world, this drunk guy on the steps of the library is proclaiming. And that's probably one of the reasons I liked existentialism so much in high school—I didn't know it was a philosophy embraced by abstract artists of Gladys's generation in the aftermath of World War II as they struggled to figure out a way to make art in a world that threatened to annihilate humanity. But in high school I was obsessed by existentialist questions about freedom.

"Hell is other people" was my favorite line from *No Exit*, Jean-Paul Sartre's most famous play, but it's also written over every interaction in *The Age of Reason*, his book that spoke to me more than any other. How I imagined myself drinking absinthe on the Left Bank in Paris like Sartre, finding other people who were doomed to question everything. Who felt they would never escape, except maybe into this doom.

I actually made a plan go to Paris for a summer with my high school friend Erik—he was the devil's advocate conservative when I was the developing radical, and somehow we bonded while arguing in class. Alienation—this we had in common. We started partying together on weekends, waiting for each other in between classes—in a different world maybe we would have been boyfriends but we didn't have that world. After graduation, we planned to go to Paris to become fluent in French, the language we both loved, but then he decided he couldn't go, why he said I don't remember, but I knew it was because he was scared. That we would fall over the edge into something too wild to recover from, yes, that was why I wanted to go.

Reading *The Age of Reason* again now, I feel a kind of anticipation, a jitteriness. I mean I can see why I loved this book—the questioning of everything and the grandiose posturing. The questioning of the grandiose posturing.

Sure, Sartre gets caught in melodrama and stereotypical tropes—the overwrought female characters, the casual racism and anti-Semitism, the disgust for bodies, the self-hating homosexuals. All of these may be stand-ins for Sartre himself, not just the more obvious stand-in of Mathieu Delarue, the central character. Delarue means "of the street," which is another irony because Mathieu is trapped in a bourgeois existence that he doesn't respect, wandering the streets in search of something else. Everyone is brilliant and horrible, except maybe Mathieu, who hates himself as much as he hates anyone. But statements like "Moreover, though I may be a pacifist, I don't respect human life, there's no such implication," this I can love just as much now.

Or: "Well, well, one is never finished with one's family, it's like the smallpox that catches you as a child and leaves you marked for life."

Do you see how it's all like a play? But the sense of play has been lost. Except in those sudden moments. I read this book during my junior year of high school, and that summer when I went to the beach with my parents and sister was when I truly felt the freedom I craved, climbing out my bedroom window to the exterior hallway of the building to get drunk on the beach with all the other wayward kids who didn't know anything about me, and so they accepted me in a way that kids like these had never done before. I mean they were middle-of-the-road jock-ish suburbanites, but they looked up to me because I could outdrink them, because I was wild, because I wasn't worried when my sister went off to make out with one of them. So they respected my wildness, but also maybe my lack of machismo?

The feeling of the wind in your hair, downing that liquor like water like breath like the stars will always stay in your eyes and the way the other kids almost didn't think I was a faggot or if they did then they weren't saying it, or when they said it I responded with enough drunken courage to make them back off. Back at home I never had access to this type of bonding because I was something else, something to stay away from. I wanted escape and here it was in that liquor bottle, but also I wanted something else and for that I would need a while longer.

I have one journal from that time period, the last few years of high school, with just a few dozen short entries, where often I write about being trapped, about never wanting to become "a clone in society," about learning to look through my parents' eyes to the wall behind their faces, about wanting to get smashed. On New Year's Day in 1990, at the top of the page I write:

FREEDOM
FREEDOM
FREEDOM

And then a few weeks later, I write: "My life is near the point of ruin." So you see how I could be a character in *The Age of Reason*. "My life is fucking predetermined. I can't stray from the path down which I am forced to go."

And I write that Gladys tells me to take risks.

I write: "I want to take risks, I do take risks, yet I don't 'follow my heart.'"

I write about starting a summer job doing environmental canvassing after my junior year in high school, and going out to a club with all the people I met. Everyone else was in college because you had to be over eighteen to work there, so I'd lied about my age. We watched a reggae band called Shiloh, and then the bar closed at 2:00 a.m. with "Don't worry 'bout a thing," and "We all went outside and talked, smoked, etc. for an hour and a half or so. It was really cool—I had this great sense of freedom—I could do anything I wanted just like the rest of the group (they all live without parents). It was so fuckin' perfection. I didn't call home and spent the night over this guy Dylan's house, but that's another story. During my college years, I definitely need to rent an apartment on my own... FREEDOM."

This journal where I'm writing in code because I know my mother reads it when I'm not home—I caught her once, sitting at my desk with my journal open. This journal where I'm lying to myself, lying to my mother, and lying to the world. How a journal is supposed to reveal hidden truths, but here I can't say anything about what is most hidden, my desire for a desire that I don't despise.

There's so much injustice in going back to a high school journal where you've hidden so much of what you were thinking and feeling. So much of what you wanted to say, it's not there, because there could never be safety.

Since this is my own journal, I know what is there and what isn't, but what about someone else reading this now, what would they imagine? I mean what wouldn't they imagine.

Is a journal always a lie, I don't know. But what does this say about history?

High school is a trap, of course. Childhood is a trap. My life began when I got away, so I was right about freedom. I needed to escape everything I was supposed to be. And Sartre helped me to see this.

Here it is, one of the moments in *The Age of Reason* that I must have loved:

> He realized, of course, that he was a wash-out: but, when all was said, in this dance-hall, at that table, among all those fellows who were also wash-outs, it did not seem to matter very much and was not at all unpleasant. He looked around...Smooth and smiling faces everywhere, but ruin in their eyes. Mathieu suddenly felt a kinship with all those creatures who would have done so much better to go home, but no longer had the power, and sat there smoking slender cigarettes, drinking steely-tasting compounds, smiling, as their ears oozed music, and dismally contemplating the wreckage of their destiny: he felt the discreet appeal of a humble and timorous happiness.

Oh how I wanted to be just that type of washout, disappearing into the bar, flailing on the dance floor, smoking slender cigarettes and drinking steely-tasting compounds, what other kind of happiness could there be?

Yes, this book is overwrought, but at the end there's something kind of masterful that happens. Daniel, the self-hating homosexual who has been enacting a viciously clever plan to manipulate Mathieu into marrying Ivich because he's jealous of his freedom—at the end, he saves Mathieu by marrying Ivich instead.

And then he declares that he is a homosexual. And Mathieu is shocked, but he says, "You are disgusted with yourself, I suppose, but not more so than I am with myself, there's nothing much to choose between us."

In this moment, Mathieu envies Daniel. "He is free," he thinks.

"What type of art do you do?" Alex, a seventh-grade cousin of Gladys's asks for a middle school class project in 2002.

And Gladys responds: "I hate to put art in a category, but if I have to put it in a category then I would say abstract."

Alex asks, "So what is abstract art like?"

And Gladys says: "Abstract art is exactly what the word means. There are two meanings of the word 'abstract'—one is the essence of an object, no matter what it is, whether it's a floral bouquet, the essence of the thing that is. Also, there's another meaning to the word abstract, meaning something that you can't reach."

Gladys is sitting at a table with Alex for this video interview with a class of seventh graders, and the way she answers the questions reminds me of how good she was with children. I mean how good she was with me.

Even if by seventh grade I didn't think I was a child anymore—I had already read *War and Peace, Crime and Punishment, The Brothers Karamazov, Buddenbrooks,* and any other book I could disappear into— these stories of decaying families, intergenerational strife, and self-conscious pondering were my salvation. But mostly I didn't think I was a child anymore because when adults said enjoy it while you can, all I could think was how dare you, how dare you lie to me like that?

And I felt a knowledge deeper than theirs—at least I recognized my pain. And I never wanted to forget this reality. I never wanted to grow into delusion.

So when I say I didn't believe I was a child anymore, also I mean that I never wanted to grow older than sixteen. Sixteen seemed like the magic number because then I could drive away, or even better I could float in invisible force fields and rescue all the kids everyone refused to see. I knew I was one of those kids, and so I knew I was trapped. But because I knew I was trapped, I was starting to figure a way out.

Watching the seventh graders ask questions in this video, and how Gladys's answers are short and straightforward and honest. When asked if there are any artists she relates to, she says, simply: "I don't think so."

How I related to her, but it wasn't really her, or it was just part of her, the part that she wanted the world to see. And how I saw it. And how I believed in it. How I believed in her.

She says: "I think that I was influenced mainly by a few artists, including Paul Klee, but I don't think that I relate to them."

She says: "I did portrait painting for about eleven years, before I finally ended up doing what I'm doing now. But you grow up. You start at one age, and each age changes, as you well know, your ideas will change again in another five years, so I grow with my own ideas."

And I think about the "as you well know"—how Gladys invites them in. She assumes that they too have a range of experiences to draw from.

Seventh grade was when I became anorexic, or actually that started in sixth grade, after my father looked at a picture of me at age two, and said: "Most fat babies grow up to be fat adults." That tone in his voice. Like he was making the funniest joke. And I internalized it all. Tightening the belt around my tiny waist to squeeze everything in, if I got it tight enough then maybe I wouldn't have to feel. Looking at my wrists, and wondering if they were getting fatter. Counting the calories in a little book, a datebook, I needed to get below one thousand. This was puberty and I was going to win.

I hated my body and I hated what it made me imagine doing. Hiding in the bathroom at recess and inhaling the smell of piss while fantasizing about all the boys who called me faggot gang-raping me in a field— to look at these kids in this video, these kids asking Gladys questions, and wonder: Which one of these kids is thinking these same things, which one?

Or: How many of them?

When asked, "What kind of messages do you try to send out in your art?" Gladys answers: "I don't really try to send out any messages, I believe that I paint for myself, and I leave it up to you to interpret the painting as you want to interpret it, and to enjoy it as you want to enjoy it."

And, perhaps most importantly: "I don't believe, in fact, that you have to tell someone how to think."

When asked, "Have you ever regretted becoming an artist?" she answers: "Never, not for one single second."

"Did your family encourage you to become an artist?" Alex asks, and Gladys says: "They didn't encourage me, but they also didn't discourage me, so I always painted. It was a lot of fun, and I'm sure all of you have painted, and I'm sure you've all enjoyed it."

And actually, I hadn't heard this before, that her family didn't encourage her, and so perhaps that's why, even though she studied painting from age nine, in a free art program at the Maryland Institute that only accepted those who excelled, even though she painted portraits for eleven years as an adult, and even though she went to Penn State to study the teaching of art, no one ever told her she was an artist, until Hobson Pittman.

"He taught me to be myself," Gladys says, "and I think that's the most important thing in painting, is to be yourself. And I think he also taught me that if you have someone that you're teaching that might be even better than you are, that's okay too, and that's a very important thing to learn. And he was happy for me, and that's what I hope I bring to my students."

She speaks to these kids about art in ways that could be just as useful to adults. She describes what a Mixografia is: "It's a mixed graphic, which means it's a procedure by which you can do more than one painting. It's a multiple. And a mixed graphic multiple has dimension whereas a print is flat, it's one surface. And I did a Mixografia collage, which is many layers of handmade paper, and also collage on top of it."

When Alex asks what Gladys teaches her students, Gladys answers: "I teach them how to think for themselves, and there are two things that one has to learn in painting. One is you have to learn how to use the medium you're working with . . . Then you also have to have something to say. I try to let them say what they want to say, and not what I want them to say."

And here she's bringing them into a sophisticated conversation about abstract art, it's an invitation, they are in this together.

And also, when asked if she ever teaches the meaning of art: "I don't think so, I think you have to find your own personal meaning to art. Art is really beauty, but beauty is what you see, and how you see it."

And, when asked about her least favorite type of art: "My least favorite type of art? Magic realism, I think, is my least favorite type of art. And I think that's a really good question. Because you have to have something that you really don't like, in order to make something that you like."

As a child, I was proud of being Jewish, even if no one in my family was observant. My parents gave me the choice to go to Hebrew school, and I loved learning to read Hebrew there, even though I was never taught what the words meant. I thought it was a beautiful act when my temple raised money every year to plant trees in the Negev Desert, since no one told me this was part of an Israeli government program to destroy Palestinian villages to make way for Israeli settlements. In fourth or fifth grade, I wrote a paper about the plight of refusenik Jews in Soviet Russia, and my teachers at regular school were so impressed that they invited me to read it to the entire school during an assembly. I didn't realize that the narrative of refusenik Jews was used to bolster Reagan's anti-Communist crusade.

I was usually the one to sing the prayers at the family Passover held at our cousins' house, which was one of the only times we would get together with our extended family. Passover celebrates Jewish liberation from slavery in ancient Egypt, but at these dinners some of my relatives would switch to Yiddish whenever they wanted to say racist things about Black people. I grew up hating Yiddish because I thought this was its primary purpose.

So many of my relatives used Jewishness as an excuse for racism, classism, upward mobility at any cost. When I was in third grade, I remember my grandmother Fran asking me: Why are all of your friends colored?

At the time I was shocked that anyone would still talk that way. But she was just the one who voiced her racist fears the most directly.

By the time of my bar mitzvah, I knew I didn't believe in God, and I was pretty sure my parents didn't either—they just didn't want to risk the social ostracism of atheism, which I embraced. Of course, there's a long history of Jewish atheists, but I didn't know this, nor did I know the history of radical Jewish resistance, so I rejected Jewish tradition outright.

Sometimes I wonder what I might have missed, but also I still feel uncomfortable, even in radical Jewish spaces. It's the way that tradition is supposed to stand for something more than tradition. Learning the history of how European Jews in Baltimore assimilated helps me to understand my discomfort.

Many of the first Jews to arrive in Maryland were convicts sent from Britain after they were sentenced to seven years of servitude in the 1700s for petty crimes, and then sold to planters alongside British goods. Most of them fled the area as soon as possible. Baltimore's growth as a commercial center both before and after the Revolutionary War also drew some Jews to migrate from Europe in search of business opportunities.

Slavery was legal in Maryland until the end of the Civil War, and Baltimore was an active port in the slave trade. The United States banned the international slave trade in 1808, but then the domestic slave trade took over, especially in Maryland and Virginia, as more than a million enslaved people were "deliberately bred for legal sale," in the words of W. E. B. Du Bois. According to Lawrence T. Brown, "Nearly every part of the nation's economy was intertwined with the commoditization of Black people's flesh and the wealth extraction of Black people's labor— particularly Black women's labor via the practice of human breeding." Black bodies and lives were monetized and commoditized to such an extent that not only their labor but their legal status as property that could be bought and sold, rented and mortgaged was essential to the nation's economic and financial systems.

More than a dozen slave traders were located on or near Pratt Street in downtown Baltimore, and they cooperated with law enforcement and advertised in local papers while running their own dockside prisons as they routinely forced men, women, and children down the street in chains and onto ships bound for the slave market in New Orleans. Baltimore also had its own slave markets, as well as agencies specializing in the slave trade. Enslaved people were also routinely auctioned off as part of estate sales, and advertised alongside furniture, dry goods, and groceries. There were more free Black people in Baltimore than in any other city, and they vastly outnumbered those who were enslaved, but free Black people were routinely sold into slavery once arrested, and children were especially vulnerable to being kidnapped and sold into slavery, so the freedom of any Black person in the city was under constant threat.

In 1826, the passage of the "Jew Bill" gave Jews the same legal rights as white Christians, but only after it was narrowed to make sure it wouldn't apply to anyone else, especially not to free Black men. By the time of the Civil War, most Jews in Baltimore were immigrants who had fled poverty and pogroms in Germany, but neither this nor their own scripture taught them the obvious lessons, and they overwhelmingly supported slavery, in alliance with the white Southern establishment.

When a mob of thousands of Confederate sympathizers attacked Union soldiers passing through Baltimore in the Pratt Street Riot in 1861, the resulting sixteen deaths became the first official casualties in the Civil War, and Baltimore was placed under martial law. An antislavery rabbi was forced to flee to Philadelphia with his family after the offices of his newspaper were destroyed by another mob. His congregation made it clear that he would only be allowed to return if he no longer made any statements against slavery.

Baltimore remained under Union occupation for the duration of the war, and during this time Jewish merchants were among those who smuggled goods to the Confederacy. Baltimore was a border city, a gateway between North and South. The segregated North, and the segregated South, and where they intersect in silence.

Violence.

Violins?

In 1908, more than forty years after the Civil War, Jewish politicians authored and supported a bill to disenfranchise Black voters, which passed the state legislature and only failed to become law because immigrant voters worried about a citizenship test that might affect future European immigrants. In 1910, Baltimore was the first US city to pass a law mandating housing segregation. In 1917, the Supreme Court struck down residential segregation laws, but private covenants and mob rule by racist white Christian homeowners continued to enforce block-for-block housing segregation in Baltimore.

Gladys's family moved from Ohio to Baltimore in 1919, when she was two years old. Now that I found their address in the census, I see their house was just above North Avenue, less than two blocks from the dividing line between white and Black Baltimore. This was a white, working-class Catholic neighborhood, within walking distance of the upwardly mobile Jews like Helen, who became Gladys's childhood best friend.

I have a picture of Gladys's father wearing his apron, standing on the steps in the back of their house, hands on his hips. Gladys kept this framed photo in her studio, it was one of the only photographs there. But she never mentioned that her father had worked at the A&P, so this outfit remained a mystery to me—for years I wondered if it was some kind of drag, since the full-body apron he's wearing looks kind of like a dress. Gladys only described him as a potter, and he did become a potter a few decades later, after he retired due to heart problems, and Gladys and Ed bought him a hundred pounds of clay. But before he retired he'd made his living scouring the city markets for produce to sell at the A&P.

Gladys grew up during a time when Baltimore was rapidly expanding due to a post-WWI boom. Tens of thousands of Black people were moving north to Baltimore as they fled systemic racist violence as part of the Great Migration. The only area where Black people were allowed to own property was not far from the one where Gladys grew up, and where many landlords and property owners were Jewish. Jews were prevented from living in much of Baltimore due to anti-Semitism, but also because they were seen as more likely to sell or rent to Black people. So when Jews started moving into a neighborhood, this would immediately instigate the flight of white Christian residents. Once Jews couldn't be kept out anymore, signs saying "No Jews or Dogs" gave way to mob violence instigated by white Christians targeting Black families.

And yet Jewish landlords and real estate speculators made money off both white flight and urban blight. Often they were the ones who initiated the blockbusting of whites-only neighborhoods—fleeing white Christian homeowners would sell their homes far below value, and then these speculators would turn around and sell them to the Black middle class at exorbitant rates and under exploitative terms. Meanwhile, in the neighborhoods where poorer Black people remained, Jewish landlords often profited from renting dilapidated apartments to Black people trapped by poverty and racist covenants.

Many of the grand downtown department stores were Jewish-owned, and they enforced the same Jim Crow policies as other department stores—no service to Black people at lunch counters, no returns, no trying on clothes, no credit. Most of the businesses on Pennsylvania Avenue, the central thoroughfare of Black Baltimore, were Jewish-owned, and while they extended credit to Black people at a time when this was difficult elsewhere, they did so at predatory rates, and refused to hire any Black employees.

At this point, wealthy and middle-class white people were moving farther and farther from the city center, to escape the possibility of Black neighbors. How did growing up in a border neighborhood shape Gladys's views, and her own racist fears, her own segregated mindset? Her own path of white flight.

The path of upward mobility for Jews was to move farther northwest, since this was the only section of the city where Jews were allowed to own property, and this was where Gladys moved after she married Abraham Oliver at eighteen, and then later, after her divorce, when she married Ed, my grandfather, a schoolteacher, in 1941, and moved to the house in Howard Park where my father grew up.

There were even prominent Jewish developers involved in Baltimore's poshest neighborhoods conceived by the Roland Park Company with investment by British colonialists—Roland Park was one of the first planned segregated suburbs in the country when it was built in 1891, and Guilford was advertised as "A Thousand Acres of Restricted Land" in 1913 because it was whites-only by covenant. All Roland Park Company developments also prevented Jews and other undesirables from moving in through an extensive neighborhood vetting process. So these Jewish developers enforced not only racist but also anti-Semitic housing exclusion. One of these developers was Joseph Meyerhoff, the hallowed patron of the Baltimore Symphony, who created a real estate empire by selling and renting housing only to white Christians. He was seen as a civic hero due to his philanthropy, even as he continued to enforce discriminatory policies at least until they were ruled illegal by the Fair Housing Act of 1968.

Gladys loved the Symphony. I don't remember her talking about segregation in Baltimore, except to say she was proud to live in Mount Washington, an integrated neighborhood, even though I never saw evidence of this integration. Perhaps she meant it was integrated because Jews were not prevented from owning property like in the wealthier neighborhoods across Falls Road, which still prohibited Jewish homeowners when she bought her house in 1964.

There had been a community of Black residents and a Black schoolhouse near Mount Washington as early as the 1800s, but in 1913, neighbors in Mount Washington opposed the plans of Morgan College, a Black university, to move nearby, forcing the school to locate elsewhere. And in 1959 they succeeded in fighting for a zoning ordinance to limit any new construction to no more than six units per acre, keeping out anyone but middle-class families and maintaining the neighborhood's status. When Gladys and Ed moved to their newly built house in 1964, it was one of only a few on a lot this small in their neighborhood. When I stayed at Gladys's house after she died, and walked everywhere, I did discover a middle-class Black neighborhood in a different part of Mount Washington, but this was not somewhere I'd known about before.

I'm thinking about the legacy of Jewish complicity in structural racism, but also the legacy of the South. I don't remember any of my relatives ever saying they came from the South, and yet three of my grandparents, including Gladys, grew up under strict Jim Crow segregation. But no one ever mentioned this. How white lies become the accepted truth. How European Jews became part of whiteness by becoming part of the lie. And how the notion of Jewish exceptionalism, the idea that Jews are somehow innately tied to social justice, hides Jewish complicity in structural racism.

Municipal parks in Baltimore like the one near the house where Gladys grew up were not desegregated until 1953, schools not until 1954, theaters and hotels not until a few years later. So, until Gladys was in her mid-thirties, Baltimore was legally segregated in almost every way. This was how she grew up. Even my father, who was born in 1943, would have gone to legally segregated schools until he was eleven. And somehow I never heard about any of this.

For so many years I've thought about how the private school in DC that I attended from second grade through twelfth, which prided itself on being the "first integrated school" in DC, was over 80 percent white at a time when DC was almost 80 percent Black. For so many years I've thought about growing up in a city that saw itself as cosmopolitan and international, and in no way connected to the South, where the legacy of segregation was so blatant. For so many years I've thought about how, when I went to Baltimore to visit my grandparents as a kid, I felt like I was going to the South, even though Baltimore is north of DC.

What does it mean not to acknowledge the obvious facts made invisible by the repetition of a lie, over and over again until it becomes an accepted truth? The agreement to lie to one another, even with the truth right there. The repetition of these white lies as family history.

There were fierce unionization battles in Baltimore on the docks and in the factories in the 1920s and '30s, and I'm wondering what kinds of conversations Gladys's family had about this. Certainly her father, who traveled to the city's produce markets on a daily basis, would have been informed. Many union organizers were Jewish, but so were many of the factory owners they organized against.

The campaign to force Jewish-owned stores to hire Black workers on Pennsylvania Avenue started near Gladys's house, in 1933, when Gladys would have been a student at Western High School. Public schools didn't desegregate for another twenty years—were there conversations about these "Don't Buy Where You Can't Work" protests at school?

Gladys went to the Maryland Institute to study art, but dropped out when she found out about Picasso—how could they not tell her about Picasso? So she was rebellious in certain ways. Would she have been curious about the Black nightlife on Pennsylvania Avenue, not far from the house where she grew up? When she returned from Florida, and moved back in with her parents as a divorcée, did she have any relationship to this bustling Black neighborhood, or was segregation a reality she never challenged?

Thinking about white flight as the engine of urban blight. How this escalated with the redlining of neighborhoods in the 1930s by federal housing agencies, banks, and insurance companies that decided who could and could not obtain a mortgage. The federal government's Home Owners' Loan Corporation, a central piece of New Deal legislation, managed to standardize the mortgage process and save a million home-owners from foreclosure, but, as part of this process, government and financial institutions not only supported segregated housing but created the financial structures that enforced it.

The Home Owners' Loan Corporation promoted racial covenants as a way of allegedly ensuring the stability of property values, and created a hierarchy of race and ethnicity to determine whether particular neighborhoods should receive mortgages. Neighborhoods known for Black residents were automatically redlined, which meant anyone in the neighborhood was generally refused housing loans, homeowner's insurance, or fire insurance. Neighborhoods bordering Black neighborhoods, often with a high percentage of Jewish residents, were given a C grade, colored yellow on the map, and seen as "definitely declining," where few insured mortgages would be available.

On the 1937 redlining map, Gladys's neighborhood was given the C grade. Two blocks south or east was the redlined neighborhood, and a few blocks north and west was a wealthier neighborhood graded B, where mortgages would still have been relatively easy to obtain.

On the notes for Gladys's neighborhood on the redlining map, the author writes, "No immediate danger of negro encroachment, but there is a heavy concentration of negros in the section adjoining." Gladys and her family moved four years later.

Until I visited my grandmother Fran in assisted living in DC in 2018, I didn't realize her family was also from Baltimore. Her parents moved to Hagerstown, Maryland, where she grew up, to open their furniture store. As a kid, Fran went to Baltimore to visit her grandparents all the time. They lived in the heart of East Baltimore, which was the neighborhood where Jewish immigrants first settled, on Pratt Street. Fran tells me she would remember the house today, if I took her there. It was right near Broadway, she says, that was such a big street.

But I'm guessing the house wouldn't be standing today—not much of that neighborhood is still standing.

What is, and what is not a project of whiteness.

I'm trying to imagine what it would have been like to grow up in Baltimore in the 1920s, right near the dividing line between white and Black. How rigid was that line? And I realize that Billie Holiday was raised in Baltimore. She was born in Philadelphia in 1915, two years before Gladys. Her mother brought her to Baltimore by the end of that year, and she lived there until she was thirteen or fourteen. In her memoir, she says that in Baltimore, "A whorehouse was about the only place where black and white folks could meet in any natural way."

This tells me everything.

Jazz was labeled "whorehouse music," in part because of the threat of racial mixing. When Billie Holiday heard Louis Armstrong playing on the Victrola at the whorehouse on the corner as a child, she was transfixed. "It was the first time I ever heard anybody sing without using any words," she says.

I don't know what Gladys would have thought of whorehouses when she was a child, but I do know she thought my writing was vulgar, and it couldn't have helped her opinion when she found out I was a whore. I started turning tricks in San Francisco when I was twenty—sex work offered me the freedom to live on my own terms, or as close as possible, and I didn't hide it from anyone because I no longer believed in hiding anything.

Actually, as a kid, I remember my father talking about whorehouses—he loved telling stories of visiting brothels with his childhood best friend Dave when they traveled across Europe together, but he was just romanticizing his own access. I can't remember the details of those stories because it always felt like they were directed at me. Did he say he wanted to take me to a whorehouse, or was that just the implication?

I'm thinking about how Gladys dismissed my work as vulgar, but it was my father who reveled in saying things like "That waitress is stacked like a brick shit house." As loud as possible. While my mother laughed and said Oh Bill.

I remember one time, when all four grandparents were over at our house for dinner, which was rare, so it must have been a special occasion, and my parents got in a dramatic fight, which was not rare. My father stormed out of the room as we were getting ready to sit down. Then he came back in, and said: Karin, let's fuck.

And then they went into their bedroom while we all waited. Gladys didn't say anything. Did anyone? Maybe this was the same dinner when everyone was obsessed with telling me that I wasn't eating enough. But that was every dinner. You see what they cared about, right.

A year or two after I became a whore, I confronted my father about sexually abusing me. And, I confronted the family. Then, instead of dealing with my father's abuse, they would meet with that false memory syndrome specialist at Gladys's house. Because the truth was the problem, not my father's abuse.

I don't know when my life as a whore became a topic of conversation, but I know my mother became obsessed with saying I was endangering myself. She didn't mention the danger she kept me in as a child. She wanted to address an imagined crisis so she didn't have to confront the real one. And sex work was one way I was freeing myself from all of them. How could it not be a threat?

Billie Holiday says that if she had heard Louis Armstrong and Bessie Smith coming through the windows of a church as a child, then she would have done anything for that minister, just to listen to the music. Or if she'd heard it at a Girl Scout jamboree, she would have loved it just as much. But she did not hear that music at a church, or a Girl Scout jamboree.

Billie grew up poor and Black in a segregated city, she was abused as a child, she was sent to reform school when she was nine, she was raped when she was eleven, and even though the man who raped her was tried and convicted she was sent to reform school again, as if she needed punishment too.

"A Depression was nothing new to us," she says, "we'd always had it." Like many kids, Holiday loved roller-skating, bike riding, and boxing, but she says she gave up these pursuits to make some money scrubbing people's steps and floors, and any other odd jobs she could find, like running errands for the women working at the whorehouse on the corner. She says she made an agreement with the women there that as long as she could stay in that front parlor and listen to Louis Armstrong and Bessie Smith, she would do their errands for free.

Sitting in that parlor, she realized how the same song could make her feel so different, depending on her mood or the time of day. How the same song was never really the same song.

Billie Holiday sings off-kilter—every word is its own universe. It doesn't matter what she's singing, she makes it hers. There's a dissonance between what she's saying and how it feels, every word on the verge of becoming something else.

Billie Holiday was the first jazz singer whose work I fell in love with, right around when I moved to San Francisco, but I felt conflicted about the misogyny of the lyrics, and the doomed narratives she invoked. A friend introduced me to the blues of Ma Rainey, Bessie Smith, and Memphis Minnie, who were Billie Holiday's predecessors, and I loved them too but it was Holiday who really took me in—maybe part of it was that sense of being trapped. I had finally escaped, but Billie Holiday knew nothing was easy—it's how she sings the words that generates the freedom to roam. Her voice bends in on itself, quivering with each extended syllable, shaking the words out of stasis.

"You can't copy anybody and end up with anything. If you copy it means you're working without feeling, and without feeling, whatever you do amounts to nothing," Holiday says in her memoir, and it's this feeling that defines her sound. And Gladys, who thought imitation was the greatest sin, would surely have agreed.

But was it feeling Gladys was after?

Billie Holiday moved to New York when she was around thirteen or fourteen, and a decade later, after she had become a fixture in the jazz scene, she sang to a packed crowd on opening night in 1938 at Café Society in Greenwich Village, known as the first integrated nightclub in New York. Café Society called itself "The wrong place for the Right people," and attracted a wild crowd of leftists, jazz aficionados, artists, and intellectuals, with celebrities mixed in among everyone else. It's where Holiday met Abel Meeropol, who showed her the lyrics for his song "Strange Fruit," and played it for her on the piano.

"Strange Fruit" became Billie Holiday's most famous song—when she sang it, she inhabited it. She did not have to convey something other than what the lyrics spelled out—and yet is her voice falling or floating, expanding or contracting into pain? She called "Strange Fruit" her personal protest, and when she sang that song the whole room would change.

In the version I have, Holiday starts by saying, "And now I'd like to sing a tune that was written especially for me," which wasn't true, but that's how much it became a part of her identity. When she clears her throat twice in a row at the beginning of this recording, you can already sense her struggle. You can sense it every time. You're there in that room.

From the first words, "Sou-uh-thern trees," where Holiday adds that extra syllable, the sinking of the "uh," you know something unexpected is about to happen. It doesn't matter how many times you've listened to this song, it doesn't matter whether you know every word already, because there's always something else. Just a subtle turn of the phrase, a flipping of the voice, a word that suddenly doesn't sound like a word at all, or not that word, what is it.

Maybe you get lost inside the sound of language made unfamiliar, even if you've listened to this song fifty or a hundred or a thousand times you still can't figure out how it all happens, how it can surprise you every time, that final series of notes, the clutching in the throat and then the opening into—opening into what. How this can still devastate you.

Holiday was under contract with Columbia Records at the time, but they refused to record "Strange Fruit," so there was controversy right from the start but she recorded it elsewhere and the song became central to her image and career. Some audience members would demand it, others would walk out of the room. She was pressured by club owners, agents, lovers, her mother, and many others to stop performing "Strange Fruit," but she persisted—even when it made her a target of federal authorities, which eventually led to imprisonment, worsening addictions, and deteriorating health. She wanted her memoir to be called "Bitter Crop," the final two words in the song, but the publisher insisted on *Lady Sings the Blues*.

Billie Holiday's memoir is known for its candor, but also its tall tales, obfuscations, half-truths, and overt lies. Like most celebrity memoirs it was written with someone else—in this case, William Dufty, a liberal white investigative journalist and jazz pianist who was married to her friend Maely. Holiday told her story to Dufty, and then he formed the narrative using her stories and published interviews. Later she claimed not to have read the book, but this was just a deflection from controversy.

When Holiday says in her memoir that she went to the whorehouse to do errands for the women working there, and this is where she first heard the music that changed her life, this may or may not be true, but here she declares her allegiance to the whorehouse as a place that formed her. She almost surely wasn't just doing errands for the women working there, though, she was one of them—turning tricks and stealing wallets and living more or less on her own, singing at the bars and after-hours joints by age eleven, staying up all night and then sleeping until the afternoon. She remained close with many of the girls she worked with, and the women who ran the houses, and would visit them whenever she returned to Baltimore.

In invoking the whorehouse, Holiday refuses segregation. Her life was always mixed—she herself was mixed race, and her close friends, lovers, and confidantes ranged across the lines of race, class, gender, and sexuality. She existed in these crossroads. She refused to exist anywhere else, even when the world punished her for this stance.

If there's one thing that's consistent in the book, it's Holiday's scathing analysis of the racism she encountered throughout her life. When she performed onstage with a band of sixteen white men in Kentucky in 1937, a racial mixing considered scandalous at the time, she describes the reaction by comparing Kentucky to Baltimore—"it's only on the border of being the South, which means the people there take their Dixie stuff more seriously than the crackers further down."

She says, "It got to the point where I hardly ever ate, slept, or went to the bathroom without having a major NAACP-type production." She wasn't courting controversy, she was just trying to live. This was two years before "Strange Fruit," but as a Black woman she was a threat onstage even when singing songs with lyrics so hackneyed that only someone with a voice and method as entrancing as hers could make you truly listen.

When traveling through the South, Holiday describes the Jim Crow racism that denied her access to restaurants, to accommodations, even to using the bathroom. After a while she didn't want to experience the same public humiliation just for basic needs, and she told the tour bus driver to stop and let her go to the bathroom in the bushes on the side of the road.

Her critiques of racism were not confined to the South—she describes the bar owners of New York's segregated white jazz scene as "plantation owners" who finally let Black musicians perform when they realized they would make more money, and she relates grotesque racist encounters from Miami to Detroit. Speaking of the segregated reality of New York in the 1930s, Holiday says, "The world we lived in was still one that white people made. But it had become a world they damn near never saw."

Billie Holiday had to sing—it was how she made a living, and it was also her life. "Although people sometimes act like they think so, a singer is not like a saxophone," she says. "When you walk out there and open your mouth, you never know what's going to happen."

The pain is real—so is the joy, the rage, the struggle to maintain. Her embrace of spontaneity, of feeling, of openness—all these traits became hallmarks for the abstract artists of the period, many of whom were directly inspired by jazz, an abstract art of its own.

Café Society was an integrated club founded by leftist Jews, and "Strange Fruit" was an anti-lynching song written by a Jewish Communist schoolteacher. I wonder what Gladys would have thought of this legacy. Did she challenge the segregated world she grew up in, or, like most white people, did she just go along?

Gladys attended the Art Students League in New York in 1941, so she could have gone to Café Society then, although by that point Billie Holiday was performing "Strange Fruit" at the jazz clubs on Fifty-Second Street, just blocks from the Art Students League, so Gladys could have heard it without venturing beyond the familiarity of a segregated venue. How would it have affected her?

Gladys grew up without much money, but when she was twelve she met a wealthy family that took interest in her as a future wife for one of their sons, and they treated her to clothing and trips to New York that would have been way above her means otherwise. This was in 1929, the year of the stock market crash that officially ushered in the Great Depression, but Gladys would have been somewhat sheltered from the impact. She turned eighteen on December 11, 1935, and shortly after that she married Abe Oliver. It wasn't what she wanted, but she was pressured by her family—surely it was a practical choice to marry the son of a millionaire during the Depression.

According to Helen, Gladys was in Florida for at least six months after her divorce, so she probably returned to Baltimore sometime in late

1938, or early 1939. Around then she met Ed, and they married in 1941. While he was attending Columbia Teachers College in the summers, Gladys lived with him on the Upper West Side and attended art classes at Columbia and at the Art Students League.

Around this time, the giants of the European avant-garde were fleeing Hitler and arriving in New York. Would Gladys have known to look for them? And what was her reaction to the surge of fascism in Europe, as a secular Jew, the second generation in her family to be born in the US? The US had not yet entered World War II—would Gladys have followed the news closely with fear and trepidation, or would she have been trying to block it out? And what about the insular world of downtown artists—would she have discovered them before they had received much public acclaim? Would she have danced with them at Café Society, an effigy of Hitler hanging from the ceiling by the coat check?

I'd like to think she would have explored every possible adventure, anything that would expand her imagination, but then I remember she told me that she never wanted to be different. And to step into an integrated nightclub in 1941 was already a stance of resistance. Many were there, but would she have wanted to be one of them?

In 1941, Gladys did not yet see herself as an artist—it would be a decade before anyone would use that word to describe her. She did not know how to claim it. The Art Students League prided itself on not limiting "the scope of its instruction to any school, method or style," which surely must have appealed to Gladys. One thing Gladys focused on was the study of anatomy, presumably so that her paintings could be more realistic. But surely as a fan of Picasso she was already thinking about abstraction.

Gladys had already been punished for claiming her autonomy. She had fled to Florida, fell in love, and then had suffered banishment again. Did this make her more cautious, or less?

The Art Students League was just around the corner from the Museum of Modern Art and the Guggenheim Foundation of Non-Objective Art, and most of the galleries in New York at the time were nearby. The League catalog also promoted a few downtown venues in their city map on the opening page, including the Whitney, which was then on Eighth Street, but I don't know how much time Gladys would have spent downtown. There were only a few dozen artists in the downtown avant-garde at that point, and they had not yet gained renown—what would Gladys have thought of this small group of mostly impoverished artists gathering at all-night cafeterias because they couldn't afford much more than coffee? Gathering to fight about ideas, to argue a future for art. The center of the art world had not yet shifted from Paris to New York, but certainly there were far more possibilities for cross-pollination in New York than in Baltimore. But regardless of what Gladys found there, it was Baltimore that remained her home for the rest of her life.

In Frank O'Hara's poem "The Day Lady Died," he learns the news of Billie Holiday's death in July of 1959 and thinks back to a summer night two years before, when he saw her sing at the Five Spot, a downtown dive bar known for a racially mixed crowd and late-night jazz, which became a haven for many of the artists who were regulars at the Cedar Tavern before it became a tourist attraction.

On that night at the Five Spot in 1957, many of these artists were in the half-empty bar, including Elaine de Kooning and Grace Hartigan, as well as Joe LeSueur and Frank O'Hara. All were fans of Billie Holiday, and they knew that ever since her conviction and imprisonment for drug possession a decade earlier, Holiday had lost her cabaret card and therefore couldn't perform in a venue that sold alcohol. But late that night she showed up unannounced with pianist Mal Waldron, and took the stage. She sang past dawn, and into the morning.

O'Hara's poem starts when he's walking around New York on another muggy July day two years later, getting "a hamburger and a malted," buying books and liquor and cigarettes, and then it ends with seeing Billie Holiday's face on the cover of the *New York Post*

> and I am sweating a lot by now and thinking of
> leaning on the john door in the 5 SPOT
> while she whispered a song along the keyboard
> to Mal Waldron and everyone and I stopped breathing

The way the end of the poem hits you like the end of a Billie Holiday song, that gasp for transcendence in the final note. And then it's gone.

Decades later, Gladys made her painting called *Night Jazz*. If there is a dance floor on the canvas it's in the saturated tones of one rectangular composition layered on top of another, and another, while the intersecting diagonals pull color through. In the lower left, a slanted grid of deep blues formed by the whites inside, shining light. Pathways of mauve, cobalt, aquamarine, gray and red and purple hues. It's those chains again, this time in paint, connecting me to you. A flash in the dark, a nighttime cry, the broken glass or a slow collapse. Everything in motion.

Yes, there is music here in this conversation through paint. But does calling it *Night Jazz* bring the emotion forward, or make it trite? After all, this was a painting Gladys made in 1988, when jazz might intrude in an elevator, but it was unlikely to cause controversy elsewhere.

But now I'm thinking about the aquamarine hues of one of the paintings behind me in the photos Gladys took when I visited her in 1993, at age twenty, with those same diagonals—here they are, framing me in a blurry photo with my shirt off. You really see the colors of my hair divided in half between purple and green, and both of these colors stand out in the painting. Even my plaid pants, now I see they are green and gray more than green and black, blending or clashing with the diagonals structured by greens and grays.

Gladys must have selected these paintings because of the colors of my hair, right? Here's another blurry one where the angle of my head bending forward is the exact angle of one of the diagonals in the painting. And then another set taken in front of a painting with similar colors, this one even blurrier, but you see a spiral behind me. The stiffness of my posture except when I'm in motion.

And then I am the spiral, dancing to the floor and now the greens and blues are visible through the window in the corner behind me. Is it the blurriness or the colors that give these photos an underwater feeling—if they were in focus would I see more, or less?

When I moved to Baltimore in 2018 to work on this book, I went there to go to familiar places and I went there to meet with people who knew Gladys and I went there to find out things about her that I didn't know, but also I just went there for whatever might come through in my day-to-day experiences.

When I was living in Baltimore, I went to Wyman Park all the time. It was the closest park to my house, so it became a part of my daily walks in the afternoon and evening. It was the first place I tried sunbathing, until I realized it was basically a swamp. But then I would walk through on the way to the Baltimore Museum of Art, or on the way to acupuncture, or on the way pretty much anywhere, since I always prefer a park to the street.

Once I figured out how to get to the health food store by walking through Wyman Park and the Johns Hopkins campus, I would pass a monument at the top of the park, but I didn't pay attention to it at first—it was a giant slab of concrete, a tiered rectangular surface that looked to me like some kind of postmodern memorial nestled among the trees. When I finally studied it closer, and pieced together the inscription on the base, I realized it had been a giant monument to Robert E. Lee and Stonewall Jackson, until the city of Baltimore removed the monument in the dead of night in 2017, less than a year before my visit.

So, until 2017, this giant monument to the leaders of the Confederacy was right there in an Olmsted Brothers park, facing the entrance to Johns Hopkins University, the most powerful institution in Baltimore, and right next to the Baltimore Museum of Art, the city's most prominent museum.

In Sabine Gruffat's 2018 film *Take It Down*, she shows Confederate loy-
alists enacting an annual ritual for *Silent Sam*, the Confederate monument on the campus of the University of North Carolina. Dressed up
in the clothes they imagine their ancestors would have worn, they sing
the North Carolina state song and explain their pride in Confederate
history to the filmmaker.

Then we see protests against the monument—one protester says, "I
poured my blood and red ink on the statue because for me this is the
completion of the statue."

The film is solarized so that positive and negative are reversed, and
everything shakes in a field of color like when you close your eyes after
looking at something too bright. As the Confederate sympathizers continue to sing the North Carolina state song, we see a series of Confederate monuments in front of stately buildings, each one shaking in a field
of saturated magentas, blues, greens, yellows, and oranges until, one by
one, they disappear in a beam of light.

There's an excitement to this banishment ritual, but also there's
the tension between literal and figurative that isn't quite resolved—the
monuments go away, but we still hear the words of the Confederate
sympathizers.

During the Q and A with the filmmakers someone says to Gruffat:
"Maybe you could have broken it up more, so the words aren't as intel-
ligible, so you don't know exactly what is happening, so both sides are
more subdued."

And I say, "Wouldn't that make it complicit?"

And then the woman who made this suggestion leaves the room.

I'm just glad I said something—this isn't just an abstract piece of art,
right, it's an intervention in a rarefied world of experimental film that so
often doesn't want to make a political stance. Here we are watching the
film in Seattle, and someone wants to make it even further away.

In another film, *Amarillo Ramp*, made by Sabine Gruffat and Bill
Brown, nature literally takes over a Robert Smithson earthwork sculpture. It's a giant ramp he constructed from the Texas desert, now decaying into the earth. But when Gruffat and Brown sent their film to

the Robert Smithson foundation in New York, the foundation said there couldn't be cow shit on the earthwork because it was behind a fence. Even though no one from the foundation had ever visited, they imagined a ramp made of dirt and rocks somehow delicately preserved for decades in the desert.

The South as the place no one from the North even wants to visit.

In *XCTRY*, a film by Bill Brown, a speaker describes the marks of the bodies on used mattresses in a motel like fingerprints awaiting analysis in the hallway. Sometimes we wonder why, and sometimes we just wonder, and sometimes we are in wonder. As I'm walking home, I gaze at the giant construction site across from Cal Anderson Park, all the obliterating lights and enormous machines, and I think: There's the next movie.

I want a history of everything that was never recorded, and all the records that have been lost. I want a history of everything left unsaid. Everything that never happened, but should have happened.

Marion Cajori: Do you begin with the landscape?

Joan Mitchell: No, I'm with it all the time.

Marion Cajori: Do you lose yourself?

Joan Mitchell: When I do it's blissful.

In "Why I Am Not a Painter," Frank O'Hara writes:

> There should be
> so much more, not of orange, of
> words, of how terrible orange is
> and life.

I stay there, between the period after "life" and "Days go by," which comes right after—and I'm shaken. By all that orange. And life. How terrible it is.

In the prologue to *Restless Ambition*, Cathy Curtis's biography of Grace Hartigan, she writes, "I discovered that Grace had entered adulthood with no goals except to escape her family."

If every biography started this way, maybe more of us would escape.

Oranges is a series of twelve paintings Grace Hartigan made in collaboration with Frank O'Hara, whose poems inspired the works. Sometimes his words are in the paintings, like in Oranges # 1 (*Black Crows*):

> THE BRIMSTONE
> ODOR OF YOUR STARS
> SNEERS
> AT OUR HOROSCOPE!

On Grace Hartigan's cover for the book, the oranges almost look rotten—the way the O of the title is an orange too, but it's not even a circle—it's collapsed into the left side of the R, the title balanced on the pile of oranges below, and somehow there's so much motion here in this not-quite-still life.

Emotion too. I'm thinking about O'Hara's poem "For Grace, after a Party," which starts, "You do not always know what I am feeling"—and then we know, right?

All the mundane details contained in the poem, the details that surround a relationship, "the eggs a little / different today" or the "ashtray, suddenly there"—and I'm suddenly there, "in rooms full of / strangers."

But no, I'm getting carried away, this poem is for Grace. After a party. "You do not always know what I am feeling," Frank declares, and in declaring this he declares his love for Grace to the world.

But maybe I'm getting stuck in New York. I forgot that I have this photo album of Gladys's from 1956.

Here's my father dressed up for his bar mitzvah, and here's Gladys, just below that photo, standing in front of her easel in the basement.

Here's Gladys looking glamorous while washing the dishes, a man who's presumably her father drying them in the background, a huge box of Special K cereal on the counter. She always did like Special K.

Here's a whole page of photos of my father's neurotically organized bulletin board of sports pennants and photos of sports heroes. And then here's my father in a plaid robe at age thirteen, cuddling in bed with his father, a scene that's hard to imagine since I don't even remember them touching.

Here's Gladys next to her own bulletin board, writing something. And here's a picture of my father painting. There are no pictures of Gladys painting.

But this was a busy time for her as an artist—her solo show at the Baltimore Museum of Art took place at the end of the year, and her New York City solo show the next year. I wonder if she didn't want anyone to document her in the act of painting, or if maybe these photos were designed to showcase a different life, the domestic one as popularly imagined in the 1950s.

All of these photos are from January and February 1956, except a page at the end, from 1958. Gladys and Ed are posing outside in a snowbank. Ed is smoking a pipe and wearing a tan fedora that matches his coat, while Gladys stands next to him in a billowing red coat with a black belt pulled tight at the waist and a scarf wrapped loosely around her head. He looks proud, and she looks happy.

But here's my favorite photo—it's Keith Martin, grinning in an armchair, a man in a suit standing behind him, also grinning. This must be Dave. Are they drunk, or are they just enjoying one another's company, I think it might be both. A portrait of gay lovers in the straight domestic setting.

And here's a cigar box filled with photos that I haven't looked at yet, mostly photos of my father in high school and college. There's something so sexual about the poses that he and his friends make, something so sexual that it scares me. What is it in their eyes, just lust and male bravado or am I only interpreting my own desire? This jock in a white shirt, chin raised slightly for the photo booth, is that my father?

This must be my father's college dorm room with the shiny curtains, because here he is making big-tits gestures for the naked pinup models on his walls. This must be his box of photos that he stored at Gladys's house, and then forgot about, and she kept them.

Here he is with a beard for the first time, trying out a look that's vaguely countercultural. He was an Oberlin student, after all. The beard he would keep for the rest of his life. Oh, but wait, next to one of the pinup models is a photo of him smoking in profile, wearing a striped blazer while he gazes at one of Gladys's paintings to the right. And to his left on the wall is a naked blonde.

But the painting, I wish I could see it more clearly. I wish I could see it in color, the way it's divided geometrically but everything is in motion across the parts.

And here's a prize—a photo of Gladys in a short-sleeved dress, sitting on the floor with a formal tea set, looking down. Is that a cigarette in one hand—is she ruminating, or striking a glamorous pose? But what dominates is one of her paintings floating above her head, perched on an easel. The photo is framed so that the top third, which is the painting, is another world, and it looks like it's coming out of Gladys's head.

I can tell this painting would dominate the room. I want to see it dominate.

Oh, another stunning photo of Gladys, standing outside in a beautiful sundress, June 1960.

And here she is inside the house, arranging dinner on the dining room table, taking something out of aluminum foil, white curtains in the background, a chandelier with fake candles. And here's Ed doing the dishes. It's good to see that he was doing the dishes.

Lots of photos of my father drunk at college. Two guys sitting on toilets. But then here's another of Gladys's paintings—a relatively small vertical work with a lot of white, swirling rectangles, if rectangles can swirl.

Do I want to look at pictures labeled "CAT AS BABY," maybe I do.

Oh, wow, this cat is tiny, sitting in my father's lap, how is he only in high school here? This jock who was my father, I mean it makes sense, but I guess I didn't really know, I didn't really know before. Where exactly his misogyny came from. Or how.

A photo of Gladys in a white nightgown, maybe she's watching TV? And here she is in the kitchen, playing with the cat on the floor. Here the cat is, coming out of a box.

I don't recognize this family and their comfort with one another, what happened to this family?

Back to college, my father posing drunkenly with a cigarette, this sexualized self-conscious pose that he's perfected.

And here he is in high school wearing his letter jacket, with his head back like he's going to fight. And then this picture of him in the basement of the house, standing in front of one of Gladys's paintings, head back and arm raised, armpit visible while gulping down a bottle of liquor. It's like he's one of those action painters.

How I get to see Gladys's studio through my father's drinking poses.

Here's the largest of her paintings that I've seen from the 1950s, behind my father and a drunk friend. I can't see much of it because they're blocking it. But in the foreground I do see a can filled with Gladys's paintbrushes.

Now we're in Colorado in 1958, where Ed taught at Colorado State College of Education in the summers and Gladys would paint. They're on a road trip, and my father, who is fifteen, is posing in front of rocks—maybe they're in the mountains.

Yes, that's ice, not rocks. Another photo, everything bleached white. Gladys is standing to the right, her skirt and hair blowing in the wind. My father, also in white, sitting on a rock next to a man I don't recognize, but could it be Dave, Keith Martin's lover?

Wait, look at this. It's like an advertisement for the artist alone in the world. Gladys sits on a rock in a sleeveless blouse, wearing dark pants that end just below the knees, her legs open with her hands between. She's sitting on a rock, in a dry landscape with other rocks, and lots of weeds. In the background is a deserted road leading to a mountain, trees on both sides of the road, but only in the background, and a sky of bright clouds.

And now a pose on the mountain—Gladys on the left, the man I don't know in the middle, my father on the right. Okay, it's Pike's Peak, that's where they are, 14,110 feet up, according to the sign.

But wait, another masterpiece. Gladys poses in the forest in a white dress with a stole wrapped around her shoulders, looking up. She's standing among the trees towering behind her, on a cliff of brambles. And I realize something about these photos of Gladys. They are so deliberately posed and framed. Clearly they're taken by an artist. And I realize that artist must be Keith Martin.

Here Keith is in a group photo, posed in front of a cabin, and in another photo he's wearing plaid short-shorts, my father standing to the right.

And here he is to the left of Gladys in another group photo, with my father in the background.

But Keith isn't in the rest of the photos, because he's behind the camera.

And I'm thinking about how Keith Martin and his lover are traveling with Gladys and Ed, and my father. Or maybe they're all living in Colorado for the summer. And then when my grandfather is working during the day, Gladys and Keith and Dave and my father head out to explore. And how Dave is in the middle in some of these photos, because Keith is behind the camera. Because otherwise wouldn't it make more sense for Gladys to be in the middle? She's the one connecting them. But not in Keith's eyes.

And then these loving portraits of my father, posed on a mountain-top. How Keith and his lover were really part of their family, at least on these trips, and what does this mean?

My father, practicing the standard trope of teenaged masculinity among these queens. Were they helping him to pose? Here he is behind the sign for the Continental Divide, right in the center, as if he's holding it up. Gladys holds the sign at the right of the photo, and Ed leans on the other side.

Gladys, her gay best friend and his lover, and my father, in the 1950s. I grew up a generation later, and there were no queer people anywhere near my parents. Even when they went to gay restaurants at the beach, they never brought me and my sister. They would tell us about the incredible food, and how much they appreciated the atmosphere, but they cautioned us that these were not places for kids. Too many fairies, my father would say.

And here I'm looking again at that gorgeous photo of Gladys on the floor, posed in front of one of her paintings, now I see that this is from 1956, because there's another photo that includes the date. I wonder if this painting was in Gladys's solo show at the Baltimore Museum of Art.

And now I'm wondering if the grand location in the background, with elaborate curtains and stylized contemporary furniture—I'm wondering if this is Keith's place. Certainly the studious staging of the photos connects them to the portraits of Gladys in the wilderness.

And here's the whole painting. It's amazing how different it looks in this photo. Much lighter. Like we could float away.

I can't remember the last time I went downtown to the Seattle Public Library to do research—maybe twenty-five years ago, in the old building? But then I was just using the image files to make postcards. The new library, a sleek glass-and-metal concoction designed by Rem Koolhaas, is a tourist attraction. I enter the soaring atrium, and at the front desk they offer the fastest route or the most interesting route to my destination.

I'm looking through *ARTnews* from 1957, in case I can find anything about Gladys's show at the Duveen-Graham Gallery. This was the most influential art publication of the time, and every issue features prominent critics and artists whose names I immediately recognize, and articles on contemporary art as well as art of the past. I do see the ads for the gallery, text-only, similar to most of the other gallery ads.

Just when I think I'm not going to find anything directly about Gladys, here it is, a review in the October issue:

> **Gladys Goldstein**, in her first New York one-man show, has an ingeniously modish way of giving atmospheres the density of abstract Cubism, used decoratively rather than structurally to denote objects. The complex paint-patterning, whether of Chinatown or the desert, tends to flow rapidly to the picture plane like things bobbing to the surface of water. With expertly modulated palette and palette-knife, Miss Goldstein creates an impression of appealing virtuosity.

It's the most glowing review on the page. The reviewer, "P.T.," has a few others that are dry and somewhat scathing. I look at the table of contents to see who this is, and—no way—it's Parker Tyler.

I'm feeling something here, what am I feeling? Oh, I'm crying. Until an architecture tourist rounds the corner to stare.

Because in the early '90s I discovered *The Young and Evil*, the novel written by Charles Henri Ford and Parker Tyler, published in 1933, and I felt a shock of recognition witnessing these queens camping it up in

New York in the 1930s, reading one another and telling tales. And here Gladys is connected to that lineage too.

The Young and Evil starts with lesbians as the center of knowledge and beauty, inviting the queen in—"yes your face is so exquisite, we thought you were a Lesbian in drag when we first saw you"—and I'm thinking that exquisite was a word Gladys would say over and over. It was her finest compliment, and did she learn this from the queens in her life?

"*Ex*quisite," with the emphasis on the first syllable.

Every conversation punctuated by cigarette smoke and the shaking of the cocktail glass and poetry, literature and art as arguments these characters are living, desire and contest and conquest. There is a deep sadness but also a glee, danger in everyday longing, a dance of desperation and bravado.

This world of bars and bad relationships, the rain on the sidewalk and the reign of the barbed wit, the camp and the cramped, the lonely grasping for something not quite as lonely, all of it here, a legacy. Whimsy as a protection from everyday brutality, all the makeup and the reading of books and backward glances.

How so much of this feels so contemporary—"ninety-five percent of the world is just naturally queer"—that's ahead of the contemporary. But Herbert Hoover is president, and this is New York City under Prohibition.

And the glory of the queen's vernacular, the prancing and dancing, the back rooms and the stage of the world, the full frontal glow, "Miss 69" and "Miss Suckoffski" taking the runway—and then afterward, "everything was all wrong ... wrong but magnetic."

This book tells us that "morality is rotten." Why? "Because it's a stage of rot. It's the skin beginning to fall off." The drunk philosophizing and the sparring of wits, the search for meaning as a meandering way to escape gloom.

"One begins to have ideas about happiness as soon as one sees that happiness is impossible."

And: "Forgive and forget are both bad words because they have grown together and thus become impossible."

At the core of the book is a love between queens, a love with "no doors nor walls." These queens weather bashings and prison and bad relationships, just as part of everyday survival.

And yet one of these queens prioritizes a doomed romantic partner over this love without walls—how people do this to me over and over, and how it always destroys me.

"Perhaps love is loneliness . . . Simple, honest loneliness."

Keith Martin graduated from the Art Institute of Chicago in 1933, the year *The Young and Evil* was published, and then he moved to Europe, living in London, Vienna, and Paris over the next few years before returning to New York. He might have discovered the book in Paris, since it was published there, and banned in both the US and Britain.

Martin was introduced to Gertrude Stein's poetry while he was in Berlin, and when he wrote to her in response she invited him to visit her in Paris, but they didn't end up meeting until the end of World War II—Martin had enlisted in the army in 1941, and was trained in painting camouflage for war purposes. He also worked on murals, lettering, and posters for the war effort, and had a solo gallery show in Paris in 1945, which Stein attended. Afterward, she invited him over to her house to look at her art collection.

Charles Henri Ford was a protégé of Stein—and Ford's lover, Pavel Tchelitchew, was the first person to design sets for Lincoln Kirstein's New York City Ballet. Keith Martin designed costumes for the New York City Ballet in 1936—I see some of these designs in the catalog for an exhibit that just closed at the Museum of Modern Art, *Lincoln Kirstein's Modern*, which includes Martin's drawings that look so much like the ones I remember from my childhood kitchen.

The catalog for *Lincoln Kirstein's Modern* includes drawings by Pavel Tchelitchew, Keith Martin, and many other gay and art-world luminaries of the time. Martin lived in New York from 1934 to 1941, so the camp world conjured in *The Young and Evil* would have been familiar to him. And, this world may not have been that different from the world of John Bernard Myers yelling to Frank O'Hara and Larry Rivers at the ballet two decades later, "Here come the divine Verlaine and Rimbaud with their lips full of blood and semen." John Bernard Myers, after all, was the managing editor of *View*, Charles Henri Ford and Parker Tyler's magazine of avant-garde art and literature.

I'm thinking about Gladys's adulation for Mikhail Baryshnikov decades later, when my sister and I would watch *The Nutcracker* every year in her bed with the electric blanket.

He's the greatest dancer in history, Gladys would say, there's never been anyone like him. Isn't he exquisite?

I wonder if this adulation of the ballet—and, Baryshnikov—was part of the legacy of her relationship with Keith. Although I never met him, he was still alive then, when I was five, six, seven, eight, and nine. What would it have been like to watch the ballet in bed not just with Gladys and my sister, but with Keith Martin too? I mean what would it have been like to have this queen in my life? My father grew up with him, but there were no queers or queens in my life. Gladys was the only person who I could look to for an example of an artistic life.

I, too, fantasized about New York, Paris, and Vienna. I, too, knew that I needed to get away. But, like most queers of my generation and before, I didn't have any queer role models until I became my own.

Learning that Lincoln Kirstein was a proponent of magic realism, I'm remembering how Gladys told that class of seventh graders that this was her least favorite style of art. Since she didn't just say realism, it must have been the addition of magic that she disliked the most. Looking at the images in the catalog for *Lincoln Kirstein's Modern*, where gay artists include overtly homosexual imagery in their work and cloak this within a surrealist aesthetic, I'm wondering if it was this magic that Gladys objected to.

My mother just reminded me of something—she said my father would never go up to Gladys's studio—she always wanted him to come up, but he refused. He told my mother that it was because Gladys was too sensitive about his feedback. I have no idea whether this was true, but now I realize that's another reason why going into her studio must have felt like a dream. Because I didn't have to worry that he would invade.

Is Gladys already in the room when I enter, or does she come in after, in any case I'm surprised to see her. She's sitting on the floor in painter's clothes, maybe not her usual clothes but someone's, and she says: As a kid I painted with Lacey.

Lacey, I ask. And she says call up Russell and ask. And I realize she means Russell Paints, Lacey must be a color.

Wait a second, I say, I need to get some paper to take notes, and I go to my desk but how many sheets do I need? I decide on three and then I'm back in the room with Gladys. And she says are Marvin and Eric going to read it? Or maybe she says Marvin and Erica.

Gladys, I say, they're not around.

I don't want to say dead, because what is she?

And she says: You can join me.

Now she's wearing a red jumpsuit with a cinched waist.

No, I can't, I say, and she slowly fades away. Outside, the loud slam of the garbage truck wakes me up, but I want to bring Gladys back. I need to have a list of questions ready for next time.

I think about how the red of her jumpsuit was close to the orange of the prison uniform, how in this dream I said I wasn't going to kill myself, and has this ever been so direct.

When someone asks what is your writing process, I think it must be to try and try and then finally, in the gap between the limits of my body and the possibility of pulling something through, somewhere in that gap—

"I thought it was a really daring step of you to write a book about women only," says Deborah Solomon, in conversation with Mary Gabriel at the Whitney.

And yet *Ninth Street Women* spends so much time on the influence of all the famous men in these women's lives. But maybe this is unavoidable when depicting the time in which these women emerged as artists. When to claim the category of woman and artist would mean dooming oneself to further obscurity.

"Not either/or, but all together" is how Gabriel describes her approach. How, as the art world solidified into the art market, women were pushed out.

I want to read a biography of all these women artists, without any mention of the men who dominated their lives. I want these men to disappear. But then I guess that wouldn't be a biography, it would be an exorcism.

But then Mary Gabriel says: "Abstract painting was a language that transcended gender."

Sometimes we know what inspires us, and sometimes we don't. But there's always something, when we're inspired. And it doesn't just come from inside. It can't. Maybe that's why we're alive.

I'm thinking about Billie Holiday's mother, trying to keep her away from men. She was fine with her sleeping with women, but she thought the men would destroy her.

Unfortunately she was right.

If you watch *Jackson Pollock 51*, the ten-minute film where Pollock paints on canvas and glass, using brushes and sticks and cans, smoking the whole time and posing with the wildness of the so-called American landscape, just after the halfway mark in the film, when Pollock is finishing the process of tacking the new canvas on the wall of his studio, you can see Lee Krasner from the back, her hair freshly coiffed, wearing all black with her hands clasped behind her.

Is Krasner a prop, or a model? She's in the corner between the black wall and the white wall, the long skinny horizontal painting and the long skinny vertical one. As the camera pans slowly from right to left, with dramatic classical music as if we are in suspense, there's Krasner, head tilted slightly to the left, gazing at the edge of the canvas.

What does she see there?

Joan Mitchell: I don't have any feeling for monumental art, except what they want me to feel is that I don't exist, and that's okay.

Marion Cajori: That's okay?

Joan Mitchell: Sure, I don't want to exist in their way.

When Elaine de Kooning writes, in a 1955 *ARTnews* article, "The private myth has become public property," I swoon. Privacy as property. The public myth. The myth of property.

Or, that's where I go, anyway. Can we go there together, Elaine?

Art criticism as philosophical inquiry. Critical analysis as a spark for poetry.

De Kooning blasts away at purity battles within Abstract Expressionism, and among abstract artists in general. She makes fun of those who say you can only paint what you see, those who say you can paint what you see as long as it doesn't look like what you see, and those who say you can only paint from the imagination. "The work of many of the painters who insist on novelty or uniqueness as the only value is beginning to seem curiously alike—with the uniform originality of a 'herd of independent minds.'"

We picture this herd of independent minds, tumbling off a cliff with the buffalo.

At this point, de Kooning has been immersed in the avant-garde New York art world for almost twenty years, since she was eighteen. She knows everyone and is able to characterize their work with just a few bold gestures. Her summaries are simple and concise, witty and directed—they circle around themselves until you are inside the paradox: "The main difference, then, between abstract and non-abstract art is that the abstract artist does not have to choose a subject. But whether or not he chooses, he always ends up with one."

No one wins, but someone loses—"A style in art, when it is vital, is a mode of thinking. When the style becomes the conclusion of its own thinking, as in decoration, it is dead. Its corpse becomes the property of commercial artists."

And just when you think that de Kooning might get stuck here, she turns around to say that even the original creator of a new form can kill that invention when it becomes formulaic. And then she turns everything around again, to say that "a dead style can be brought to life—sometimes a larger life than it had originally by a living subject. The reason that artists can be endlessly enthralled by previous styles of painting is that they can bring new motives to them, and thereby confiscate them."

Confiscation as a tool for the imagination—to steal from the dead, in order to make something alive.

So the enemy of art is that which makes the gestures of creativity into a commodity instead of inspiring new ways of thinking. In this way, I'd like to think that de Kooning challenges the notion of property itself—or, at the very least, the notion that anything creative can become commoditized. She's against purity, against ideology, and against drawing battle lines because this means someone is always left out. She's writing in the exact moment when Abstract Expressionism is becoming canonized, and monetized—I don't know if she's making enemies here, or making friends, as she skewers every hierarchy, and every trap.

Gladys's relationship with the Duveen-Graham Gallery in New York started shortly after the publication of Elaine de Kooning's article, so she was entering the art world de Kooning describes. In July 1955, Gladys writes to Albert Duveen to thank him for the opportunity to show at his gallery, adding, "I painted for a long, long time before even submitting to shows—painting means much too much to me to try for something just for a moment of glory."

Indeed, she had been painting for a long time. Her father even claimed that "she was drawing before she could walk," a quote included on a gallery release. Later she was pursuing teacher education at Johns Hopkins, where Henry Roben advised her to focus on fine art and study in New York, and that's when she went to study at the Art Students League and afterward painted portraits for an income. In 1951, she went to Penn State to study with Hobson Pittman for the summer, and he convinced her to focus on her painting. Penn State then gave her a studio for two more summers, where she sometimes painted fourteen hours a day, seven days a week.

In Gladys's correspondence with the Duveen-Graham Gallery, she alternates between nervousness and confidence. In February 1956, she admits:

> The truth of the matter of my not bringing all the ten
> oils and fifteen gouaches that I did last summer in for
> you to see is that I am always petrified to show anything.

I always do what is expected of me, and appear when I
must, but it never ceases to be a frightening experience.
If I can deliver my work and then disappear, it is much
easier; and, although I was most anxious for you to see
more of my work, I never quite got up enough courage
to bring it in.

This must be the work Gladys created during one of her summers
in Colorado. Many of the paintings are titled with names drawn from
the Western landscape, such as *Arroyo* or *Aspen*. These were exhibited
alongside paintings evoking an urban landscape, such as *Wall Street* and
42nd Street. And those with titles in between, such as *January* or *Stilled
Motion*.

In April 1956, after the opening of a successful show of hers in Baltimore, Gladys writes to Albert Duveen that *Baltimore Sun* art critic
Kenneth Sawyer "called me after he had seen the show and said that
he doesn't know why he never noticed it before—but now it is very
clear to him (and he's always given me good notices)—he said that I am
<u>extending</u> impressionism—just as de Kooning is extending cubism—and
that my signature is in every brush stroke. He was very excited—and so
was I."

Perhaps Gladys had not yet seen the paper, because, the day before
her letter, Kenneth Sawyer's article in *The Baltimore Sun* describes her
as "perhaps Baltimore's most awarded painter of the season," mentioning the Popular Prize from the Baltimore Museum's Maryland
Regional show, and "Best in Show" at the Smithsonian's Penwomen
biennial. He writes: "Mrs. Goldstein's origins are quite clear: she is an
Impressionist—the only Impressionist I know of who is continuing the
tradition without repeating it. Her central preoccupation is matter contained in light, but it's matter not light that holds the canvas."

Duveen writes back to Gladys that he "feels perfectly in tune with"
Kenneth Sawyer's words about her work. And, since Gladys mentioned
that her work had been selling well, including nearly half of the work on
display at her recent show, he writes, "I hope you see that we're keeping
pace with Baltimore."

How interesting for a New York gallery owner to write about keeping pace with Baltimore, a city often described as a backwater where an

artist could never develop a career. And yet, in 1956, Gladys's art career is flourishing. At the end of April, she writes, "For the first time in my life, the bins are getting low."

And then, in September: "My sales since January '56 have more than tripled—from everywhere, including Baltimore—what's happening?"

Anticipating the opening of her solo show at the Baltimore Museum of Art, she writes, "I am not nervous about my paintings—I <u>know</u> they are <u>special</u>—and completely mine—it's being there on December 2 that bothers me—all those people!"

So Gladys emphasizes her vulnerability and prowess at the same time. If she may be trying to impress Duveen, the gallery is also wooing her. Joan Washburn, Albert Duveen's secretary, writes to Gladys about the 1957 biennial at the Corcoran Gallery in Washington, a competition which thousands entered:

> Congratulations on getting in the Corcoran! The competition is very stiff and you should be very pleased . . . This is to say that we do need more of your pictures. What with the constant requests from museum lending libraries and various other benefits sales, etc., plus the ones which we have sold, our stock in Goldsteins is becoming very low. Mr. Duveen and Mr. Graham are planning to stop in Baltimore on the way to Washington when they go down to the opening of the Corcoran show. They would like to pick up some new paintings at that time if you have anything left from your shows. They will let you know definitely when to expect them.

One of the only points of contention seems to be over a particular painting, *January*. Gladys writes to Duveen in March 1957, to say, "You got me all upset when you didn't like my large gray painting *January*—but I do think my studio is not the best place to see the big ones."

In the next sentence, Gladys adds: "Anyhow—word just arrived that <u>it</u> shall receive the Berkeley T. Ruben Miller Memorial Prize 'for original work in a progressive direction' in the Maryland Regional."

In *The Baltimore Sun*, Kenneth Sawyer mentions the rigor of the selection process for the Maryland Regional, which chose only seventy-six paintings out of fifteen hundred that year, noting, "What makes it distinct from past Regionals is the obvious efforts of the jury, composed of Betty Parsons, New York painter and gallery owner, Ibram Lassaw, sculpture [sic] and Edgar C Schenk, director of the Brooklyn Museum, to maintain the highest critical standards. The result is that while the number of entries was higher than in former years, the number of works finally selected was noticeably smaller."

He then goes on to praise *January* as "a daring, spacious gray and white oil which reveals considerable gains over the work in her recent Museum show."

In the brochure accompanying Gladys's solo show at Duveen-Graham, Albert Duveen writes, "Her canvases offer an ideal medium for the lover of the pictorial and realistic to enter the challenging world of the abstract." This is when you can still see figurative elements in her work—in about a third of the paintings in the show, there are recognizable trees, and even sometimes a building or cityscape. In *White Church*, which Gladys made while studying at Penn State, there is, in fact, a white church. But many of the paintings are completely abstract, including *January*, which does end up in the show.

And, in the first letter from Robert Graham, the co-owner of Duveen-Graham, he encloses a review by Dore Ashton in *The New York Times*, where she praises *January*, and he adds, "I think it is particularly interesting that she liked JANUARY as that is my favorite picture too. I like the transparency or lucidity which I had never noticed in any of your painting until this time."

If this transparency in Gladys's work was new at the time, I can see why she was attached to people noticing it—after all, it was this effect of light coming through the picture that Gladys would perfect throughout her life. When Kenneth Sawyer says she's "the only Impressionist I know of who is continuing the tradition without repeating it," maybe he means that her methods—thickly applied paint, big gestures, the use of the palette knife as brush, the intensity of the colors, the channeling of the unconscious, the refusal of a central focus, the painting off the canvas—are more current to a time when Abstract Expressionism is in ascendance.

No matter how smooth a painting of Gladys's looks, when you get up close the texture is there. Always the deliberate clumping of the paint, the bumps, the shifting thickness to emphasize imperfection.

In her *ARTnews* article, Elaine de Kooning uses the term "Abstract-Impressionist" to describe painters who "keep the Impressionist manner of looking at the scene but leave out the scene." Could this be what Sawyer means when he says Gladys is an Impressionist? De Kooning writes, "As the Impressionists attempted to deal with the optical effects of nature, the followers are interested in the optical effects of spiritual states, thereby giving an old style a new subject."

A term like Abstract Impressionism might connote Europe and delicacy, whereas Abstract Expressionism immediately meant New York and manliness. Maybe this is why, once Abstract Expressionism became a school that became a commodity that became a brand that became history, it was a disparate group of artists who were included—fiercely independent and rarely collaborative, still they all ended up under this label. Critics even argued about who was first generation, and who was second.

As a kid, I was obsessed with Monet's water lilies—I went to the Monet retrospective at the National Gallery, and bought a large *Nymphéas* poster that remained on the blue wall above my bed for years, until, sometime in high school, I painted the wall gray and replaced the water lilies with a Romare Bearden poster. Monet's water lilies were starting to seem cliché, even if I can still remember the awe at seeing them on a trip to Paris with my parents and sister when I was in high school. But somehow we never made it to Giverny, where Monet painted.

Wait, I can actually picture myself walking over that bridge, so we must have been there. Or am I just picturing myself in a painting?

No, I remember a train through the suburbs, and once we arrived the water lilies weren't doing that well. Or am I thinking of the water lilies in Volunteer Park, where I go almost every day now, watching the ducks in the koi ponds?

Joan Mitchell bought the house next to Monet's former estate in Giverny where he painted the water lilies, and then she lived there in drunken seclusion and painted her own water lilies, although she never called them that. And no one calls her an Abstract Impressionist. Because that never became a brand.

Elaine de Kooning writes, in 1955, that there are twice as many Abstract Impressionists as Abstract Expressionists in New York, although they are rarely mentioned. And I wonder who she includes under this umbrella. Her precise description of Abstract Impressionism as painting the scene but leaving out the scene makes me think she isn't only saying this in jest.

Gladys was drawn to abstraction, but she was not afraid to paint from nature, even if it was an internal nature she most wanted to reveal. She painted from inside, like the Abstract Expressionists always claimed to be doing, but she also painted from outside, as with older European avant-garde traditions. Maybe this is what Duveen-Graham was pointing to when they promoted her work as an ideal starting point for someone branching out into the realm of abstraction—her work does not claim purity, its loyalties are mixed.

Gladys wasn't a formalist who believed that the role of the artist should be moot, an ideology de Kooning pokes fun at when saying that even Mondrian, who strove for impersonality, signed his art, like anyone else, in the lower right corner, and that when doing so "he is just as involved with the question of his own identity as he is with the identity of the subject." Gladys believed that all her art was personal, like Lee Krasner.

During Gladys's 1957 show at Duveen-Graham, she writes to the gallery in a more confident tone, to advise them about a potential visit from the collector Edward J. Gallagher Jr.:

> He "buys"—but usually names—Pollock, Tobey, Graves, etc. He keeps NOTHING—he is now buying for the new modern section at the Met. He is the one who bought my BIG CITY for the University of Arizona—gave them 50 paintings and built the "museum" to house them . . . He has little confidence in his own judgment and likes to be told how great something is. He also likes a bargain. He couldn't get a reduction from Sidney Janis on a Pollock so he went to Mrs. Pollock and bought the "best" Pollock. He bought my Big City from a show and I was advised to let him have it for less than marked but it didn't matter to me since I'd

already gotten over 150.00 in prize money for it and I priced it higher for the show anyhow. I tell you this so that you can understand him and if you want to quote higher prices, do so.

I'm thinking about Gladys's place as an insider and an outsider. Here she comes across as very savvy about the art market and its politics. She's speaking in detail about this collector because she knows the stakes. She also knows that he liked her work enough to have included it in a major collection. And now he's become her student: "I met him only the one time when he bought my painting—until last Wednesday when he showed up in one of my classes," she writes.

In the Gallagher Collection, Gladys's work is placed directly in context with the canonized and soon-to-be canonized artists of her generation, and the generations that preceded it—Jackson Pollock, Willem de Kooning, and Mark Rothko are all there, as are Mark Tobey, Theodoros Stamos, and Larry Rivers. And even many of the Europeans who inspired them—Picasso, Chagall, Miró, Matisse, Klee, Fernand Léger, Ernst Kirchner.

Gladys's painting, *Big City*, which is one of the largest in the collection, is located in the catalog above Arshile Gorky, since the images are arranged alphabetically. I see the Gorky painting in dialogue with a Jean Arp at the beginning of the catalog, as well as a William Baziotes painting with similar movement. And I like thinking about Gladys's painting in conversation with Joseph Falzone's *Twin Cities*, which is pictured on the previous page. You could look at her painting and already know it showed a city, the buildings blending into abstraction, whereas with his you need the title for this interpretation.

And also Gerhardt Wind's *Composition*, the way the geometry rises through. Or Anna Bonetti's paintings that contain geometry within Impressionist landscapes. Or Jun Dobashi's *Late Afternoon*, with the white lines coming through. Or I. Rice Pereira's paintings that take the geometry forward, into another dimension. I can see all of these together, as a tour of modernist cityscapes into landscapes into abstraction.

The white lines in each, and what they allow to come through. The gradients. The shading. I can't see the colors, because all the reproductions are black-and-white. But this allows me to see the structure more clearly. To foreground or surround, to open and close. What I mean is that I'm sensing a dialogue here. And Gladys must have loved being part of this conversation through her work, that's what I imagine.

Except somehow this collection is not mentioned in Gladys's bios. It is not even mentioned in the University of Maryland catalog, even though they mention *White Church*, her painting purchased by Pennsylvania State around the same time. But *Big City*, painted just slightly later, is a more developed work, and one that shows her moving toward full abstraction in a more direct way. Was there a reason Gladys didn't want it on her record? It's hard for me to imagine why. I know she always wanted her newest work to stand out, but then why mention *White Church*?

Back in 1957, though, clearly Gladys wanted Gallagher to purchase her work for the Metropolitan Museum of Art. As a Baltimore artist, Gladys was several steps removed from the center of the art world in New York. But she also had influential allies. Betty Parsons, who chose *January* for the award at the Maryland Regional show, was the gallerist, after all, who was famous for representing Jackson Pollock. And Dore Ashton, who reviewed her show in *The New York Times*, was one of the most powerful art critics. And there was Parker Tyler, who reviewed her show in *ARTnews*.

And then there was the Baltimore Museum of Art—her solo show was in 1956, and a year later the museum opened a new wing housing the Cone Collection, with its extensive collection of Matisses. Most major museums were vying for this collection, so it must have raised Baltimore's profile, at least temporarily.

But it's Keith Martin who might be the most influential person in Gladys's art career. When Gladys first meets him in the 1950s, he has been exhibiting his work for two decades—in the 1930s, his work has already appeared in several New York shows and he has designed costumes for the American Ballet. In the 1940s, he had solo shows at galleries in London, Paris, and New York, as well as solo museum shows in the US. His show at the Baltimore Museum of Art took place three years before Gladys's, and he started showing at the Duveen-Graham Gallery in 1955, just before her. In fact, in September of 1955, he writes to Albert Duveen, "I am very pleased you decided in favor of Gladys Goldstein. I feel the work is outstanding in these parts. She, too, is very happy with the arrangement."

I don't have a record of Gladys's exhibitions before the mid-1950s because she didn't save any information in her scrapbook. To Albert Duveen, she writes, "Unfortunately, it wasn't until my friends got after me that I even saved press notices and catalogs. I always fret that yesterday's news was not news at all."

When she did start saving press clippings, many of the most glowing reviews were from Kenneth Sawyer, the *Baltimore Sun* art critic, who was receiving awards for his criticism. Gladys writes to Albert Duveen that Sawyer "is a very perceptive critic, unfortunately we shall not be able to keep him in Baltimore—he is getting many wonderful offers."

Sawyer was also a champion of Keith Martin's work, and it's possible that he found out about Gladys through Keith. In a 1956 *Baltimore Sun* article with the headline "Keith Martin—An Artist Of Stature." Sawyer opens, "Any exhibition of paintings by Keith Martin would be a welcome one," and goes on to write, "It would be both inaccurate and unjust to describe Mr. Martin as a Baltimore artist; rather, he is a painter of international reputation who, by chance, happens to live in Maryland. His work belongs to no region or movement—it is the personal expression of a man whose vision is at once vast and particular."

Sawyer praises Martin's collages in particular, writing, "Like all master collagists, he invests his materials with an additional force—with a life beyond their ordinary uses." And, since Martin has already been exhibiting his collages in the 1950s, he must have also influenced Gladys in that direction.

Kenneth Sawyer describes Martin as "a Baroque painter (if, indeed, the word has any meaning outside its historical context)," which might indicate that he likes to make improbable categorizations, such as when he describes Gladys as an Impressionist. And, if Gladys loves this comparison, she's not as happy with Dore Ashton's highly positive write-up of her Duveen-Graham show in *The New York Times*.

Within a few sentences, Ashton goes from describing some of Gladys's paintings as using a "modified cubist scheme, with an angular division of form" to her storm pictures "flecked with swirling movements more expressionist in temper" and saying her "most promising work is in a lyrical vein" with "softly rendered drifts of color, freely moving over a luminous base."

It's an evocative assessment, but Gladys is unimpressed. She responds only that "I do wish that critics would not try to put one in a category—someday they'll invent a new one for me."

It's the anniversary of Frank O'Hara's death, and his *New York Times* obituary from 1966 is circulating. But wait—Frank O'Hara was born in Baltimore? How did I not realize this before?

His parents fled Massachusetts for Baltimore because they didn't want their conservative Irish Catholic families to realize that Frank's mother was already three months pregnant when they married. They were in Baltimore for eighteen months before the family came down to convince Frank's father to move back. Frank's mother didn't want to return, she even fantasized about moving to Florida, where cheap land in the 1920s was inspiring a mass migration.

Because of this family history, would Frank have seen added symbolism in Grace Hartigan moving to Baltimore—not to escape tradition, but in search of it?

"I don't give a fuck for families," O'Hara once wrote to his brother. "I think that people should treat each other as they feel."

In 1953, seven years before Grace Hartigan moved to Baltimore, artist Amalie Rothschild created the Outdoor Art Festival in Druid Hill Park. She was frustrated that there weren't enough opportunities for artists to exhibit their work in Baltimore, and so she established this annual fair where artists could display and sell their work along the fence surrounding the reservoir. These artists included Keith Martin, Betty Cooke, Rothschild herself, Gladys, and many others. Gladys and Amalie also exhibited together in a number of gallery shows, at least as early as 1960.

The Outdoor Art Festival attracted more artists and attendees each year, until it ended in 1968. Druid Hill Park was close to the neighborhood where Gladys grew up, and as a child she would go there regularly. Baltimore parks were desegregated in 1953—was this why Rothschild began the festival in that year? And it ended in 1968, presumably after the assassination of Martin Luther King and the resulting uprisings.

Rothschild was born in Baltimore one year before Gladys. Both studied art at the Maryland Institute as children, and both enrolled there after graduating from high school. Both Gladys and Amalie were Jewish women and mothers with long art careers who chose to remain in Baltimore for almost their whole lives.

After Rothschild died, her namesake daughter preserved her entire body of unsold work, fourteen hundred pieces left in the house and studio. She documented and contextualized everything meticulously, piece by piece. And this allowed her to map her mother's trajectory from fashion illustration to portraits and landscapes, to her discovery of abstraction and sculpture. With Gladys I don't know exactly when she started painting abstractly, or whether any of her early experiments survive.

Gladys did not acknowledge a tension between her role as artist and mother, but Amalie described a sense of fragmentation that led to panic attacks. In her daughter's 1974 film, *Nana, Mom and Me*, she asks Amalie where she got the idea for a painting called *Cyclops*, which consists of four panels, each six feet high by three feet wide—stripes of reds and oranges turning to purples and blues, brighter and then darker, swirling up to cross around a red circle until the circle is black inside the swirl, which forms another circle. "From the open form till it closes up," Amalie says, although she also says someone else saw it as fulfillment of life.

"We don't know where ideas come from," she says. "We certainly know that they're related to personal experience, and I know exactly what was behind this, it's quite personal and it has to do with an eye problem, and we'll leave it at that."

When her daughter asks why it's shameful to reveal something that's bothering her and that expresses itself through her work, she ends up asking herself, "And why am I making a film, and why are we here together in the first place, why am I trying to get something out of you, when I'm not even sure what it is?"

And Amalie tries to answer her daughter's rhetorical question.

This conversation between mother and daughter, both artists, a conversation oriented around the content of the work and its motivation, but also the experience of living and making art. The process. A philosophical conversation that becomes the movie itself. And the joy in this conversation, how Amalie comes alive when she says to her daughter behind the camera, "Why are you asking me these questions, I should be asking you."

When I return to the beginning of this scene, I see how Amalie's studies for *Cyclops* are on the wall behind her as she pulls out each of the four parts of the painting to arrange them.

The more you watch something, the more you can see. This film was made between 1972 and 1974, so this scene was shot either right before I was born, or right after. If I watch Amalie moving her art, and listen to her talking about her art, can I see Gladys in the frame too?

"But how did you resolve the conflict between your work and the family?" her daughter asks. And Amalie says, "I have not fully resolved it, other than a compromise, and I know that you're probably questioning it because you're going to be confronted with the same problems."

When I was a child, Gladys wanted to give me freedom. Once I became an adult, she tried to take that back. Returning to the photos she took of me when I was twenty, I realize I'm standing in front of one of Gladys's paintings that's in the same color palette as Amalie Rothschild's *Cyclops*.

In Gladys's painting, the circles are muted within the red that dominates, but in another photo, when the camera moves up close, it's squares I see, not circles.

No, this must be a different painting, suffused in a wash of purple, a watery glow. Yes, here it is in another photo, it's a much smaller work. So these two must be part of a series. I kind of want to place them with Amalie's work to create a whole room of red and purple—how geometry can delineate and how it can blend. Amalie's pieces with sharper lines so precise they could be mistaken for graphic design from afar, and Gladys's layering of color where the form pushes through. A conversation between paintings, these purples and reds, an opening and a closing off.

I'm sitting in front of Gladys's painting, the squares softening around me and becoming Amalie's rounded pathways up and around. If *Cyclops* is now part of the collection of the ophthalmology department at Sinai Hospital, does this mean that Amalie's conversation with her daughter for this film allowed her to make the inspiration for the painting more public?

How does it change with pupils dilated, the opening and the closing. I wonder how often it can be both.

When I mention the book about Amalie Rothschild to my mother, how she asked her daughter to ensure her legacy and the intense dedication with which her daughter pursued every element of this task, when I mention this to my mother, she says: That's what I was supposed to do for Gladys.

But that wasn't fair of her to ask of you, I say. You were not an artist. You did not know about the art world. This was a game. It was a test. She knew you would fail.

Or was Gladys just desperate, and grasping for anyone she could reach? She had alienated so many of the people who could help her with this task, over the years when she was busy removing herself from the art world.

And yet still there were others, like Marilyn Maupin Hart, who invited her to establish the permanent collection of her work at the University of Maryland. Or Joel, her next-door neighbor, who helped her to catalog her work. Gladys didn't need to involve my mother.

Or did my mother involve herself? Whatever it was that emerged between them after my father's death, it was a struggle for control.

Control was my father's game, and did he learn this from Gladys?

Certainly my mother learned the game from him. A circle of control—a cycle of anger repressed and expressed.

Gladys divorced her first husband at age twenty, in 1937, in the midst of the Depression, leaving a life of guaranteed wealth for something precarious.

She knew she had to save herself.

To become herself.

When I was nineteen, I dropped out of college and moved to San Francisco.

To save myself.

To become myself.

Did this threaten Gladys so much because it reminded her of her own choices?

Sometimes the best writing is the writing about not writing. How telling the definitive story reveals that the story can never quite be definitive.

Inside the exhaustion there are words, and on the other side there is language. Sometimes all it takes is a few sentences, and then I feel like another person. Expansive and awake, alert to the possibility of language activating the body. Please let it stay this way.

"The painting has to work, but it has to say something more than that the painting works," Joan Mitchell says, in a profile in the same issue of *ARTnews* where Parker Tyler reviews Gladys's 1957 Duveen-Graham show.

Mitchell rejects the categorization of art into "good" and "bad," hates the word "nature" and yet paints from it, the nature that's in her mind while facing a wall.

"I carry my landscapes around with me," she says. "Other people don't have to see what I do in my work.'"

Grace Hartigan: "You are inside yourself, looking at this damned piece of rag on the wall that you're supposed to make a world out of. That is all you are conscious of ... Inside yourself, you're looking at this terrifying unknown and trying to feel, to pull everything you can out of all your experience, to make something."

I keep thinking about the Amalie Rothschild sculpture *For Jeff*, which she made in 1994 for her friend Jeff Duncan, founder of Dance Theater Workshop, who died of AIDS in 1989. It's a fifty-four-inch-tall pink triangle that operates a full musical scale that can be played on the eight metal rods that hang from an orange circle that forms a structure inside the pink triangle.

I wonder what this sounds like.

And then there's the shadow the sculpture makes on the wall behind it, another instrument. The way that as soon as you play the scale, the past comes into presence. And then it's gone again. Another kind of history.

Grace Hartigan: "It doesn't interest me to think of myself in a retrospective way. One doesn't want to be one's own history."

To stay in the present moment offers its own legacy. How do we tell history in this way, each individual gesture building into something it did not anticipate?

What if a collective is not the sum of its parts. What if a collective experience is barely an experience.

If one doesn't want to be one's own history, does it become someone else's?

In high school, my favorite movie was *The Unbelievable Truth*. The scene I remember the most is when two young women are lying in the grass, talking to one another while looking up at the sky.

That's the only scene I remembered until an hour ago, when I started to watch the movie again. I was relieved to find that I might still love it.

And now I know that when they lie in the grass and look up at the sky, we never see the sky.

First they ride together on a bike, sharing the seat and talking excitedly while leaning into one another. They are not lovers, but they are in love at this moment. How could they not be, with the way the light shines onto their faces?

A romance that isn't a romance, which is always the kind of romance I've believed in.

When someone says history repeats itself, this phrase has already been repeated so many times that it's hard not to nod your head in agreement. But does the repetition of this phrase make the persistence of structural injustice sound inevitable, neutral, or coincidental? Does this conceal the bias of the discipline of history, everything left out that continues to remain invisible?

I'm sitting here looking at the map of Baltimore. I'm trying to find the intersection where Freddie Gray was arrested on April 12, 2015, leading to his death in police custody. How do I describe the feeling when I realize that Mount Street, where he was apprehended, is just two blocks east of McKean Avenue, where Gladys grew up? How do I describe the feeling when I realize that Freddie Gray was arrested just five blocks from the house where Gladys grew up?

History is everything we remember, and everything we forget.

When I asked Gladys if she ever went back to the neighborhood where she grew up, she said: You can't.

The path of white flight is the path of complicity.

I know very little about what this neighborhood was like when Gladys moved there with her family when she was two years old, in 1919, almost a century before Freddie Gray was murdered. I know very little about this neighborhood, because Gladys told me nothing. It was somewhere you couldn't go, and somewhere you couldn't imagine. Maybe because to imagine would mean you could go.

This neighborhood was only about a fifteen-minute drive from the house in Mount Washington where Gladys lived for the last forty years of her life, six and a half miles away, in the same city, and yet she never went back. Because the people who were living there were like Freddie Gray.

But Freddie Gray was the one who was murdered.

How white fear informs policy.

Abandonment. Flight. Disengagement. Blight.

Helen said it was a nice neighborhood, just twelve blocks away from where she lived. She and Gladys would walk to each other's houses, they would play in the woods. Children on their own, from an early age. In

Gladys's sketchbook autobiography, she writes about walking all the way downtown with her brother when they were little kids, going to travel agencies to ask for brochures.

When I go to an independent bookstore, often the first thing I do is to search the front tables for independent press titles. Sometimes I can't find any, or only a few, and this was the case when I went to the Ivy Bookshop in Baltimore, not far from the house where Gladys lived in Mount Washington. But then I noticed *The 2015 Baltimore Uprising: A Teen Epistolary*, a thick four-by-six-inch book of tweets about the uprising after Freddie Gray's murder, and I rushed to the counter to get a copy.

The book is professionally produced and designed, but no author or publisher is credited. There is an ISBN and barcode for scanning the price at stores, but no title page or publishing information. All Twitter handles are blacked out, as are any facial features for protesters, so the publishers were thinking about the safety of the authors of these tweets.

"RIP Freddie Gray . . . Cops killed him during an arrest by breaking his spine while he was in cuffs on April 19th" is how the book opens, and it ends with "The riots aren't over." In between there's an outpouring of unfiltered emotion. Someone tags the Baltimore Police Department to say "@BaltimorePolice murderers rapist racist thugs gang members."

The first photo of the mass protests accompanies a tweet that says "This ain't the television stuff no more it's right here in Baltimore City." On the next page, a child sitting on someone's shoulders holds a sign that says "JUSTICE Black Lives Matter Fuck the Police."

"Let ppl protest how they please, fuck being embarrassing, it's about getting a point across #NoJusticeNoPeace," says one person. Another: "Y'all worried about how we 'look' We are laid out in the street dead, then handcuffed in cold blood. That's how we look." "Shit Real Dwntwn" accompanies a photo of someone running from a phalanx of cops. "For 2 weeks we have held peaceful protest still no answ ers ! remember that."

Most of the posts appear to be by, for, and addressed to Black youth. There is one series of posts that celebrates a white teacher who "was helping destroy one of the cars," "was the one who had me attend my first protest in the tenth grade to fight for education funding," and has "been protesting for Black people before we were even born," according to three posts. Later, a news story accompanying the tweet, "Yo Mr Bleich is the realest nigga !!" shows this teacher holding up a piece of the Confederate flag that he ripped off the antenna of a car when the driver tried to run protesters over. Then the protesters lit the flag on fire.

All of this takes place during high school prom, and one tweet says, "This riot doesn't excuse these ugly ass prom dresses on my TL." In a photo, someone stands on top of a cop car with smashed windows while someone else tries to kick in the windshield. "Burn down the JAIL," someone says. "So if the police get arrested what gets changed?" asks someone else. "Niggas want change, locking up a few officers ain't change," says another. "Police been doing fucked up shit to us for centuries!" says another.

On April 27, the day of Freddie Gray's funeral, the police presence makes "Mondawmin look like a Call of Duty mission." And, as a result "they throwing bricks at the police," "niggas goin dislocate them shoulder throwing all them rocks," and "Niggas on the police cars bringing the A Town stomp back."

"They canceled people proms," someone says, and someone else tweets a screen capture that says "Baltimore police say gangs 'teaming up' to take out officers," with the heading "we're trending."

"Everybody keep saying violence is not the answer but CAN'T TELL ME WHAT THE FUCK THE REAL ANSWER IS!" And: "Baltimore protested peacefully for a week before they started this , but I bet the news won't show that." And, someone else: "all CNN keeps saying is gang, gang, gangs, gangs, gang." And: "they keep hollerin bout gangs, WE DON'T EVEN HAVE GANGS LIKE THAT NOMORE."

On the destruction of a CVS by protesters, someone says: "I feel bad for the ppl who lost their jobs bc of the CVS but I feel worse for ppl who lost their family bc of police brutality." Photos of people carrying stolen goods. Commentary on mayor Stephanie Rawlings-Blake, "Stephanie keep calling yall thugs she wanna be white so bad." And: "Someone take away her Black card." And: "Stephanie Rawlings Blake needs to be impeached ! I can't deal with this dumb ass curfew shit." And: "dear stephanie Rawlings Blake if we get all our chores done early this week can we stay out a little later Saturday to watch the fight."

And back to a post about the white teacher from Polytechnic High School, protesting with his Black students, "YASSSS MR.BLEICH FUCK IT UP #POLYPRIDE." "Meanwhile over east . . ." is a caption for a huge fire in the distance, and "keep that fire shit over west," and, "Yooo that fire BIG AS SHIT."

"Everything they destroying can be replaced Stores, houses, cars, etc but once you take someone's Life they gone forever." And: "you niggas is dumb !! !! go burn down a fucking courthouse or a fucking jail not no CVS." And: "40 years of peaceful protesting got us absolutely nothing, no recognition. As soon as we riot, every news channel and celebrity got opinions."

And: "Believe it or not the riot bringing Baltimore together, that's a fact." And: "Riding through my city, I'm confused like do we live in Baltimore or Iraq." And: "only people upset about the looting is the privilege ones, people struggling don't really care what y'all say."

Two days after Freddie Gray's funeral, when the media reports that his death was accidental: "HOW THE FUCK CAN YOU BREAK YOUR OWN SPINE." And: "Please don't do this to that man family." And: "if the police don't admit the truth Baltimore going be a war zone."

Celebrations when the officers are charged, but also, "CHARGES DOESN'T MEAN CONVICTED." And: "How do you feel about the charges? 'I just feel like fuck the police,' teenager says. His mom laughs and shoos him away."

And then the book ends with a post from April 30, with a picture of Freddie Gray and his coffin, "R.I.P. Freddie Gray 4/19/2015 Don't scroll down without typing 'R.I.P.'"

And then eight pages of R.I.P.

There's something about reading this history formed by tweets that feels so visceral and personal and intimate that I wake up and I'm still thinking about those two weeks. I can picture the houses on those blocks, the fires in the distance, the sound of the police sirens, the running to and running from, the smashing of windows, the jumping on top of cop cars, the celebration and desperation, the rage and fear and the sense that something is happening, something big. All these gestures of anger and humor and hopelessness and empowerment, collective and individual, spontaneous and imaginative and silly, practical and creative.

And, I wake up thinking about how white flight becomes urban blight—none of this is inevitable. None of this is accidental. The subway station and transit hub where the protests erupted was on the exact spot as the grand movie theater Gladys went to as a kid. The high school where the protesters came from is located in the same building where Gladys went to high school. Then it was a legally segregated public high school for girls. Now it is a coed public high school that is almost entirely Black, segregated by disinvestment.

Gladys loved kids, she believed they were great artists. What if she had visited that high school, or the neighboring elementary school— what kind of art would she have found there, what creative magnificence?

Maybe a different way to say history repeats itself would be to say history never resolves itself. History is a lesson, this may be true, but, as with any other lesson, the people who need it the most rarely listen.

To Gladys, this was a neighborhood where you could no longer go. But what was it like for her growing up? I go back to that sketchbook where she starts her autobiography. Her earliest memory is of the death of her aunt Rose in 1920—she died in her pink nightgown on the brown leather sofa. "And I knew that I was no longer a child," Gladys thinks. At age three.

And I'm reading again about this walk with her brother for miles, going downtown to get travel brochures, a three-year-old and a five-year-old on their own, "I never felt lost or frightened because Lon was there to protect me." And then, when he started school, and the neighborhood kids would start to bully him, "Now it was my turn to protect him."

She would go on adventures with Roland, her first love, whose father died of the flu when he was a child, and whose mother died when Gladys was thirteen—they would ride bikes and shower under the sprinklers and go to movies at the Met.

The Metropolitan Theatre was a movie palace with seating for 1,450 people, as well as a bowling alley and a billiards hall. It stayed in business until 1977, and was demolished in 1978 to build the Penn-North subway station. That the city would demolish such a grand theater to build a subway station says something about how they saw the neighborhood.

Like the corner where Freddie Gray was arrested, this subway station was exactly five blocks from the house where Gladys grew up. It was also the fourth stop for the police vehicle that drove in a circle with Freddie Gray inside before bringing him to the station, where he was treated by paramedics before he was taken to the hospital in a coma.

Gladys's bedroom was in the back of the house, facing her friend Doris's house. Doris died when she was ten or eleven. Then there was another Doris, who was hit by a car on the corner, and Donald, whose twin brother was hit by a car...

I only have thirty pages of this handwritten autobiography, but I'm thinking again about all these deaths, and the others Gladys describes—in World War II, or of multiple sclerosis, or of unnamed illnesses. Gladys grew up during the Depression, she was familiar with sudden death from an early age, she grew up between the two world wars, she came of age as the Nazis gained power. She was familiar with trauma.

And the people who grew up in her neighborhood—her family, and the families like hers, fled as Black people moved closer. They saw this as a threat. But their lives were not that different—or they didn't have to be different. These white homeowners and renters could have reached out to their new neighbors, they could have shared stories of resilience and strategies for survival or connected through shared trauma, but instead they fled.

Gladys left in 1941 after she married Ed, about three years before Black people started to move into houses across the Fulton Avenue line that had divided Black and white in a rigidly segregated city.

Once white people fled, city services went with them. Discriminatory housing policies, from racist federal government redlining to predatory lending and exploitative leases, doomed the possibilities for sustainable neighborhoods. Urban removal and forced neighborhood demolition furthered displacement. After Martin Luther King was assassinated in 1968, the resulting uprisings left charred buildings that were never rebuilt. The Fair Housing Act, passed shortly after King's assassination, may have technically outlawed housing discrimination, but this had little effect in areas already targeted by decades of racist exclusion. Here escalating police repression led to mass incarceration and dispossession in traumatized neighborhoods undermined by structural violence and calculated abandonment.

Decades of disinvestment later, Freddie Gray would play basketball with his friends on Fulton Avenue in the summer—they would make a milk crate into a basketball hoop, and practice their alley-oops, even if these got a little painful. When the sun went down, he would race his friends to get to the corner store to buy ice cream. He would sit on his aunt's steps and watch dirt bike races. He sang along to music videos, and sang in the children's choir at church. He ran track, and liked to chat with his friends on the phone.

What if Gladys had returned to her old neighborhood to teach art? What would she have learned from these kids?

Tomorrow Is Another Day, the Mark Bradford show I saw in Baltimore, was originally created for the 2017 Venice Biennale. The US pavilion there, built in 1930, was modeled after Monticello, Thomas Jefferson's grandiose home and plantation, built with enslaved labor and maintained by two hundred enslaved people. "After all, tomorrow is another day" is the last sentence in *Gone with the Wind*, the bestselling 1936 novel that romanticized the last days of the Confederacy, which was adapted into the highest grossing movie in US history three years later.

The US pavilion in Venice, built during the Great Depression, invokes Jefferson's storied role as a founding father of the United States without indicting his active participation in slavery. Bradford planned to obliterate the courtyard imitating the manicured lawn for white visitors to Monticello and gut the interior of the grand portico—in the life-size model of the pavilion he constructed in LA, the sundial floor appears to be chipped apart, the walls and ceiling covered in paper as if crumbling from neglect.

In the final work, the walls and floor appear mostly intact, so it's the ceiling that stands out, wrapped in layers of oxidized paper that snake around the perimeter like the black and gold coils that form the *Medusa* sculpture in the show.

In the catalog, though, created before the Biennale, it's Bradford's model of the pavilion that's pictured, where on the walls you can read "Save Up to 70%," "Receive Calls On Your CELL PHONE," "From JAIL From JAIL From JAIL," over and over again, in what would generally be an elegant entryway to slavery's vision of democracy or art or American prosperity.

In *Black Reconstruction in America*, published in 1935, W. E. B. Du Bois points to the ways that workers around the world are "paid a wage below the level of decent living; driven, beaten, prisoned and enslaved in all but name." Du Bois was one of the founders of the Niagara Movement, a Black civil rights organization that first met in 1905 near Niagara Falls. They took the name Niagara to invoke the famous waterfall as the fight for racial justice pouring over the nation. The 1953 film *Niagara* stars Marilyn Monroe, and features what has been described as the longest walk in the history of cinema. When Mark Bradford recreates this walk in his video installation for the Venice Biennale, instead of Marilyn in her familiar glamour it's a Black queen walking the everyday runway of survival in a basic men's tank top and exercise shorts, seen only from the back.

As a child, Mark Bradford was beaten up daily for being a sissy—he learned to run all the way home from school or take the alleys to avoid the neighborhood boys. His mother, a hairdresser, had many queer friends, and once she realized why he was running they moved from a middle-class Black neighborhood in South Los Angeles to mostly white Santa Monica. Going to a predominantly white public high school in an affluent liberal neighborhood gave him a place to create art, but still he found himself abandoned by his friends as a teenager for being queer. At age fifteen he found a new world of pageantry in dressing up and going out to the gay clubs of LA in the 1970s.

Bradford came of age in that nightlife world, but as the devastation of the AIDS crisis emerged he sold his car to buy a plane ticket and then he wandered across Europe off and on for six years—there, racism did not call him out, no one commented on his sexuality, and AIDS had not yet taken such a toll. Eventually he returned to Los Angeles, enrolled in art schools, still roaming the streets for solace and inspiration. When Bradford says "the grid saved my life," he means the organization of squares on the canvas that became a home for the brain to rest.

The Sirens, Bradford's giant trio of works created by the layering of translucent black rectangles on the canvas, this is the grid. Bradford used end papers for the hair salon to generate this shimmering effect—in the salon, they protect the hair during a chemical treatment. On the canvas, they allow the light to come through.

I'm thinking again of Gladys's Emotional Squares. How much emotion can be allowed in, and how much can be allowed out?

In Bradford's show at the Baltimore Museum of Art, you go from the Sirens to another trio of huge works that look like paintings, but all the colors and textures come from industrial paper layered onto the canvas—in these works the grid explodes, implodes, melts. They are cut up and sprawling, cracking open. *Tomorrow Is Another Day* is in the middle. This was the one that first captivated me—an expansion in the chest, an opening of the arms, is this breath or is it a scream. To want both. To need both. How to make tomorrow today.

My grandfather Ed worked for Baltimore City Public Schools for most of his adult life. He started as a schoolteacher, and worked his way up to become the director of finance. But I only know this from listening to an oral history interview with Gladys at the Jewish Museum of Maryland, which she starts by asking: "Do I have to tell the truth?"

As a child I was never quite sure what my grandfather did for the public school system. Gladys described Ed as assistant to the superintendent, and my father said he was a phys ed teacher. He worked for the school system when it was officially segregated, perhaps for as long as two decades, and he worked there for more than three decades after the school system was legally desegregated in 1954 in response to the Supreme Court decision in *Brown v. Board of Education.* The resulting policy of "free choice" adopted in Baltimore immediately after the Supreme Court ruling led to white flight that gutted the school system, which crumbled under decades of racist disinvestment.

Now the Black middle class has also fled the neighborhoods left in ruin by white flight. "Value is determined by perception," lawyer Dominique Moore says. Her great-uncle Isaac Joseph Bacon, a Black World War II veteran, bought a comfortable rowhouse near Druid Hill Park in 1950 with help from the GI Bill. His new neighborhood was just a few blocks from where Gladys grew up, and was still almost entirely white when he moved in. Four years of white flight later, when he married, the neighborhood was almost entirely Black.

Bacon lived in that house for over sixty years, until he and his wife were forced to move into assisted living in 2011 after he got sick and needed more support. Even though their three-bedroom home was well-kept and included elegant architectural detail, they couldn't even convince a relative to live there for free because the area was now known for poverty and crime, with blue-light police cameras surveilling everyone outside. When the Bacons' house went into foreclosure, the only potential buyers were predatory investors with offers which, when adjusted for inflation, were far less than the $6,300 Bacon originally paid in 1950.

Gladys left the neighborhood in 1941 when she married Ed, a decade before she went to Penn State to study with Hobson Pittman. While she was studying with Pittman, Ed was finishing his doctorate in education at Columbia, which he received in 1952.

Ed would not yet have known that in two years *Brown v. Board of Education* would lead to the legal desegregation of schools, or that this would accelerate white flight, but once he became director of finance at Baltimore City Public Schools, what was his relationship to policy? The school system is only required to keep records for seven years after an employee's departure, and so they offer no information on his tenure. Who does this serve?

When the schools desegregated in 1954, my father was eleven. He remained in public school until he graduated from high school in 1960. I know Gladys and Ed believed that education was the most important thing for any child, so they must have kept their faith in the public school system. And they remained in Baltimore when they bought their new house in 1964, although in a mostly white enclave not far from the county line.

In a 1965 *Baltimore Sun* article about their house that features Gladys's studio, it says that Ed was the administrative assistant to the superintendent of schools, which doesn't sound like a job where he would have influence over policy. Since that's also what I remember from my childhood in the '80s, I'm still not sure when he was director of finance.

Mark Bradford says, "I'm interested in the history of abstraction, of unpacking the '50s. What does it mean to unpack that moment, when both Emmett Till and Jackson Pollock were on magazine covers? Abstraction was becoming this huge thing at the time of civil rights. It's fascinating. I don't know what I really feel about it."

Emmett Till was a Black fourteen-year-old who was lynched in Mississippi in 1955 after he was accused of flirting with a white woman. His mother, Mamie Till, insisted on an open-casket funeral after her son's body was discovered floating in the river. By showing the results of the murder in all its brutality, this funeral helped to launch a new wave of the civil rights movement.

Billie Holiday died four years later, in 1959, at age forty-four, after twenty years of persecution by federal authorities. She became a target of the drug war before it was called the drug war, starting right after she began performing "Strange Fruit" in 1939. *Gone with the Wind* was released at the end of that year, and so Holiday must have performed

"Strange Fruit" while people were flocking to theaters across the country in droves to see a nearly four-hour epic that not only did not hide its racism but spelled it out in giant white letters across the screen at the beginning: "There was a land of Cavaliers and Cotton Fields called the Old South ... Here in this pretty world Gallantry took its last bow ..."

Gone with the Wind was a lavish production with elaborate costumes and sets that left nothing unadorned in its quest to make enslavers into heroes. Billie Holiday's performance of "Strange Fruit" took the opposite aesthetic strategy—just before she sang her "pastoral scene of the gallant South" at Café Society, all the lights would go off and the house would go completely silent before a spotlight shone just on Holiday's face. When she finished the song the room would go pitch dark again, and she would walk offstage without saying a word, no matter how much applause filled the room.

These were Barney Josephson's stage directions—he wanted to heighten the political and emotional impact of the song. Later, though, he claimed that Billie Holiday didn't understand the song when she first started singing it, but this kind of racist arrogance only casts doubt on his vision of integration.

Holiday continued to make "Strange Fruit" her finale after Café Society, and it became a political touchstone for both white antiracists and the Black political class—it was even sent to every member of the US Senate in 1939 as part of a campaign for federal anti-lynching legislation. Holiday said that she always considered herself a race woman, and with this song her allegiance was recognized. Unfortunately it wasn't just those against lynching who paid attention.

Much has been made of Billie Holiday's addictions, and not enough about the conditions that fostered these addictions. She refused the confines of a racist world, and was punished for this. She struggled to survive a series of relationships with extremely abusive men. She led a life of gender, sexual, and social fluidity at a time when nuclear war gave birth to the nuclear family. For two decades she was harassed by police and federal officials who imprisoned her, took away her primary means of making a living, and then continued to target her in New York and across the country. Given these conditions, how could her addictions not escalate?

In 1959, at age forty-four, she collapsed in her apartment due to malnourishment, and was hospitalized for cirrhosis of the liver, which had affected all her vital organs. In the hospital she began to recover, and there was a festive atmosphere in her room among friends who were visiting, and even a movie deal. But then she was arrested for drug possession while in her hospital bed—she was interrogated in the hospital, and then her door was guarded twenty-four hours a day by the police. Only her abusive husband was allowed to visit. The hospital confiscated her record player, radio, flowers, and telephone. She died in that hospital bed.

When Mark Bradford says he wants to unpack the '50s, I think about Billie Holiday rising out of that bed. I think about Emmett Till, alive today, celebrating his eightieth birthday. As an abstract artist, Mark Bradford's primary aim is not political intervention, but whenever he has a show he partners with a local arts organization. In Venice for the 2017 Biennale, it was a social collective to train women prisoners to make bags using recycled PVC from advertising billboards. I bought a few of these at the Baltimore Museum of Art gift shop—the repurposed ads now form abstract patterns on practical waterproof carrying cases.

For Bradford, working with the prisoners in Venice was not just a one-time act of charity, it was part of a larger project to create a sustainable support system for these women once they get out of prison. He is now a hugely successful artist of international renown, but he rejects the market-based notion of the artist as a lone figure without ties to the world that created him. He wants to provide the skills, training, and camaraderie for people without traditional access to create their own art. While this may not be possible in prison, a support system can create access, and access can create a support system.

In Baltimore, the Maryland State Arts Council recently designated a Black Arts and Entertainment District along Pennsylvania Avenue. On the website for this Black Arts District, it says, "Start Your Journey at Pennsylvania Avenue and North Avenue," which is the same corner where Gladys went to the movies as a kid. That theater isn't mentioned, but the Black Arts District does dream of rebuilding the Royal Theatre, a 1,200-seat palace on Pennsylvania Avenue where Billie Holiday first performed in 1937. Two blocks away was the 2,000-seat Regent Theatre, which was right next to the Penn Hotel, the first Black-owned hotel in Baltimore, where Black entertainers would stay when they were prevented by segregation from staying elsewhere. There were once dozens of other bars, restaurants, theaters, clothing stores, and shops nearby, but most of these businesses also closed long ago. In 1985 a giant bronze statue of Billie Holiday was erected on Pennsylvania Avenue, but aside from a few murals there is not much evidence now along boarded-up storefronts and vacant lots that this was once the central thoroughfare of Black prosperity.

"We want to make sure we are not gentrifying out the folks who currently live in the community," spoken word artist Lady Brion Gill, the founder of the Black Arts District, says, in an interview in *Baltimore* magazine in July 2019. "We want to protect the area to ensure that the demographics remain as they are now." But has this happened with any of the other Arts and Entertainment Districts in Baltimore?

I'm thinking of Station North, a mile and a half to the east, with the $18.5 million Parkway Theatre, the $19 million renovation of the Centre Theatre for the MICA and Johns Hopkins film programs, and all the other highly funded arts organizations nearby, and yet what about basic services for the people already living in that neighborhood and suffering from decades of neglect? Most of the bars and restaurants that have emerged in Station North since the area was declared an Arts and Entertainment District are primarily venues for white newcomers. As rent and property taxes skyrocket, how many Black people who've lived in the neighborhood for generations have lost their homes, and how many are struggling to maintain?

The new Black Arts District along Pennsylvania Avenue is meant to offer a different model for rebuilding, one where investment in the arts helps Black people already there, instead of serving as cover for real estate exploitation and white consumption. But how much of that neighborhood is already owned by corrupt white landlords who keep their properties in substandard conditions, or banks and other institutions that have facilitated the neighborhood's deterioration by keeping boarded-up buildings vacant and crumbling as they wait for the moment when they might prosper from the neighborhood's rebound? And how much of the deterioration is the responsibility of a city that routinely confiscates houses for a few hundred dollars of unpaid property taxes?

I worry that the goals of the Black Arts District will be co-opted when I watch a news segment saying the new district is "vying for a slice of Baltimore's multibillion-dollar tourism industry." Or when, in this news segment, a white firefighter, seemingly out of nowhere, says this will create two thousand jobs. When Baltimore mayor Jack Young talks about courting businesses from out of town, including an unnamed restaurant in Washington, DC, that he says anyone would recognize, I think about Busboys and Poets, the chain of restaurants anchored by a social justice–oriented bookstore. The original location is on Fourteenth and V Streets, not far from where my mother lives. This was once the heart of Black DC, with theaters and jazz clubs like those that once existed on Pennsylvania Avenue in Baltimore. But the neighborhood is now primarily a place for people like my mother—white, and well-off.

Is Busboys and Poets, with a vibrant multiracial crowd, a counterpoint, or just cover for more displacement? The expansive restaurant is located in a building called the Langston Lofts, continuing the reference to Langston Hughes, the famed poet of the Harlem Renaissance who once worked as a busboy, but the rest of the building consists of posh condos catering to white affluence, and in other locations Busboys and Poets also partners with new developments emblematic of gentrification.

There are now eight branches of Busboys and Poets—I see that they opened one in Baltimore in 2021. It's on a block right near Johns Hopkins where almost everything was torn down to build upscale new apartment buildings and create a buffer zone between the wealthy campus and the rest of the neighborhood. When I found Keith Martin's address in the Baltimore Museum of Art archive, I realized it was right around the corner, which must have been convenient when Dave worked for the Baltimore Museum of Art in the 1960s and 1970s, and they would entertain their friends in the art world. So I walked over to look for their spacious rowhouse with a big front porch, but I couldn't find anything because not even the street address remains.

In 2016, two years before my Baltimore stay, Christopher Bedford became the director of the Baltimore Museum of Art. At the same time he was the commissioner for the Venice Biennale, so this was when he was working with Mark Bradford on *Tomorrow Is Another Day*. In 2018 the Baltimore Museum of Art made headlines by selling seven works of art by famous white male artists in order to purchase twenty-three works by women artists and artists of color. That sale generated $16.2 million, and in 2020 the museum announced an even bigger sale to fund pay equity among staff, and further racial and gender equity in the collection. This sale, expected to generate $70 million, was halted after controversy.

Andy Warhol's *The Last Supper*, which anchors the museum's contemporary wing, was the most well-known of the three works expected to raise $70 million. It consists of two silk-screened images based on Leonardo da Vinci's renowned mural, side-by-side in black ink on a twenty-five-foot-wide canvas painted technicolor yellow. When the museum originally bought the painting at auction for $682,000 in 1989, the most it had ever paid for a work of art, this created a scandal among members of the museum and the larger public who did not consider Warhol's work worthy of space in the museum at all. A few decades later, the museum caused controversy in the art world when it announced the impending sale of what had become a cornerstone of its collection.

Warhol made over one hundred works using multiples of *The Last Supper* in various media, but in spite of this, *The Last Supper* was predicted to sell for $40 million or more in 2020. Arguably the work itself, which he made in 1986 in the midst of a frenzied art market, could be seen as commentary on the value of art, but this possibility was not highlighted in the controversy, which focused on whether it was ethical to raise funds for a museum by selling off major works in the collection.

Christopher Bedford's efforts to bring racial and gender equity to the Baltimore Museum of Art are notable, especially coming from a straight white man who, due to his own privilege, may have more power than others to make this happen. In his pitch he emphasized that the museum was already in a strong financial position, and so it was the spectacle of a museum participating so openly in the crass commercialism of the market that bolstered the opposition to his plans.

Brenda Richardson, the former curator who spearheaded the purchase of *The Last Supper*, said she was "horrified" by the impending sale, but the most dynamic response came from Black queer performance artist Monsieur Zohore, who reenacted the Warhol painting in three dimensions by staging *The Last Supper* across the street from the Baltimore Museum of Art with twelve other artists, many of them also queers of color. Dressed in black choir robes and pale button-down yellow shirts, with bright yellow paint dripping down their faces—noses and mouths covered by black face masks to prevent the spread of COVID-19, they reenacted *The Last Supper* as a satirical pizza party during a pandemic.

Their unsanctioned location across the street from the museum also called attention to the ways in which, even when local artists of color are exhibited at the Baltimore Museum of Art, their work is rarely collected by the museum, which still focuses almost entirely on established artists outside of Baltimore. The table for this last supper may have been across the street from the museum, at the edge of Wyman Park, but in photos it's as if the performance is taking place right in front of the grand 1920s museum designed by Charles Russell Pope with its stately columns reminiscent of the dominant institutions of power in Washington, DC. When Zohore connects Warhol's *The Last Supper*, made by a famous gay artist in 1986, to the AIDS crisis, it's hard not to feel an emotional pull between deadly pandemics furthered by government inaction.

I'm thinking of Mark Bradford, telling Christopher Bedford that he wandered across Europe for six years in the '80s to escape "death, death, death, death, more death."

When Christopher Bedford characterizes Mark Bradford as an artist and a social activist, Bradford replies: "I really actually just think that I'm an artist. I think we have to expand the possibilities of what an artist can do."

When Brenda Richardson moved to Baltimore in 1975 to become a curator at the Baltimore Museum of Art, she says, "I was completely shocked. It was a ghettoized city—Jew-gentile, Black-white, total separation."

This was the Baltimore where Gladys grew up. Where she remained.

Brenda Richardson was hired to bring contemporary art to Baltimore, as if it couldn't have existed there otherwise.

Gladys always saw herself as a contemporary artist, up until her last days. But did she realize she was living in a city of total separation?

I've never written a book that involves so much research. I could just keep going. And going. And going.

I'm not trying to write a history, and yet I'm caught. In the sudden overlap of knowledge. What this might reveal.

So when I learn that some of the first Jews in Maryland were sentenced by the British to seven years of convict labor for committing petty crimes in London, and then sent across the ocean for stealing a wig or a silver tankard or a sword, I want to know more. And when I read that Jews in London in the 1700s exhibited "a precapitalistic, lower-class disdain for both the work ethic and the personal morality of respectable folk," I think oh, these are my people.

Or when Billie Holiday helps me to understand segregation in Baltimore, and then I read seven books about her, each one building on and contradicting the others. I could read seven more.

When to get lost, and when to emerge. How to emerge from loss.

I'm still waiting for the University of Maryland to figure out a way to digitize the Beta tapes that may or may not be the interviews with Gladys for their catalog, but the last time I heard from the librarian there was two years ago. In the catalog, there are quotes from Gladys's notebooks in the Arts Program Archive, but the Arts Program tells me they do not have any papers archived. I could make a list of everyone else I'm waiting to hear from, like Grace Hartigan's executor who probably doesn't want to talk to me, but should I try again?

I listen to a fifty-part public radio series on inequality in Baltimore. In the first episode, Sheldon Caplis talks about his father who worked for the post office—he died in 1964 of a heart attack, when Sheldon was thirteen, and one day when forty or fifty of his Jewish family members and friends were gathered in mourning in the house, the doorbell rang and there were two Black men at the door, which Sheldon says was very unusual in 1964, so when they came inside everyone got quiet.

These two men introduced themselves, and said they'd worked with Joseph at the post office, and one of them said to his wife Jennie, "We want you to know that without your husband we wouldn't own our own homes."

Because Joseph Caplis had cosigned their loans.

And Jennie started crying.

I cry every time I listen to this episode.

Gladys bought her house in 1964. When I went there after she died in 2010, that's when I realized how much it would have meant to me if she'd engaged with my work. I wanted to stay there as long as possible, to feel this loss. To feel everything.

But my mother refused to let me stay in the house alone, so I had to argue with her instead. She finally left when my other grandfather suddenly died, and she had to go to the funeral in DC. I thought of going to the funeral too, but I was never close to him, and what I needed was to feel Gladys's loss. In her house. Alone.

I wanted Gladys's house to become a residency for other artists. Maybe then I would be there now, writing this.

Gladys's diaries must have still been in the house then, all her papers, everything my mother later threw away. There is always more to art than art. But you can't wonder too much about what has been lost, or then there will only be loss.

I found a new place to hang Gladys's art, above my refrigerator. It's a small space right next to a cabinet, and I thought it might look too cramped with art there, but actually the foil in this collage pulls the light up into that corner so it's like the light is shining down.

This is one of Gladys's candy wrappers, but it's the only one I've seen like this—foil shaped almost into pick-up sticks in two uneven overlapping rows on black, and then a few of the pick-up sticks push up and out from the rest, a silver and a pink and a gold and a blue, so there's a three-dimensional effect that's immediate.

I never paid attention to that corner above the refrigerator before, but now I look over at all different times of the day, searching for what the light reveals. That part of a Reese's Peanut Butter Cup label, or when I notice that the whole collage bends forward and back, each flattened tube of crinkled foil collapsing over the other. That shimmering green—oh, that shimmering green.

How art is never just art. How art is never just.

We used to play pick-up sticks—Gladys loved that game. The arrangements that the sticks would make. Look at that, she would say, isn't that something.

And I would look.

ACKNOWLEDGMENTS

As always, I want to thank the brilliant and generous writers, artists, and friends, friends, artists, and writers who gave me crucial feedback on the manuscript—Katia Noyes, Jessica Lawless, Jennifer Natalya Fink, Corinne Manning, Carolyn Case, Miss tree turtle, Cara Hoffman, a million thanks to all of you for such deep engagement!

For helping with research at the Baltimore Museum of Art: Emily Rafferty, Helene Grabow, Morgan Dowty, Mary Alessi, and Sarah Dansberger. And to everyone there, really, since the museum itself became part of the book. And to other archivists and institutions that played a role in my research—Christina Menninger at Loyola Notre Dame, Katherine Cowen at Maryland Institute College of Art, Lorie Rombro at the Jewish Museum of Maryland, and the staff of the Seattle Public Library, Syracuse University Special Collections, and the Archives of American Art. And Oliver Sage helped to track down the Dore Ashton review of Gladys's 1957 New York show.

Thanks to Eric Key for welcoming me to the Gladys Goldstein Gallery at the University of Maryland Global Campus, and John West-Bay for giving me a tour of the collection beyond what's on display. Brian Young offered crucial insights on Baltimore art history, and art in general, and Bobby Donovan shared his experiences with Gladys with welcome candor.

Gladys's friends and former students were an invaluable resource, and this book benefits in particular from conversations with Fran Taylor, Janet Mishner, Pam Berwager, Effie Gereny, and Claudia DeMonte. Her next-door neighbors, Joel and Norma Cohen, welcomed me into their home and hearts—Joel shared so much about his relationship with Gladys, and Norma provided the brief sketchbook autobiography by Gladys that otherwise I never would have found.

Thank you to Janet Mishner for saying, in a social media comment, that if Gladys were alive today, "in these times, not in her time, she would be amazed at you."

I read dozens of books while researching *Touching the Art*, and all contributed to my knowledge, but three I think were especially important. Mary Gabriel's *Ninth Street Women* changed my perspective on Abstract Expressionism, offered intellectual and historical grounding, and led me to many of the other books that became crucial to me. While I read many books about Baltimore, Lawrence T. Brown's *The Black Butterfly* may have impacted me the most with its political, historical, and structural analysis (thanks to Miss tree turtle for recommending this title, and nine other books). And Paige Glotzer's *How the Suburbs Were Segregated* led me to the legacy of Cross Keys.

I found George Ciscle through an interview by Michael Anthony Farley in *BmoreArt*, and am grateful for his depth of knowledge, and in particular his insights into Keith Martin's life and legacy. Raoul Middleman shared his experience of learning about Gladys through reviews in *The Baltimore Sun* and conversations with Jewish collectors in northwest Baltimore when he was a young artist in the 1950s. Amalie R. Rothschild shared details about her mother and her legacy, both in correspondence, and in the stunning book she created about her.

Several relatives shared their memories of Gladys, as well as family histories, including Eileen Abels, Jonas Goldstein, Barbara Goldstein, and Michelle Kaplan, who shared a video she made when visiting Gladys's house as a teenager. Eileen shared an invaluable video of her daughter, Alex Abels, interviewing Gladys for a middle school class in 2004. And, of course, my sister, Lauren Goldstein, was there with me for so much of the time I spent with Gladys as a child.

My mother, Karin Goldstein, was skeptical of this project at first, but became a crucial resource when I was moving to Baltimore to continue working on the book. Spending time with her collection of Gladys's work in her home in DC offered an intimate setting for her candid memories of Gladys, my father, and me, and she surprised me with her enthusiasm when I read all the parts where she plays a role to her on the phone, including the uncomfortable truths. Her only complaint was that she wanted to hear me read the whole book.

And my other grandmother, Fran Saturn, surprised me with her own Baltimore family history as she was spending her last days in assisted living.

In Baltimore, Lynne Price and Karen Shavin helped me to keep my body at least somewhat balanced (thanks to Andrew Sargus Klein and Dav Clark for the referrals), and Karen shared her decades of knowledge about Baltimore in informal conversations after Feldenkrais sessions. Ananda La Vita and Jules Rosskam provided queer camaraderie and drove me on excursions into Gladys's past (and to the health food store). Catherine Mayhew first accompanied me to the neighborhood where Gladys grew up, and made the connection that this was where Freddie Gray was murdered. Jessa Crispin, Rahne Alexander, Mark Gunnery, Kate Drabinski, and Gabriel Hedemann offered wisdom and charm.

For tangibles and intangibles: Kevin Darling, Andy Slaght, Joey Carducci, Tony Radovich, Jed Walsh, Sarah Schulman, Temmy Smith-Stewart, Jesse Mann, Dana Garza, Yasmin Nair, Alyssa Harad, Matthew Schnirmann, Eric Stanley, Kristen Millares Young, Jason Sellards, Karen Maeda Allman, Elissa Washuta, Zee Boudreaux, Steve Zeeland, Keidy Merida, Devyn Mañibo, Madeline ffitch, David Naimon, Maggie Nelson, Jory Mickelson, Michael Silverblatt, Jack Curtis Dubowsky, Jeannie Vanasco, Hedi El Kholti, Brian Lam, Jenna Johnson, Bill Clegg, Betty Cooke, Peter Valente, Benoît Loiseau, Christina Sharpe, Joe Osmundson, Catherine Lacey, Rabih Alameddine, Bruce Nauman, Mark Bradford, the Parkway Theatre, Billie Holiday, Frank O'Hara, Grace Hartigan, Joe LeSueur, and anyone else I may have inadvertently forgotten—in spite of the length of this list, I'm sure there are many.

To Jesse Jimenez, Jason Porter, and Jen Till at the Seattle Art Museum for getting this party started in the ideal space.

To my editor at Soft Skull, Sarah Lyn Rogers, for taking on this manuscript and working so closely and intimately on every aspect—what a dream to work with you, let's do this again, please.

To Mensah Demary, Soft Skull editor in chief, for bringing everything to fruition, and assuring a smooth editorial and production process—I'm honored to be part of your roster. To everyone else at Soft Skull/Catapult—Megan Fishmann, Rachel Fershleiser, Lena Moses-Schmitt, Cecilia Flores, Nicole Caputo, tracy danes, Selihah White, Miriam Vance, Kira Weiner, Wah-Ming Chang, and anyone who I may not have worked with directly but who worked on this book. And thanks to Lexi Earle for the stunning book cover that utilizes Gladys's candy wrapper collages in exactly the way I imagined.

To my agent, Rebecca Friedman, for accompanying me on this journey—to more magic and mayhem, please. And, to my new speaking agent, Leslie Shipman, as we embark on an adventure together.

For publishing excerpts of this book, in earlier forms: *Local Knowledge* and *The BitterSweet Review*.

No writer is a writer without other writers, and so I'm thankful for all of you, really. Let's do this together.

NOTES

11   **"I'm much better than Jackson Pollock"**: Mattilda Bernstein Sycamore, *Pulling Taffy*. San Francisco: Suspect Thoughts Press, 2003, p. 142.

27   **"To get away from being too emotional"**: Laura Nelson, *Capturing the Essence: The Art of Gladys Goldstein*. Adelphi, MD: University of Maryland University College, 2004, p. 38.

27   **"a piece of paper left to the elements will rot"**: Nelson, p. 40.

51   **"The papers on the surface"**: Nelson, p. 38.

51   **"Even as a young child"**: Nelson, p. 10.

71   **Hopkins has a security force**: Lawrence Jackson, *Shelter: A Black Tale of Homeland, Baltimore*. Minneapolis: Graywolf Press, 2022, p. 249.

104   **But now I learn that before Cross Keys became**: Information about the history of Cross Keys comes primarily from two sources, Paige Glotzer, *How the Suburbs Were Segregated: Developers and the Business of Exclusionary Housing, 1890–1960* (New York: Columbia University Press, 2020), and Jim Holechek, *Baltimore's Two Cross Keys Villages* (Lincoln, NE: iUniverse, 2004).

110   **Raoul Middleman wanted to study with Gladys in the 1950s**: From a phone conversation with Raoul Middleman in 2018.

151   **"When the museum acquired it"**: Quotes on this page are from letters between Gladys and Brenda Richardson that are housed in the Baltimore Museum of Art archive.

155   **"It wasn't apathy"**: Mary Gabriel, *Ninth Street Women: Lee Krasner, Elaine De Kooning, Grace Hartigan, Joan Mitchell, and Helen Frankenthaler: Five Painters and the Movement That Changed Modern Art*. New York: Little, Brown and Company, 2018, p. 199.

158   **"I never knew anyone"**: All quotes on this page from Joe LeSueur, *Digressions on Some Poems by Frank O'Hara: A Memoir*. New York: Farrar, Straus and Giroux, 2003, p. 104.

160   "That he preferred men sexually": Gabriel, p. 10.

160   "It's nice that Frank has a sex life": LeSueur, p. 151.

160   "Grace, upon counsel of her cornball shrink": LeSueur, p. 152.

162   "headstrong, stubborn, contentious": LeSueur, p. 102.

162   "a vulgarity of spirit": LeSueur, p. 153.

163   "I have found my 'subject,' it concerns": Robert Saltonstall Mattison, *Grace Hartigan: A Painter's World*, New York: Hudson Hills Press, 1990, p. 9.

164   "that Frank was a homosexual": Marjorie Perloff, *Frank O'Hara: Poet Among Painters*. Chicago: University of Chicago Press, 1998, p. 210.

166   "I have never taught in my life": From an interview with Hartigan in Cindy Nemser, *Art Talk: Conversations with 12 Women Artists*. New York: Charles Scribner's Sons, 1975, p. 163.

166   Grace "was a diva": Quoted in Cathy Curtis, *Restless Ambition: Grace Hartigan, Painter*. New York: Oxford University Press, 2015, p. 220.

166   "no contemporary arts scene to speak of": Curtis, p. 197.

167   Grace might offer her opinion: From a lecture at Skidmore College, quoted in Curtis, p. 272.

167   "one is working out of nature": Curtis, p. 206.

167   "Nature is art, that's what it is": "Oral History Interview with Gladys Goldstein," Jewish Museum of Maryland, June 25, 2007.

167   "I can't keep repeating the same thing": "Oral History Interview with Gladys Goldstein," Jewish Museum of Maryland, June 25, 2007.

168   "It's embarrassing": "Oral History Interview with Gladys Goldstein," Jewish Museum of Maryland, June 25, 2007.

171   "Moreover, though I may be a pacifist": Jean-Paul Sartre, *The Age of Reason*. Originally published as *L'Âge de Raison*. Paris: Éditions Gallimard, 1945. Translation by Hamish Hamilton, 1947. Reprint. London: Penguin Classics, 2001, p. 104.

171   "Well, well, one is never finished with one's family": Sartre, p. 109.

173   "He realized, of course": Sartre, p. 167.

173   "You are disgusted with yourself, I suppose": Sartre, p. 295.

173 **"He is free"**: Sartre, p. 295.

174 **"What type of art do you do?"**: Quotes in this section come from Alex Abel's video interview with Gladys for a class project at Eastern Middle School in Silver Spring, Maryland, in 2002.

178 **Many of the first Jews to arrive in Maryland were convicts**: Eric L. Goldstein and Deborah R. Weiner, *On Middle Ground: A History of the Jews of Baltimore*. Baltimore: Johns Hopkins University Press, 2018, p. 22.

178 **Slavery was legal in Maryland until**: For historical details in this section, I'm drawing from a number of sources, including Lawrence T. Brown, *The Black Butterfly: The Harmful Politics of Race and Space in America* (Baltimore: Johns Hopkins University Press, 2021); Ralph Clayton, *Cash for Blood: The Baltimore to New Orleans Domestic Slave Trade* (Westminster, MD: Heritage Books, 2007); W. E. B. Du Bois, *Black Reconstruction in America, 1860–1880* (New York: Harcourt, Brace, 1935; reprint, New York: Free Press, 1998); Eric L. Goldstein and Deborah R. Weiner, *On Middle Ground: A History of the Jews of Baltimore* (Baltimore: Johns Hopkins University Press, 2018); Antero Pietila, *Not in My Neighborhood: How Bigotry Shaped a Great American City* (Chicago: Ivan R. Dee, 2010); Richard Rothstein, *The Color of Law: A Forgotten History of How Our Government Segregated America* (New York: Liveright Publishing Corporation, 2017); Harry A. Ezratty, *Baltimore in the Civil War: The Pratt Street Riot and a City Occupied* (Charleston, SC: History Press, 2010); Elizabeth Fee, Linda Shopes, and Linda Zeidman, *The Baltimore Book: New Views of Local History* (Philadelphia: Temple University Press, 1991); P. Nicole King, Kate Drabinski, and Joshua Clark Davis, *Baltimore Revisited: Stories of Inequality and Resistance in a U.S. City* (New Brunswick, NJ: Rutgers University Press, 2019); Paige Glotzer, *How the Suburbs Were Segregated: Developers and the Business of Exclusionary Housing, 1890–1960* (New York: Columbia University Press, 2020).

178 **The United States banned**: Lawrence T. Brown, *The Black Butterfly: The Harmful Politics of Race and Space in America*, Baltimore: Johns Hopkins University Press, 2021, p. 33.

178 **in the words of W. E. B. Du Bois**: W. E. B. Du Bois, *Black Reconstruction in America, 1860–1880*. New York: Harcourt, Brace, 1935. Reprint. New York: Free Press, 1998, pp. 42–43.

178 **"Nearly every part of the nation's economy"**: Brown, p. 34.

178 **More than a dozen slave traders**: Scott Shane, "The Secret History of City Slave Trade; Blacks and Whites Alike of Modern-Day Baltimore Have Ignored the Story of the Jails That Played a Key Role in the U.S. Slave Trade of the 1800s," *Baltimore Sun*, June 19, 1999.

179 **An antislavery rabbi was forced to flee**: Goldstein and Weiner, p. 91.

181 **with investment by British colonialists**: Paige Glotzer, *How the Suburbs Were Segregated: Developers and the Business of Exclusionary Housing, 1890–1960*. New York: Columbia University Press, 2020, p. 30.

186 **And I realize that Billie Holiday was raised in Baltimore**: For details about Billie Holiday's life, I draw primarily from Billie Holiday, with William Dufty, *Lady Sings the Blues* (New York: Doubleday, 1956; reprint, New York: Harlem Moon, 2006); Julia Blackburn, *With Billie: A New Look at the Unforgettable Lady Day* (New York: Pantheon, 2005; reprint, New York: Vintage Books, 2006); Donald Clarke, *Wishing on the Moon: The Life and Times of Billie Holiday* (New York: Viking, 1994); David Margolick, *Strange Fruit: The Biography of a Song* (New York: Ecco Press, 2001); Billie Holiday Project for Liberation Arts, Coursework II: Baltimore's Billie Holiday, "'I'm from Baltimore, I don't know nothing.': Billie Holiday's Baltimore," Johns Hopkins Krieger School of Arts and Sciences.

186 **"A whorehouse was about the only place"**: Billie Holiday, with William Dufty, *Lady Sings the Blues*. New York: Doubleday, 1956. Reprint. New York: Harlem Moon, 2006, p. 10.

186 **"It was the first time I ever heard anybody sing"**: Holiday, p. 9.

187 **"A Depression was nothing new to us"**: Holiday, p. 35.

188 **"You can't copy anybody"**: Holiday, p. 53.

190 **"it's only on the border of being the South"**: Holiday, p. 80.

190 **"It got to the point where I hardly ever"**: Holiday, p. 84.

191   "**plantation owners**": Holiday, p. 112.

191   "**The world we lived in**": Holiday, p. 46.

191   "**Although people sometimes act like**": Holiday, p. 197.

194   "**and I am sweating a lot by now and thinking of**": Frank O'Hara, *The Selected Poems of Frank O'Hara*, edited by Donald Allen. New York: Vintage Books, 1974, p. 146.

201   "**Do you begin with the landscape?**": *Joan Mitchell: Portrait of an Abstract Painter*, director Marion Cajori. Arthouse Films, 1993.

203   "**There should be**": O'Hara, p. 112.

203   "**I discovered that Grace had entered adulthood**": Cathy Curtis, *Restless Ambition: Grace Hartigan, Painter*. New York: Oxford University Press, 2015, p. x.

204   "**You do not always know what I am feeling**": O'Hara, p. 92.

212   "**yes your face is so exquisite**": Charles Henri Ford and Parker Tyler, *The Young and Evil*. Paris: Obelisk Press, 1933. Reprint. New York: Gay Presses of New York, 1988, p. 11.

212   "**ninety-five percent of the world is just naturally queer**": Ford and Tyler, p. 159.

212   "**Miss 69**" and "**Miss Suckoffski**": Ford and Tyler, p. 162.

212   "**everything was all wrong . . . wrong but magnetic**": Ford and Tyler, p. 169.

212   "**morality is rotten**": Ford and Tyler, p. 173.

212   "**One begins to have ideas about happiness**": Ford and Tyler, pp. 173–174.

212   "**Forgive and forget are both bad words**": Ford and Tyler, p. 97.

212   "**no doors nor walls**": Ford and Tyler, p. 194.

213   "**Perhaps love is loneliness**": Ford and Tyler, p. 175.

214   **Keith Martin graduated from the Art Institute**: Details about Keith Martin's life come from Keith Morrow Martin Papers, Syracuse University Special Collections.

214   "**Here come the divine Verlaine and Rimbaud**": Larry Rivers, *What Did I Do?: The Unauthorized Autobiography*. New York: Thunders Mouth, 1992, pp. 243–244.

219   "**I thought it was a really daring step**": "Ninth Street Women: Mary Gabriel in Conversation with Deborah Solomon | Live from the Whitney," October 3, 2018.

221 **"Abstract painting was a language that transcended gender"**: "Ninth Street Women: Mary Gabriel in Conversation with Deborah Solomon | Live from the Whitney," October 3, 2018.

225 **Joan Mitchell: I don't have any feeling for monumental art**: This page quoted from *Joan Mitchell: Portrait of an Abstract Painter*, director Marion Cajori. Arthouse Films, 1993.

226 **"The private myth has become public property"**: All Elaine de Kooning quotes here from Elaine de Kooning, "Subject: What, How or Who?" *ARTnews*, April 1955, p. 29.

227 **"I painted for a long, long time"**: All correspondence between Gladys and the Duveen-Graham Gallery from James Graham & Sons Gallery Records, Archives of American Art, Smithsonian Institution.

228 **"perhaps Baltimore's most awarded painter"**: Kenneth Sawyer, "Goldstein and Binebrink Exhibitions," *Baltimore Sun*, April 22, 1956, sec. A, p. 7.

235 **"Any exhibition of paintings by Keith Martin"**: Kenneth Sawyer, "Keith Martin—an Artist of Stature," *Baltimore Sun*, October 2, 1955, sec. A, p. 2.

235 **"modified cubist scheme"**: Dore Ashton, "Two First Displays of Abstraction," *New York Times*, September 27, 1957.

237 **"I don't give a fuck for families"**: Frank O'Hara, quoted in Brad Gooch, *City Poet: The Life and Times of Frank O'Hara*, New York: Alfred A. Knopf, 1993.

244 **"The painting has to work, but it has to say something more"**: All Joan Mitchell quotes on this page from Irving Sandler, "Mitchell Paints a Picture," *ARTnews*, October 1957.

245 **"You are inside yourself, looking at this damned piece of rag on the wall"**: Nemser, p. 170.

247 **"It doesn't interest me to think of myself in a retrospective way"**: Nemser, p. 172.

258 ***Tomorrow Is Another Day*, the Mark Bradford show**: Details about Mark Bradford's life come primarily from Katy Siegel and Christopher Bedford, eds., *Mark Bradford: Tomorrow Is Another Day*. Baltimore Museum of Art and Gregory R. Miller, 2017.

258 **"paid a wage below the level of decent living"**: Du Bois, p. 15.

259 **"the grid saved my life"**: "Like a Loose Shawl: Christopher

Bedford and Mark Bradford," Katy Siegel and Christopher Bedford, eds. *Mark Bradford: Tomorrow Is Another Day*. Baltimore Museum of Art and Gregory R. Miller, 2017, p. 114.

260   **The resulting policy of "free choice"**: Howell S. Baum, *"Brown" in Baltimore: School Desegregation and the Limits of Liberalism*. Ithaca, New York: Cornell University Press, 2010, pp. 71–75.

260   **"Value is determined by perception"**: *The Lines Between Us*, Maryland Morning on WYPR, Episode 10: "The Wealth Gap," November 30, 2012.

261   **In a 1965 *Baltimore Sun* article about their house**: Anne Louise Hitch, "An Artist's Home That Fulfills Her Dream," *Sunday Sun Magazine*, March 14, 1965, pp. 32–33.

261   **"I'm interested in the history of abstraction, of unpacking the '50s"**: Alina Cohen, "AIDS, Abstraction, and Absent Bodies: A Conversation with Mark Bradford," *Hyperallergic*, December 9, 2015.

264   **"We want to make sure we are not gentrifying out the folks who currently live in the community"**: Angela N. Carroll, "What Pennsylvania Avenue's Official Arts District Designation Means for the Community," *Baltimore* magazine, July 16, 2019.

264   **"vying for a slice of Baltimore's multibillion-dollar tourism industry"**: "Pennsylvania Avenue Corridor Designated as Black Arts and Entertainment District," WBALTV 11, July 23, 2019.

266   **"horrified" by the impending sale**: Sebastian Smee and Peggy McGlone, "Baltimore Museum of Art Hopes to Raise $65 Million by Selling Warhol's 'Last Supper' and Two Other Paintings," *Washington Post*, October 2, 2020.

266   **the most dynamic response**: Information on Zohore's performance comes from Cara Ober, "Monsieur Zohore's 'The Last Supper' at the BMA," *BmoreArt*, December 23, 2020.

267   **"death, death, death, death, more death"**: "Like a Loose Shawl: Christopher Bedford and Mark Bradford," in Katy Siegel and Christopher Bedford, eds. *Mark Bradford: Tomorrow Is Another Day*. Baltimore Museum of Art and Gregory R. Miller, 2017, p. 109.

268   **"I really actually just think that I'm an artist"**: "Like a Loose Shawl: Christopher Bedford and Mark Bradford," in Katy Siegel

and Christopher Bedford, eds. *Mark Bradford: Tomorrow Is Another Day*. Baltimore Museum of Art and Gregory R. Miller, 2017, p. 124.

269 **"I was completely shocked. It was a ghettoized city"**: "Oral History Interview with Brenda Richardson," Archives of American Art, Smithsonian Institution, June 29–30, 2011.

270 **"a precapitalistic, lower-class disdain"**: Todd M. Endelman, *Jews in Georgian England: Tradition and Change in a Liberal Society, 1714–1830*, quoted in Eric L. Goldstein, *Traders and Transports: The Jews of Colonial Maryland*. Baltimore: Jewish Historical Society of Maryland, 1993, p. 28.

270 **"We want you to know that without your husband we wouldn't own our own homes"**: *The Lines Between Us*, Maryland Morning on WYPR, Episode 1: "Song for My Father," September 28, 2012.

SELECTED BIBLIOGRAPHY

Books, Exhibition Catalogs, Articles

The 2015 Baltimore Uprising: A Teen Epistolary.

Art Students League of New York, 1939–1940.

Art Students League of New York, 1940 –1941.

"Artists Denounce Modern Museum." *New York Times,* April 17, 1940.

Ashton, Dore, "Two First Displays of Abstraction." *New York Times,* September 27, 1957.

Balder, Alton Parker. *Six Maryland Artists: A Study in Drawings.* Baltimore: Balboa Publications, 1955.

Baum, Howell S. *"Brown" in Baltimore: School Desegregation and the Limits of Liberalism.* Ithaca, New York: Cornell University Press, 2010.

Blackburn, Julia. *With Billie: A New Look at the Unforgettable Lady Day.* New York: Pantheon, 2005. Reprint. New York: Vintage Books, 2006.

Brown, Lawrence T. *The Black Butterfly: The Harmful Politics of Race and Space in America.* Baltimore: Johns Hopkins University Press, 2021.

Burney, Lawrence. "Soul of the City." *Baltimore* magazine, February 2022.

Canaday, John. "Sometimes You Feel Sorry." *New York Times,* March 21, 1965.

Carroll, Angela N. "What Pennsylvania Avenue's Official Arts District Designation Means for the Community." *Baltimore* magazine, July 16, 2019.

Clarke, Donald. *Wishing on the Moon: The Life and Times of Billie Holiday.* New York: Viking, 1994.

Clayton, Ralph. *Cash for Blood: The Baltimore to New Orleans Domestic Slave Trade.* Westminster, MD: Heritage Books, 2007.

Cohen, Alina. "AIDS, Abstraction, and Absent Bodies: A Conversation with Mark Bradford." *Hyperallergic*, December 9, 2015.

Curtis, Cathy. *Restless Ambition: Grace Hartigan, Painter.* New York: Oxford University Press, 2015.

Davis, Angela Y. *Blues Legacies and Black Feminism: Gertrude "Ma" Rainey, Bessie Smith, and Billie Holiday.* New York: Random House, 1998.

De Kooning, Elaine. *The Spirit of Abstract Expressionism: Selected Writings.* New York: George Braziller, 1994.

De Kooning, Elaine. "Subject: What, How or Who?" *ARTnews*, April 1955.

Denmead, Tyler. *The Creative Underclass: Youth, Race, and the Gentrifying City.* Durham, NC: Duke University Press, 2019.

De Veaux, Alexis. *Don't Explain: A Song of Billie Holiday.* New York: Harper and Row, 1980.

Dorsey, John. "BMA Acquires 18 Warhols." *Baltimore Sun*, May 5, 1994.

Du Bois, W. E. B. *Black Reconstruction in America, 1860–1880.* New York: Harcourt, Brace, 1935. Reprint. New York: Free Press, 1998.

Ezratty, Harry A. *Baltimore in the Civil War: The Pratt Street Riot and a City Occupied.* Charleston, SC: History Press, 2010.

Fee, Elizabeth, Linda Shopes, and Linda Zeidman. *The Baltimore Book: New Views of Local History.* Philadelphia: Temple University Press, 1991.

Ford, Charles Henri, and Parker Tyler. *The Young and Evil.* Paris: Obelisk Press, 1933. Reprint. New York: Gay Presses of New York, 1988.

Forestra, Merry A. *A Life in Art: Alma Thomas 1891–1978.* Washington, DC: National Museum of American Art, 1981.

Friedman, Samantha, and Jodi Hauptman. *Lincoln Kirstein's Modern.* New York: Museum of Modern Art, 2019.

Gabriel, Mary. *Ninth Street Women: Lee Krasner, Elaine De Kooning, Grace Hartigan, Joan Mitchell, and Helen Frankenthaler: Five Painters and the Movement That Changed Modern Art.* New York: Little, Brown and Company, 2018.

Glotzer, Paige. *How the Suburbs Were Segregated: Developers and the Business of Exclusionary Housing, 1890–1960.* New York: Columbia University Press, 2020.

Goldstein, Eric L. *Traders and Transports: The Jews of Colonial Maryland*. Baltimore: Jewish Historical Society of Maryland, 1993.

Goldstein, Eric L., and Deborah R. Weiner. *On Middle Ground: A History of the Jews of Baltimore*. Baltimore: Johns Hopkins University Press, 2018.

Gooch, Brad. *City Poet: The Life and Times of Frank O'Hara*. New York: Alfred A. Knopf, 1993.

Gruen, John. *The Party's Over Now: Reminisces of the Fifties—New York's Artists, Writers, Musicians, and Their Friends*. Wainscott, New York: Pushcart Press, 1989.

Herman Maril: An Artist's Two Worlds. Provincetown, MA: Provincetown Art Association and Museums, 2008.

Hirschland, Ellen B., and Nancy Hirschland Ramage. *The Cone Sisters of Baltimore: Collecting at Full Tilt*. Evanston, IL: Northwestern University Press, 2008.

Hitch, Anne Louise. "An Artist's Home That Fulfills Her Dream." *Sunday Sun Magazine*, March 14, 1965.

Hobbs, Robert Carlton, and Gail Levin. *Abstract Expressionism: The Formative Years*. Ithaca, NY: Cornell University Press, 1978.

Holechek, Jim. *Baltimore's Two Cross Keys Villages*. Lincoln, NE: iUniverse, 2004.

Holiday, Billie, with William Dufty. *Lady Sings the Blues*. New York: Doubleday, 1956. Reprint. New York: Harlem Moon, 2006.

Jackson, Christine. "The BMA Deaccessioning Scandal, Explained." *Baltimore* magazine, October 22, 2020.

King, P. Nicole, Kate Drabinski, and Joshua Clark Davis. *Baltimore Revisited: Stories of Inequality and Resistance in a U.S. City*. New Brunswick, NJ: Rutgers University Press, 2019.

Kligman, Ruth. *Love Affair: A Memoir of Jackson Pollock*. New York: Cooper Square Press, 1974, 1999.

La Moy, William T., and Joseph P. McCaffrey, eds. *The Journals of Grace Hartigan, 1951–1955*. Syracuse, NY: Syracuse University Press, 2009.

Lanahan, Lawrence. *The Lines Between Us: Two Families and a Quest to Cross Baltimore's Racial Divide*. New York: New Press, 2019.

LeSueur, Joe. *Digressions on Some Poems by Frank O'Hara: A Memoir*. New York: Farrar, Straus and Giroux, 2003.

Levin, Gail. *Lee Krasner: A Biography.* New York: William Morrow, 2012.

Levitov, Karen. *Collecting Matisse and Modern Masters: The Cone Sisters of Baltimore.* New York: Jewish Museum, 2011.

Magee, Michael. "Tribes of New York: Frank O'Hara, Amiri Baraka, and the Poetics of the Five Spot." *Contemporary Literature,* Winter 2001.

Margolick, David. *Strange Fruit: The Biography of a Song.* New York: Ecco Press, 2001.

Martin, Keith, and Brenda Richardson. *Keith Martin: Collages: An Exhibition, September 13–October 30, 1977.* Baltimore: Baltimore Museum of Art, 1977.

Mattison, Robert Saltonstall. *Grace Hartigan: A Painter's World.* New York: Hudson Hills Press, 1990.

McDougall, Harold A. *Black Baltimore: A New Theory of Community.* Philadelphia: Temple University Press, 1993.

McGlone, Peggy. "State Asked to Halt Sale of Three Baltimore Museum of Art Paintings." *Washington Post,* October 15, 2020.

Miller, Hallie. "Group Looks to Rehab Baltimore's Pennsylvania Avenue into Thriving Black Arts and Entertainment District." *Baltimore Sun,* March 29, 2019.

Mitchell, Margaret. *Gone with the Wind.* New York: Macmillan Publishers, 1936.

Moore, Anne Elizabeth. *Gentrifier.* New York: Catapult, 2021.

Moskowitz, P. E. *How to Kill a City: Gentrification, Inequality, and the Fight for the Neighborhood.* New York: Nation Books, 2018.

Myers, John Bernard. *Tracking the Marvelous: A Life in the New York Art World.* New York: Random House, 1983.

Nelson, Laura. *Capturing the Essence: The Art of Gladys Goldstein.* Adelphi, MD: University of Maryland University College, 2004.

Nelson, Maggie. *On Freedom: Four Songs of Care and Constraint.* Minneapolis: Graywolf Press, 2021.

Nelson, Maggie. *Women, the New York School, and Other True Abstractions.* Iowa City: University of Iowa Press, 2007.

Nemser, Cindy. *Art Talk: Conversations with 12 Women Artists.* New York: Charles Scribner's Sons, 1975.

New, Elisa. *Jacob's Cane: A Jewish Family's Journey from the Borderlands of Lithuania to the Ports of London and Baltimore.* New York: Basic Books, 2009.

Ober, Cara. "Artists and Curators Weigh in on Baltimore Museum's Move to Deaccession Works by White Men to Diversify Its Collection." *Hyperallergic*, May 8, 2018.

Ober, Cara. "Monsieur Zohore's 'The Last Supper' at the BMA." *BmoreArt*, December 23, 2020.

O'Hara, Frank. *The Selected Poems of Frank O'Hara*, edited by Donald Allen. New York: Vintage Books, 1974.

O'Meally, Robert. *Lady Day: The Many Faces of Billie Holiday*. New York: Arcade Publishing, 1991.

Perloff, Marjorie. *Frank O'Hara: Poet Among Painters*. Chicago: University of Chicago Press, 1998.

Pietila, Antero. *Not in My Neighborhood: How Bigotry Shaped a Great American City*. Chicago: Ivan R. Dee, 2010.

Pryor-Trusty, Rosa. "Rambling Rose." *African-American Community, History and Entertainment in Maryland: Remembering the Yesterday's 1940–1980*. Reisterstown, MD: Xlibris, 2013.

Pryor-Trusty, Rosa, and Tonya Taliaferro. *African-American Entertainment in Baltimore*. Charleston, SC: Arcadia Publishing, 2003.

Rivers, Larry, with Arnold Weinstein. *What Did I Do?: The Unauthorized Autobiography*. New York: Thunder's Mouth Press, 1992.

Rizzo, Mary. *Come and Be Shocked: Baltimore Beyond John Waters and The Wire*. Baltimore: Johns Hopkins University Press, 2020.

Rothschild, Amalie R., and Angelo Pontecorboli. *Amalie Rothschild*. Florence: Angelo Pontecorboli Editore, 2012.

Rothstein, Richard. *The Color of Law: A Forgotten History of How Our Government Segregated America*. New York: Liveright Publishing Corporation, 2017.

Row, Jess. *White Flights: Race, Fiction, and the American Imagination*. Minneapolis: Graywolf Press, 2019.

Russeth, Andrew. "At Baltimore Museum of Art, Christopher Bedford Creates a New Kind of Institution." *ARTnews*, January 14, 2020.

Sandler, Gilbert. *Jewish Baltimore: A Family Album*. Baltimore: Johns Hopkins University Press, 2000.

Sandler, Irving. "Mitchell Paints a Picture." *ARTnews*, October 1957.

Sartre, Jean-Paul. *The Age of Reason*. Originally published as *L'Âge de Raison*. Paris: Éditions Gallimard, 1945. Translation by Hamish Hamilton, 1947. Reprint. London: Penguin Classics, 2001.

Sawyer, Kenneth. "Goldstein and Binebrink Exhibitions." *Baltimore Sun*, April 22, 1956.

Sawyer, Kenneth. "Keith Martin—an Artist of Stature." *Baltimore Sun*, October 2, 1955.

Schloss, Edith. *The Loft Generation: From the de Koonings to Twombly: Portraits and Sketches, 1942–2011*. New York: Farrar, Straus and Giroux, 2021.

Shane, Scott. "The Secret History of City Slave Trade; Blacks and Whites Alike of Modern-Day Baltimore Have Ignored the Story of the Jails That Played a Key Role in the U.S. Slave Trade of the 1800s." *Baltimore Sun*, June 19, 1999.

Siegel, Katy. *Abstract Expressionism*. London: Phaidon Press, 2011.

Siegel, Katy, and Christopher Bedford, eds. *Mark Bradford: Tomorrow Is Another Day*. Baltimore Museum of Art and Gregory R. Miller, 2017.

Smee, Sebastian, and Peggy McGlone. "The Baltimore Museum of Art Backed Out of a Plan to Sell Three Paintings from Its Collection." *Washington Post*, December 6, 2020.

Smee, Sebastian, and Peggy McGlone. "Baltimore Museum of Art Hopes to Raise $65 Million by Selling Warhol's 'Last Supper' and Two Other Paintings." *Washington Post*, October 2, 2020.

Stewart, Kitria. *Freddie Gray, My Childhood Friend*. CreateSpace Independent Publishing Platform, 2016.

Swed, John. *Billie Holiday: The Musician and the Myth*. New York: Viking, 2015.

Sycamore, Mattilda Bernstein. *Pulling Taffy*. San Francisco: Suspect Thoughts Press, 2003.

Tomlinson, R. R. *Children as Artists*. London and New York: King Penguin Books, 1947.

Wije, Michele, ed. *Sparkling Amazons: Abstract Expressionist Women of the 9th Street Show*. Katonah, NY: Katonah Museum of Art, 2019.

Film, Video, and Audio

Agnes Martin—Beauty Is in Your Mind, directed by Lindsey Dryden for TateShots. Available on YouTube.

Agnes Martin—Before the Grid, directors Jina Brenneman and Kathleen Brennan, 2016.

Amarillo Ramp, directors Bill Brown and Sabine Gruffat, 2017.

Artists Work, director Mary Lance, 1982.

Artworks This Week, Maryland Public Television, 2004.

Five Minute Histories: The Billie Holiday House. Baltimore Heritage. Available on YouTube.

Goldworks: The Art of Gladys Goldstein. Videotaped and Edited by Paul E. Gittelsohn, 1988.

Gone with the Wind, director Victor Fleming, 1939.

Inside New York's Art World: Lee Krasner, 1978. Interviewed by Barbara-lee Diamonstein-Spielvogel. Available on YouTube.

Jackson Pollock, director Kim Evans, 1987.

Jackson Pollock 51, director Hans Namuth, 1951.

Joan Mitchell: Portrait of an Abstract Painter, director Marion Cajori, 1993.

The Lines Between Us, Maryland Morning on WYPR. September 28, 2012–October 4, 2013. Available online.

Meet Grace Hartigan, Smithsonian American Art Museum. Available on YouTube.

Nana, Mom and Me, director Amalie R. Rothschild, 1974.

The New York School, director Michael Blackwood, 1972.

Ninth Street Women: Mary Gabriel in Conversation with Deborah Solomon | Live from the Whitney, October 3, 2018. Available on YouTube.

"Oral History Interview with Brenda Richardson," Archives of American Art, Smithsonian Institution, June 29–30, 2011.

"Oral History Interview with Gladys Goldstein," Jewish Museum of Maryland, June 25, 2007.

Painters Painting, director Emile De Antonio, 1973. Arthouse Films.

Peggy Guggenheim: Art Addict, director Lisa Immordino Vreeland, 2015.

"Pennsylvania Avenue Corridor Designated as Black Arts and Entertainment District," WBALTV 11, July 23, 2019.

Shattering Boundaries: Grace Hartigan, director Murray Grigor, 2008.

Strange Fruit: The Biography of a Song, director Joel Katz, 2002.

Take It Down, director Sabine Gruffat, 2018.
Woo Hoo? May Wilson, director Amalie R. Rothschild, 1969.
XCTRY, director Bill Brown, 2018.

Archives

Archives of American Art, Smithsonian Institution
Art Students League of New York
Baltimore Museum of Art
Maryland Institute College of Art
Loyola Notre Dame of Maryland
Syracuse University Special Collections

Online Resources

Billie Holiday Project for Liberation Arts, Coursework II: Baltimore's Billie Holiday, "'I'm from Baltimore, I don't know nothing.': Billie Holiday's Baltimore." Johns Hopkins Krieger School of Arts and Sciences.
The Lines Between Us, Maryland Morning, WYPR Radio.

© Jesse Mann

MATTILDA BERNSTEIN SYCAMORE is the award-winning author of *The Freezer Door*, a *New York Times* Editors' Choice, one of *Oprah Magazine*'s Best LGBTQ Books of 2020, and a finalist for the PEN/Jean Stein Book Award. Winner of a Lambda Literary Award and an American Library Association Stonewall Honor Book, she's the author of three novels and three nonfiction titles, and the editor of six nonfiction anthologies, most recently *Between Certain Death and a Possible Future: Queer Writing on Growing Up with the AIDS Crisis*. Sycamore lives in Seattle.